WITHDRAWN

KNIT KNIT KNIT KNIT

tenknet

PROFILES + PROJECTS
FROM KNITTING'S NEW WAVE

Sabrina Gschwandtner

Photography by **Kiriko Shirobayashi**

STC Craft/A Melanie Falick Book
Stewart, Tabori & Chang New York

This book is dedicated to my grandmothers:

"Omi" Maria Gschwandtner, who sent me elaborate hand-knit sweaters every year from Thalgau, Austria, and Janice Fleschner, who expressed her love through fine art.

Published in 2007 by Stewart, Tabori & Chang
An imprint of Harry N. Abrams, Inc.

Text copyright © 2007 by Sabrina Gschwandtner
Photographs copyright © 2007 by Kiriko Shirobayashi unless otherwise noted (see page 176).

Library of Congress Cataloging-in-Publication Data
Gschwandtner, Sabrina.
    KnitKnit: Profiles + Projects from Knitting's New Wave /
    by Sabrina Gschwandtner.
    p. cm.
  Includes index.
  ISBN-13: 978-1-58479-631-2
  ISBN-10: 1-58479-631-6
  1. Knitting. 2. Knitting—Miscellanea.
  3. Knitters (Persons)—Miscellanea. I. Title.

TT820.G84 2007
746.43'2041—dc22
2006101807

Editor: Melanie Falick
Designer: Kevin O'Neill
Production Manager: Jacquie Poirier

The text of this book was composed in Akzidenz-Grotesk, Rockwell and Helvetica Rounded.

Printed and bound in China.
10 9 8 7 6 5 4 3 2 1

HNA
harry n. abrams, inc.
a subsidiary of La Martinière Groupe

115 West 18th Street
New York, NY 10011
www.hnabooks.com

Foreword

I first met Sabrina Gschwandtner after encountering her work on the Internet as part of a research project looking at new uses for traditional materials and techniques. I immediately ordered a copy of her publication *KnitKnit,* and contacted her to set up a meeting to learn more about her somewhat strange but lively and engaging world. I was aware of the growing popularity of knitting as a pastime internationally, among young people in particular and, in contrast to many people's expectations, among both females and males. Living in New York one cannot avoid seeing an astonishing number of needle-wielding devotees laboring happily away on buses and subways, and in parks and coffee shops.

Through Sabrina, I was soon to become much more intimately aware of the parallel rise of knitting as a vehicle for artists, in addition to those individuals who simply wanted a handmade scarf or sweater. The other happy surprise for me was to become more aware of the ways in which the community of knitters was structured. Having been involved in the world of craft mediums used by artists for many years, I saw how important the sharing of knowledge—of materials, techniques, ideas—was to the makers. In the world of traditional craft, such knowledge was passed on freely from one person to another or from one generation to another. The "making" of things by hand, often in collaboration with others, expresses other deeply felt, personal, and social needs and visions. Sharing provided a true sense of belonging, and the making of things for oneself or to give to others enhanced a sense of individual self-esteem and social connection. Our daily lives tend to be dominated by technology and the computer, and a sense of fragmentation or isolation is commonplace. Knitting has become an important way to reassert the tactile and social pleasures we all crave.

At the core of Sabrina's book is this sense of community. The artist/knitters who are profiled represent the diverse approaches to the technique, and also the diversity of intentions that give such vibrancy to the knitting community. There are, of course, the knitters who are making beautiful things to wear, with designs that represent traditions as well as stylistic innovations and aberrations from the elegant to the extreme. Another group uses the technique to communicate humor, irony, satire, and even biting social commentary. Finally, there are knitters who create imposing pieces of sculpture, architectural interventions, and performance works. Linking them all together is this book, which celebrates knitting as a vital and ever-evolving form of expression.
—David Revere McFadden
Chief Curator / Museum of Arts & Design, New York

Introduction

I started knitting to stop thinking. It began as a way to make things without over-deliberating their artistic value or semiotic meaning, which is what I was learning how to do in my college classes. Back then, in between bouts of dense reading, I would knit in total silence, thinking of nothing and completely concentrated on making small, repeated loops. I knit clothing instinctually and just grabbed whatever yarn most appealed to me when I felt like using a new color or texture. When I wore knit hats and sweaters to the film class for which I was a teaching assistant, a couple of students asked me to make them clothes. I started selling hats and mittens, first to some of those students, then to boutiques in downtown Manhattan, and finally to a few large department stores uptown. I made all the clothes myself, and each item was one of a kind.

After focusing on making clothing for two years after college, my knitting veered away from a profession, and moved into the periphery. I took a part-time job as an assistant to the installation artist and sculptor Sarah Sze, and when she commissioned me to knit something for her, I made a white winter hat that could tie around her long hair, with a matching pair of gloves that I thought reflected what I had observed about the way she worked with her materials—light, deliberate, experimental. I got a second part-time job as the screening manager of the American Museum of the Moving Image, where I would knit in between movies while sitting at the front desk chatting with the regulars—also known as the cineastes, most of them painfully shy people who were more comfortable speaking to me when I looked down at my knitting and not up at them. At the museum, knitting was not about what I was making, it was about the act of making. A daily dialogue I never initiated would develop when people saw what I was doing. "Why are you knitting in that color purple?" "Can you teach me how to knit?" "How did you learn to knit?" "Will you make me something?" "Do you know when the spring screening schedule will be printed?" "If I learned to knit, do you think I could knit while watching movies?"

Meanwhile, Jim Drain was making mind-numbingly psychedelic machine-knit outfits for music shows performed by his art group Forcefield, and Jamie Peterson was crocheting with used plastic grocery bags. These were friends of mine who had come to handcraft, like me, from other artistic pursuits. Riding my bike home from Prospect Park one day in the fall of 2002, I thought, I'm going to interview Jim and Jamie, and make a zine about handcraft and conceptual art. As I was riding, pushing down on each pedal, I thought, knit, knit, knit, knit. *KnitKnit* became the name of a zine, a new art project, and a way of exploring the link between knitting and fine art practices like sculpture and performance.

It started as a photocopied booklet with spray-painted, fabric covers that I bound on a sewing machine and mostly gave away. I dropped off one for review at Printed Matter, a nonprofit artist's book organization in Manhattan, and they took in ten copies to sell. Michael Gillespie, an art dealer, asked me to launch *KnitKnit* issue #2 as part of a summer event at his gallery that included music and art performances. When the third issue was ready, I organized a reception at Printed Matter, showcasing the work of various contributors. *The New Yorker* listed the event as an "unraveling gathering." I started a spreadsheet for sales. My friend Sara Grady made a website. It grew.

Six issues later, the publication now sells at yarn shops, art galleries, bookstores, and fashion boutiques across the United States and in stores in England, Ireland, Canada, France, and Australia. Making the publication and organizing *KnitKnit* launch events and art exhibitions were methods of creating a community of people interested in pushing the boundaries between art, craft, and fashion. In showcasing people who knit the unpredictable, I was able to explore the ways in which handcraft can express the unconventional, the philosophical, the obsessive, the political, the inventive, the intellectual, and the extreme.

Four years after I started *KnitKnit,* knitting had so permeated American culture that I no longer felt a minority in my welcoming of the knitted extreme. Melanie Falick, editor at Stewart, Tabori & Chang and author of the 1996 epic *Knitting in America,* is to be credited for encouraging me to conduct a survey of knitting today—to cull together a group of people whose work reflected knitting's current ideas, venues, and forms.

The people included in this book are not the only creative people working with knitting today, but are the ones who I have come to know and work with through *KnitKnit,* the knitters I have long admired who were available to take part in the project, or the knitters I found through a very pleasant research process. I met with yarn store owners. I talked with hobbyists at Church of Craft meetings. I went to art galleries. I called *KnitKnit* distributors. I followed countless links on a countless number of knit blogs. I looked through various fiber arts and knitting magazines and books. I posted a submission call on my website. I wanted to find a broad spectrum of knitters, the ones who, as a group, would represent a wide range of knitting's possibilities.

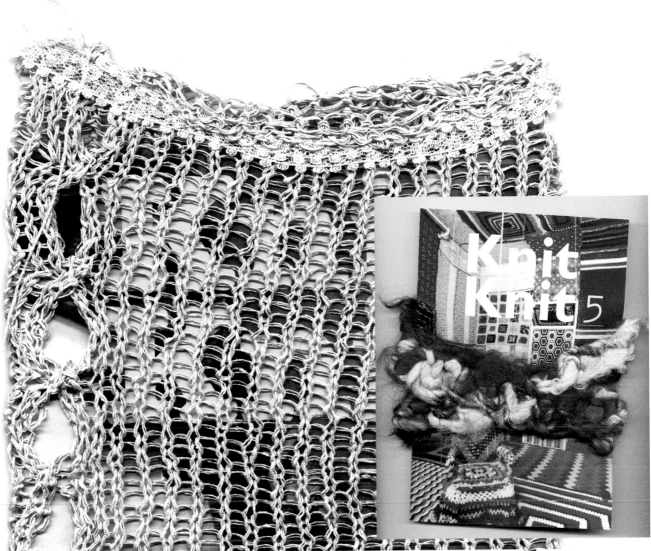

Traveling to meet this group of knitters—to see where they work, to meet those closest to them, to try on the knit items they had described to me over e-mail, to look at the views from their windows, to check out their yarn supplies, to get fed by them or take them out to lunch—was an immersive, exhilarating, and intimate experience. I got to hear what drew them to knitting, to understand how their work had developed, and to guess with them at why knitting has gotten so popular.

Kiriko Shirobayashi, a fine art photographer I befriended during an art residency, traveled with me to take photographs in settings that represent where and how these knitters live and work. She and I collaborated with each person to create a visual record of who they are today. Kiriko felt she needed to know how to knit to take pictures of knitters, so she got free lessons from Debbie New and Cat Mazza.

I asked everyone who participated to design something readers could make, and I gave no restrictions. All of them—even the knitters who work at an unusual scale, or with difficult materials, or in a conceptual fashion—have contributed. Each pattern has an introduction written by the knitter, in his or her own voice. Kiriko and I used their friends or family as models, to represent how knitting fits into real lives.

This book is not just a presentation of knitters and their projects; it is also a profile of a medium as it exists today. Knitting can be clothing, gift, sculpture, therapy, protest, graffiti, or performance … you choose.

Left to right
KnitKnit #4 covers were knitted by Liz Collins (page 44).

David Gentzsch (page 70) and his wife, Terri, e-mailed me because they had heard about KnitKnit **on a radio program while driving. They sent me a sample of their yarn, and I asked them for a donation so that artist Josh Faught could crochet covers from it for** KnitKnit #5.

Lisa
Anne
Auerbach

Lisa Anne Auerbach has a website for her knit works, and it's named after the notorious counterculture book by political activist Abbie Hoffman. The home page of StealThisSweater.com urges readers to "Get all cozy and radical. Stop making scarves. Start making trouble." In a tone as incendiary as Hoffman's *Steal This Book,* Lisa details the various purposes and processes of her many knit projects, most of which declare her political opinions. Take, for example, her description of a biking sweater she machine-knit in 2005:

"This is a sweater specifically about riding in Los Angeles. I made it with set-in sleeves and high ribbing both on the body and the sleeves … The front says 'Bike Los Angeles Always.' I was thinking about how BikeSummer shouldn't be the only time we ride LA. We should ride LA always! The back says 'On my bike, Los Angeles is mine.' That's my handwriting and I really do feel that way about how the relationship of bikes to the street defines a rider's urban landscape. I made this sweater a little long, so that when I lean over to grab my bars, it won't ride up. Awesome! Get on your damn bike, already!"

Although in writing Lisa incites readers to follow her pursuits, in person she's a self-described misanthrope who generally prefers to knit alone. Yet Lisa is as comfortable speaking her opinions as she is knitting them. Outspoken, blunt, and passionate, Lisa has heated views on a wide range of subjects, from food (she's a vegan), transportation (she travels by bike as much as possible), and clothing (pink pants and a favored pair of Clogmaster clogs) to current political events and the price of wool. Since 2004, when she knit a group of outfits stating her choice for president, Lisa has been using her knitting as a platform for a political call to arms rather than a form of community building. "Chart your message, and wear it proudly," Lisa encouraged in "Knitting for a New Millennium," an essay she wrote for *KnitKnit* #6. "The revolution is at hand and knitting needles are the only weapons you'll need."

Lisa means this literally, having developed a knitting method wherein she writes a message, charts it, knits it, and then wears it. Sometimes her work is all hand-knit; other times, she scans her handwriting and creates a chart through a computer program called Win Crea. Her knitting machine, a Passap e6000, is hooked up to her PC through a cable so that the designs are automatically integrated into the knitting. Her projects can take anywhere from a couple of days to a few months to design and complete, depending on how much time she has to spend on them. "Machine stuff takes more time to design and finish than actually knit," Lisa says. Her projects usually begin with a political statement. Then she develops imagery around the selected text, often incorporating classic knitting elements, like traditional Fair Isle and Scandinavian patterning. Lisa is especially fond of sweaters, but she has made a wide range of clothing, including hats, ponchos, skirts, leg warmers, gloves, vests, and sashes. She also creates banners that concretize present-day political phrases like "Quagmire," "Shoot to Kill," and "Freedom is Messy," and can either be worn over her shoulders or hung on exhibition walls.

Although she's been showing her knitted pieces in galleries and museums since 2004, Lisa began knitting after she graduated with an MFA in photography from the Art Center College of Design in Pasadena, California, in 1994. She no longer had darkroom access but wanted to stay productive, and she had always wanted to make herself a sweater that stated "Lisa Anne, Lisa Anne" upside down, inspired by a knit pullover with similarly inverted letters that spelled out "Cheap Trick," worn by Rick Nielson, the band's lead guitarist. Lisa checked out a knitting book from her local library and taught herself. She recalls that she wanted to investigate a friction between the liveliness of language and the permanence of an important medium like a sweater.

Lisa's childhood was spent in Illinois, which may reveal why she would call a sweater an important medium. She now lives in south Los Angeles, where she teaches photography at the University of Southern California and at Los Angeles City College. She continues her

photography practice by taking photographs of over-looked landmarks, or herself, posing in her knitted garments. Many of her self-portraits appear in her numerous self-published zines.

She does her knitting and zine-making inside a small back unit behind her house; her husband Louis grows corn, tomatoes, kale, lettuce, Swiss chard, watermelon, and zucchini in their front yard. Some of Lisa's many zines have included *Saddlesore,* about riding her bike around Los Angeles; *The Casual Observer,* which she started while working at the Griffith Observatory; *American Homebody,* a contemporary counterpart to the 1970s publication *Women's Household;* and *Last Week in the Project Space,* which details her days as an artist-in-residence at the Headlands Center for the Arts in Sausalito, California. Entries from *Last Week in the Project Space* read something like the following: "August 24. Ate lasagna. Knit. Finished panel and washed it downstairs. I'm having trouble getting things to dry up here. It takes days."

Though quotidian events are quickly forgotten after they've been read in zines or even in national newspapers, Lisa thinks the impact of language knit into clothing might endure. "T-shirts represent something you can just throw away when you don't believe in them anymore," Lisa states emphatically when describing a machine-knit pro-Kerry sweater that she made in 2004. "Sweaters are forever. Sweaters with messages become historic." A sweater that Lisa made right after the 2004 presidential election records her ambivalence. The front reads "Things can only get better" and the back reads "Things can only get worse." She signed her initials on the sleeves.

Promoting the wearing—even the making—of knitted clothing as a daily performance, Lisa once hand-knit an orange hat in the shape of a traffic safety cone to wear during "Walktober," the month she decided she would do a lot of walking in the hopes of convincing others to commute without cars. She freely distributes a pattern on her website for a pair of hand-knit Body Count

mittens that memorialize the number of American soldiers killed in Iraq at the time the mittens are made. Her left mitten, for example, is dated March 23, 2005, and lists the number of American soldiers killed by that date as 1,524. She started work on the second mitten on March 31, 2005, by which time the number of American troops killed in Iraq had risen to 1,533. Worn together, the pair shows the increase in the number of soldiers killed over that particular eight-day period. Lisa tells people that it's a great project to knit in public, because it will encourage conversation about the war. "Wear history sadly and thoughtfully," she writes at the conclusion of the mitten instructions, "let the memories and unfathomable statistics keep you warm."

Lisa's work suggests that knitting can be a new form of broadcasting—handmade, personal, and slow, yes; but also fashionable, empowered, and enduring.

Clockwise from top
Lisa's zine, *Last Week in the Project Space*, was created while she was an artist-in-residence at the Headlands Center for the Arts in Sausalito, California.

Lisa wears her General Jinjur skirt, which says "Aqua Alert, Buttercup Alert, Pansy Alert, Poppy Alert," along with her Interlopers Hiking Club panel as a warm underskirt (peeking out from underneath), and two sashes that say "Bikewinter" (blue one) and "Walktober." She is also wearing her favorite Clogmaster clogs.

"Shoot to Kill" reads the other side of this banner.

Saddlesore, Lisa's zine about riding her bike around car traffic in Los Angeles.

The Sundown Lid: A Geodesic Hat

Fritz Haeg invited me to be part of a knitting event at his fancy geodesic dome home, so I made a hat based on the structure of his house. I figured that if Buckminster Fuller could design astounding architecture out of the humble triangle, the least I could do was bring some geometry into my knitting. The hat ended up looking like a space-age multicolored knit helmet, perfect for wearing wherever you might encounter triangles, and a great gift for that Bucky-obsessed person in your life.

— Lisa Anne Auerbach

FINISHED MEASUREMENTS
Approximately 21" circumference

YARN
Artfibers Kyoto (69% silk / 25% super kid mohair / 6% extrafine wool; 110 yards / 50 grams): 1 hank each #30 brown (A), #27 gold (B), #35 orange (C), #18 red (D), and #44 blue (E) (optional)

NEEDLES
One pair straight needles size US 5 (3.75 mm)
Change needle size if necessary to obtain correct gauge.

NOTIONS
Crochet hook size US F/5 (3.75 mm)

GAUGE
15 sts and 17 rows = 3" (7.5 cm) in Stockinette st (St st)

NOTES
To resize the hat, or to use a different number of triangles at the crown, first determine what the desired circumference will be (21" for this hat), then divide that number by the number of triangles to be sewn together to make the crown of the hat (6 for this hat). This gives you the width of each side of this equilateral triangle (c). The triangle can be divided into two right triangles by dividing the base (c) of the triangle by 2. This gives you the width of the base of each right triangle (a). To determine the height of each triangle (b), use the Pythagorean Theorem as follows: $c^2 - a^2 = b^2$ (see drawing).

Once you have these numbers and the stitch and row gauge of the yarn you will be using, you can determine how many stitches to cast on (multiply c by the stitch gauge—round to an even number) and how many rows it will take to get to the end of your triangle (multiply b by the row gauge—round to an odd number). Now determine how many stitches you will need to decrease per row (1 or 2 stitches each side), and how often (every row, every other row, etc.), to get to 2 stitches on the next-to-last row. You are now ready to work your custom hat!

Adventurous knitters might also try combining different colors and stitch patterns for a dramatically different look. Or try using double-pointed needles and fine yarn, working in-the-round on 3 needles with the same number of stitches per needle, decreasing one stitch at the end of each needle until 3 sts remain. This will give you a triangle worked from the outside in; when you get to 1 st remaining per needle, break the yarn, thread it through the remaining loops, pull tight and fasten off.

HAT
Triangle (make 18)
Using color of your choice, CO 18 sts.

Begin Pattern:
Row 1: (RS): Knit.
Row 2: P2tog, purl to last 2 sts, p2tog–16 sts remain.
Repeat Rows 1 and 2 seven times–2 sts remain.
(RS) K2tog. Fasten off.

Earflaps (optional)
Make 8 additional triangles, 4 for each Earflap.

FINISHING
Sew triangles together as indicated on the Assembly Diagram, beginning either with the brim or the crown triangles. Sew on Earflap triangles (optional). *Note: To retain elasticity in the Hat, make sure that the stitches of each triangle are running vertically, not at an angle.*

Using crochet hook and color of your choice, work 1 rnd single crochet around base of entire Hat.

Embellish Hat with pompoms, crochet chains, I-cords, ribbons, or tassels if desired (see Special Techniques, page 172).

Weave in all loose ends.

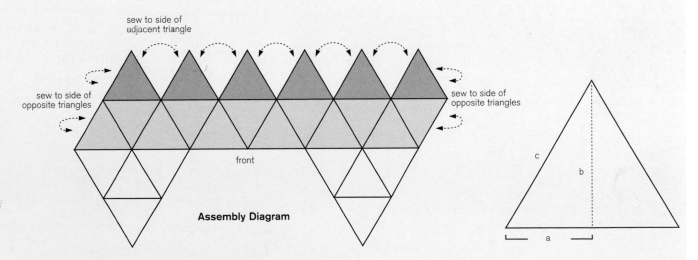

sew to side of adjacent triangle

sew to side of opposite triangles

sew to side of opposite triangles

front

Assembly Diagram

NOTE: Dark gray shaded triangles form the crown of the Hat, medium gray triangles form the brim, and light gray triangles form the optional Earflaps.

Anna
Bell

In the autumn of 2004, Anna Bell's husband suggested that she start a blog. She looked at him blankly and asked, "What is that, and why would I want one?" Despite her initial ambivalence, Anna followed his advice. She started by posting thoughts about missing elements to her wardrobe, like chic exercise outfits and jodhpurs, alongside personal photographs. Before long Anna began to realize that the creative act of online journaling could be a form of pleasant therapy—just like knitting, a childhood hobby that she had recently rediscovered as she emerged from a ten-year depression.

Anna's blog, Amelia Raitte: My Fashionable Life, was named after the main character in a short story that her husband wrote before they were married; "Amelia Raitte" signifies *ameliorate,* which means to make or become better. "Being well is like feeling the sun on my face after the longest, coldest winter," reads her online description. Anna decided never to post angst or trauma, and because her family and coworkers read her blog, it's not the place she goes to confide. She only writes about what she calls "the nicer things in life," and after she discovered the immense network of online knitting blogs, she was inspired to post pictures and text about her own enjoyable projects in progress. Anna was welcomed into the virtual community of knitters, and when she posted progress of her very first knit design, its members cheered her on.

Before the blog, Anna hadn't thought about designing her own handknits, though she admits to a lifelong habit of sketching clothing in her notebooks. To begin to learn the design process, she read Maggie Righetti's book *Sweater Design in Plain English.* "The basics of building a stocking-stitch sweater are not difficult to grasp—to me, the more creative act is in coming up with designs," says Anna, an admirer of Jean Paul Gaultier's couture knits and Vivienne Westwood's hand-knit sock designs.

In just a year, Anna's blog started getting, on average, well over two thousand hits a day. Though a few of her patterns appeared in online magazines, people mostly discovered Anna's site through links from other bloggers. Her second knit design (Sgt. Pepper, which was sold to Alchemy Yarns and republished as The Rebel) was celebrated and linked to by countless bloggers, and being nominated for a Best of Blogs award in the knitting/craft category (an award sponsored by One by One Media) gave Anna another boost in readership.

The steady stream of comments and e-mails from her readers motivates and encourages Anna to come up with new designs. She often thinks of the clothes she covets—most of them inspired by movies, books, fashion magazines, and catwalk shows—and then creates her own interpretations, which develop along the way. Her aesthetic is a self-described "closed-up, dusty dressing box locked up in the nursery of an old-forgotten house … where the clothes are taken out and rediscovered." She chooses childish, naïve shapes that are quintessentially English, and creates elaborate backstories for her garments. "I look at them and wonder, 'Are they sensible, restrained, authoritative?'" She then examines the particular character traits exhibited by each of her designs, and names them accordingly. Jess is a useful, between-seasons jacket while Pippa is "perfect for any occasion when one wants to look a little more than casual." Anna drapes herself in her newest knit designs and posts self-portraits onto her blog to show them off.

More reserved in person than her photos might suggest, Anna leads a quiet, patterned lifestyle. She and her husband live in West London, in a two-story, cottage-style house visited four mornings a week by a milkman. Their backyard—huge by city standards, about sixty feet long by twenty-five feet wide—is host to a small vegetable garden and an ancient pet tortoise named Lucien. Anna works as a copywriter for a charity fundraising agency by day, knitting on the way to and from work, then after dinner until she goes to bed. Every Monday night, Anna goes to a pub near her house to flick her sticks with a group of six to eighteen knitters.

Having transitioned from a knit hobbyist to a knitwear designer, Anna now sells her designs as downloadable PDF files from her blog, and has also launched a new site called Needle and Hook, from which she sells her hand-knitted garments. "My progression from knitter to designer has happened very quickly," Anna says. "I consider myself very lucky that I've found a creative channel that I enjoy so much, and that my designs have proved quite popular in such a short time." Anna imagines that she might publish a book of her own designs one day, but remains so satisfied by the sales and compliments she receives from her reliable, generous audience that she may prefer to just keep blogging.

Facing page
Anna in the living room of her London home.

Above
Anna's sketch for Bridie, an asymmetrical cardigan (see page 16).

Below
Anna's design Daisy closes with a concealed fastening of pearl buttons and sewn button loops. "I once heard of a diamond ring lined on the inside with jewels," Anna describes, **"and I enjoyed thinking about secret treasures while finishing the precious details."**

Bridie

It all started in a meeting at work, where I was sat opposite a red-haired beauty wearing a divine camel-colored cardigan with an asymmetric opening. It was a fine, silky, machine-knit, in a classic style, but the way the opening whipped across to the hip, sloping sharply from the solar plexus, gave it a hint of the warrior. Or that could have been its wearer's bearing. Either way, my instincts were twitching.

And even before then I had been planning a variation on an earlier design, which had been doing great service in my wardrobe. So I straightaway ordered the yarn (Karabella Margrite) and, while waiting for the parcel post, mulled and sketched.

The original inspiration had the lower half of the front opening, if you can picture it, veering off to the right. It looked gorgeous fastened, but cardis can be so pretty worn with the top two or three buttons done up and the rest open, and asymmetry there might lead to odd shapes at the hem. The twist moved upwards to the bust.

— **Anna Bell**

SIZES
X-Small/Small (Small, Small/Medium, Medium, Medium/Large, Large)
To fit bust sizes 32 (34, 36, 38, 40, 42)"

FINISHED MEASUREMENTS
34½ (36½, 39, 41, 43, 45½)"

YARN
Karabella Yarns Margrite (80% extra-fine merino / 20% cashmere; 154 yards / 50 grams): 7 (8, 8, 9, 9, 10) balls #6

NEEDLES
One pair straight needles size US 5 (3.75 mm)
One pair straight needles size US 6 (4 mm)
Change needle size if necessary to obtain correct gauge

NOTIONS
Removable stitch markers; stitch holder; eight ⅜" pearl shank buttons

GAUGE
22 sts and 34 rows = 4" (10 cm) in Lattice Pattern using larger needles

NOTES
Each piece has 1 edge st at each side, which will always be worked in St st. All increases should be worked within the edge sts, and all increased sts should be worked in Lattice Pattern. First and last repeats of Lattice Pattern may not be complete.

STITCH PATTERNS
Twisted Rib
(multiple of 2 sts + 1; 2-row repeat)
Row 1 (RS): K1-tbl, *p1, k1-tbl; repeat from * across.
Row 2: P1, *k1-tbl, p1; repeat from * across.
Repeat Rows 1 and 2 for Twisted Rib pattern.

Lattice Pattern (see Chart)

CARDIGAN
Back
Using smaller needles, CO 83 (89, 95, 101, 107, 113) sts.

Begin Twisted Rib (RS): K1 (edge st, keep in St st), work Twisted Rib to last st, k1 (edge st, keep in St st); work even until piece measures 3½" from the beginning, ending with a WS row.

Begin Lattice Pattern (RS): Change to larger needles. K1 (edge st, keep in St st), work in Lattice Pattern to last st, beginning with st# 1 (6, 3, 8, 5, 2) of Chart, k1 (edge st, keep in St st). Work even for 9 rows.

Shape Body (RS): Continuing in Lattice Pattern, increase 1 st each side this row, then every 10 rows 6 times, as follows: K1, m1, work to last st, m1, k1—97 (103, 109, 115, 121, 127) sts. Work even until piece measures 13 (13, 13¼, 13¼, 14, 14)" from the beginning, ending with a WS row.

Shape Armholes (RS): BO 3 (3, 4, 4, 5, 5) sts at beginning of next 2 rows, 3 sts at beginning of next 2 rows, then decrease 1 st each side every row 3 (3, 5, 5, 7, 7) times, every other row 1 (1, 2, 2, 3, 3) times, then every 4 rows 0 (2, 0, 2, 0, 2) times– 77 (79, 81, 83, 85, 87) sts remain. Work even until armhole measures 7 (7½, 8, 8½, 9, 9½)", ending with a WS row.

Shape Shoulders (RS): BO 7 sts, work 18 (19, 19, 20, 21, 21) sts, join a second ball of yarn and BO center 27 (27, 29, 29, 29, 31) sts, work to end. Working both sides at same time, BO 7 sts at beginning of next 3 rows, then 3 (4, 4, 5, 6, 6) sts at beginning of next 2 rows, and at the same time, BO 4 sts at each neck edge twice.

Right Front
Using smaller needles, CO 41 (45, 47, 51, 53, 57) sts.

Begin Twisted Rib (RS): K1 (edge st, keep in St st), work Twisted Rib to last st, k1 (edge st, keep in St st); work even until piece measures 3½" from the beginning, ending with a WS row.

Begin Lattice Pattern (RS): Change to larger needles. K1 (edge st, keep in St st), work in Lattice Pattern to last st, beginning with st# 2 (4, 3, 1, 4, 2) of Chart, k1 (edge st, keep in St st). Work even for 9 rows.

Shape Body (RS): Continuing in Lattice Pattern, increase 1 st at end of this row, then every 10 rows 6 times, as follows: Work to last st, m1, k1, and, AT THE SAME TIME, when piece measures 11 (11, 11½, 11½, 12, 12)" from the beginning, ending with a WS row.

Shape Neck Edge
Row 1 (RS): K1, m1, work to end.
Row 2: Work to last st, m1p, p1.
Repeat Rows one and two 8 (8, 8, 9, 9, 9) times, then Repeat Row one 0 (1, 1, 0, 0, 1) times–66 (71, 73, 78, 80, 85) sts. Work even until piece measures same as for Back to armhole shaping, ending with a RS row.

Shape Armhole (WS): BO 3 (3, 4, 4, 5, 5) sts at armhole edge once, 3 sts once, then decrease 1 st at armhole edge every row 3 (3, 5, 5, 7, 7) times, every other row 1 (1, 2, 2, 3, 3) times, then every 4 rows 0 (2, 0, 2, 0, 2) times–56 (59, 59, 62, 62, 65) sts remain. Work even until armhole measures 3 (3, 3½, 3½, 4, 4)", ending with a WS row.

Shape Neck (RS): BO 27 (28, 28, 31, 30, 33) sts at neck edge once, 3 sts twice, then decrease 1 st at neck edge every other row 6 (7, 7, 6, 6, 6) times–17 (18, 18, 19, 20, 20) sts remain. Work even until armhole measures 7 (7½, 8, 8½, 9, 9½)", ending with a RS row.

Shape Shoulders (WS): BO 7 sts at armhole edge every other row twice, then 3 (4, 4, 5, 6, 6) sts once.

Left Front
Using smaller needles, CO 41 (45, 47, 51, 53, 57) sts.

Begin Twisted Rib (RS): K1 (edge st, keep in St st), work Twisted Rib to last st, k1 (edge st, keep in St st); work even until piece measures 3½" from the beginning, ending with a WS row.

Begin Lattice Pattern (RS): Change to larger needles. K1 (edge st, keep in St st), work in Lattice Pattern to last st, beginning with st# 3 (2, 3, 2, 3, 2) of Chart, k1 (edge st, keep in St st). Work even for 9 rows.

Shape Body (RS): Continuing in Lattice Pattern, increase 1 st at beginning of this row, then every 10 rows 6 times, as follows: K1, m1, work to end, and, AT THE SAME TIME, when piece measures 10½ (10½, 11, 11, 11½, 11½)" from the beginning, ending with a WS row.

Shape Neck Edge
Decrease Row 1 (RS): Work to last 3 sts, k2tog, k1.
Decrease Row 2: P1, p2tog, work to end.
Repeat Rows one and two 8 (8, 8, 9, 9, 9) times, then Repeat Row one 0 (1, 1, 0, 0, 1) times, and AT THE SAME TIME, when piece measures same as for Back to armhole shaping, ending with a RS row.

Shape Armhole (RS): BO 3 (3, 4, 4, 5, 5) sts at armhole edge once, 3 sts once, then decrease 1 st at armhole edge every row 3 (3, 5, 5, 7, 7) times, every other row 1 (1, 2, 2, 3, 3) times, then every 4 rows 3 (5, 3, 5, 2, 5) times–17 (18, 18, 19, 20, 20) sts remain. Work even until armhole measures 7 (7½, 8, 8½, 9, 9½)", ending with a WS row.

Shape Shoulders (RS): BO 7 sts at armhole edge every other row twice, then 3 (4, 4, 5, 6, 6) sts once.

Sleeves (make 2)
Using smaller needles, CO 51 sts.

Begin Twisted Rib (RS): K1 (edge st, keep in St st), work Twisted Rib to last st, k1 (edge st, keep in St st); work even until piece measures 3½" from the beginning, ending with a WS row.

Begin Lattice Pattern (RS): Change to larger needles. K1 (edge st, keep in St st), work in Lattice Pattern to last st, beginning and ending with st# 1 of Chart, k1 (edge st, keep in St st). Work even for 8 rows.

Shape Sleeve (RS): Continuing in Lattice Pattern, increase 1 st each side this row, every 8 (8, 8, 6, 6, 6) rows 10 (11, 12, 7, 7, 11) times, then every 8 rows 0 (0, 0, 6, 7, 4) times, as follows: K1, m1, work to last st, m1, k1–73 (75, 77, 79, 81, 83) sts. Work even until piece measures 18 (18, 18½, 18½, 19, 19)" from the beginning, ending with a WS row.

Shape Cap (RS): BO 3 (3, 4, 4, 5, 5) sts at beginning of next 2 rows, 3 sts at beginning of next 2 rows, decrease 1 st each side every row 3 (3, 5, 5, 7, 7) times, every other row 3 times, every 4 rows 4 (4, 2, 2, 0, 0) times, every other row 3 (4, 4, 5, 5, 6) times, every row 3 times, then BO 3 sts at beginning of next 4 rows–17 sts remain. BO all sts.

FINISHING
Block all pieces to measurements. Sew shoulder seams.

Left Front Band / Neckband
Note: To ensure a perfect fit, sew piece AS YOU WORK IT to Left Front, Back neck shaping, and Right Front neck shaping.
Using smaller needles, CO 9 sts.

Begin Twisted Rib

Row 1 (RS): K1 (edge st), work Twisted Rib to last st, k1 (edge st).

Row 2: Slip 1 (edge st), work Twisted Rib to last st, p1 (edge st). Work even until piece measures ½" less than for Left Front to beginning of neck shaping, ending with a RS row.

Shape Band

Rows 1 (WS) and 2: Work 2 sts, wrp-t, work to end.
Rows 3 and 4: Work 3 sts, wrp-t, work to end.
Rows 5 and 6: Work 4 sts, wrp-t, work to end.
Rows 7 and 8: Work 5 sts, wrp-t, work to end.
Rows 9 and 10: Work 6 sts, wrp-t, work to end.
Rows 11 and 12: Work 7 sts, wrp-t, work to end. Work even until piece measures ½" less than for Left Front to end of neck edge shaping, ending with a WS row.

Shape Band (RS)

Repeat Rows 1-12 of Band Shaping. *Note: You will begin working on a RS row, instead of a WS row.*
Work even until piece measures ¼" less than for Left Front to shoulder seam, ending with a WS row.

Shape Left Shoulder (RS): Repeat Rows 1 and 2, 5 and 6, and 9 and 10 of Band Shaping. Work even until piece measures ¼" less than to right shoulder seam, ending with a WS row.

Shape Right Shoulder (RS): Repeat Rows 1 and 2, 5 and 6, and 9 and 10 of Band Shaping. Work even until piece reaches along Right Front neck shaping and across BO neck sts. Break yarn, leaving a 6' tail for finishing Band. Transfer sts to holder. Place markers for 8 buttons, with first and last buttons ½" from bottom and top, and remaining 6 buttons evenly spaced (see photo).

Right Front Band

Note: To ensure a perfect fit, sew piece AS YOU WORK IT to Right Front.
Using smaller needles, CO 9 sts.

Begin Twisted Rib

Row 1 (RS): Slip 1 (edge st), work Twisted Rib to last st, k1 (edge st).
Row 2: P1 (edge st), work Twisted Rib to last st, p1 (edge st). Work even to first button marker, ending with a WS row.
Buttonhole Row 1 (RS): Slip 1, k1-tbl, p1, ssk, yo, k1-tbl, p1, k1-tbl, k1.
Buttonhole Row 2: P2, k1-tbl, p1, k1, p1, k1-tbl, p2.
Working buttonholes opposite button markers, work even until piece measures ½" less than for Right Front to beginning of neck shaping, ending with a RS row.

Shape Band (WS)

Work Rows 1-12 of Band Shaping as for Left Front Band. Working buttonholes as established, work even until piece measures ½" less than for Right Front to end of neck edge shaping, ending with a WS row.

Shape Band (RS)

Repeat Rows 1-12 of Band Shaping. *Note: You will begin working on a RS row, instead of a WS row.*
Work even until piece is even with BO neck sts. BO all sts.

Finish Left Front Band / Neckband

Rejoin yarn to sts on holder. Work even until piece measures approximately ½" from edge of Right Front Band, ending with a WS row. Work Buttonhole as for Right Front Band. *Note: Buttonhole should line up over buttonholes from Right Front Band.* Work even until piece reaches edge of Right Front Band. BO all sts. Sew side edge to top of Right Front Band.
Set in Sleeves. Sew side and Sleeve seams. Sew on buttons at markers. Weave in all loose ends.

Lattice Pattern

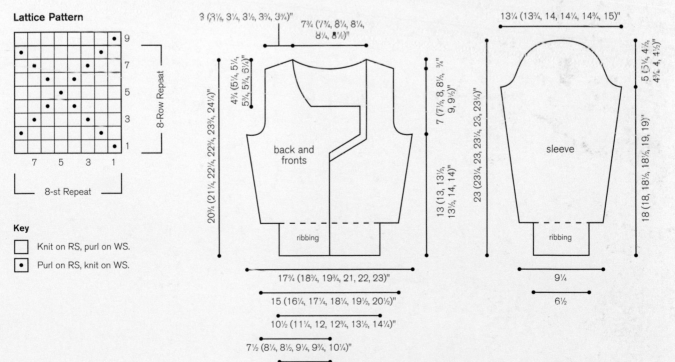

Key

☐ Knit on RS, purl on WS.

⊡ Purl on RS, knit on WS.

3 (3¼, 3¼, 3½, 3¾, 3¾)"

7¾ (7¾, 8¼, 8¼, 8¼, 8½)"

13¼ (13¾, 14, 14¼, 14¾, 15)"

4¾ (5¼, 5¼, 5¾, 5¾, 6¼)"

5 (5¾, 4½, 4¾, 4, 4½)"

7 (7½, 8, 8½, 9, 9½)"

¾"

20¾ (21¼, 22¼, 22¾, 23¾, 24¼)"

back and fronts

sleeve

13 (13, 13½, 13½, 14, 14)"

23 (23¾, 23, 23¼, 23, 23¾)"

18 (18, 18½, 18½, 19, 19)"

ribbing

ribbing

17¾ (18¾, 19¾, 21, 22, 23)"

15 (16¼, 17¼, 18¼, 19½, 20½)"

10½ (11¼, 12, 12¾, 13½, 14¼)"

7½ (8¼, 8½, 9¼, 9¾, 10¼)"

5¼ (5¾, 6, 6½, 6¾, 7¼)"

9¼

6½

Isabel
Berglund

Facing page
Isabel sits in Rachael Matthews' London house (see page 112).

Left
Knitwear from the Berglund autumn/winter 2004 collection.

Isabel Berglund works in a small, raw space in the center of Copenhagen. It's packed with dress forms, several knitting machines, a couple of sewing machines, and a long table that sits below a big board with research photos and drawings. Although about forty other artists have studios nearby, her space sometimes has a lonely feeling, so she turns on the television for a sense of presence when she works alone late at night. Isabel knits and draws out plans for her artwork in the evenings, after long days of what she calls "money work"—designing her own line of high-end knitted clothing and teaching textile design. Isabel calls herself a poor artist, but she doesn't look the part, dressing as she does in clothes of her own design, extravagantly deconstructed knit tops and sweaters made from fine wool and waxed linen. Though her knitwear designs have earned Isabel renown—and an income—her passion is art, particularly creating large-scale knitted installations, like a knitted room that can actually be worn, and other knits that elude any defining categorization.

Isabel's sense of comfort outside the mainstream can be traced to her upbringing in Jutland, Denmark, where she spent the first seventeen years of her life, from 1971 to 1990, within a hippie compound. A self-sufficient community with schooling and farms run cooperatively by seventy-five people, the commune was located in a very rural part of Denmark that's connected to the European mainland. Living as she did in an environment where everyone was encouraged to visually express themselves at will may have infused Isabel's opinions of craft: "The word craft doesn't seem serious. It sounds like you are just doing something at home, making something without thinking about what you are doing," she says, and she applies that definition to the notion of craft held by those in the compound, too. "My dad actually moved away from the commune because he was with all these people who thought they were so creative, but they weren't," she explains. "It just was raw expression without any really developed aesthetic."

Isabel's formal training in textiles began in college. Though she studied drawing, printing, and weaving at the Danish Design School in Copenhagen, she also taught herself how to do machine-knitting in hopes of creating her own fashion designs. Students weren't allowed to design clothing at the school—the teachers believed that fashion should be kept separate from

other uses of textiles—so after graduating Isabel applied to a fashion knitwear master's degree program at Central Saint Martins College of Art and Design in London. "Textiles in Denmark were cozy and safe," she says of the experience. "Saint Martins was not safe. I got pushed really hard. There was more competition at Saint Martins, and you had to design excellent garments in addition to making knit samples." Isabel learned how to hand-knit at Saint Martins so that she could create long, thick loops of waxed linen she pulled through holes in denser, machine-knit fabric made from light, soft wool. The collection she presented at the end of her degree program was an all-black group of machine- and hand-knit clothing, "a mixture of hard and soft, heavy and light, with lots of holes," she explains. "I like to play with the body. I like to see the skin poking through."

After she graduated in 2000, Isabel took a job at a company that produced machine-knit samples for lines like DKNY. "It was not me at all!" she says. "I think more in terms of the whole garment, and I wanted to make real collections." After seven months, Isabel quit to start her own label with her friend Katrine Henriksen. For about a year, Berglund/Henriksen produced a mix of machine- and hand-knitted clothing that followed the design style set forth in Isabel's thesis show. "It was very avant-garde; quite mad, some of it, like a jumper made out of elastic, knitted with open loops so it looks like a net under one arm, but knit with tight loops under the other arm," Isabel explains. "We contrasted things like hard yarns with soft; open loops with tight closed ones; and so on."

After about a year, when Isabel and her collaborator split up to pursue their own visions, Isabel continued to design hand- and machine-knit clothes with increasing success. Her designs called for giant pockets, lengthy sleeves, and plunging necklines; she generally used the purl side of fabric for its rounded shape. "Wovens are so stiff," she says. "I like knitting because you can make many angles." Isabel was doing fashion fairs in cities like Paris and successfully selling her line to stores in Tokyo, Berlin, Rotterdam, Stockholm, and New York within the first year out on her own, and she found it hard to keep up with the fast pace of the industry. "Knitwear production is so consuming," she says. Because she wanted to slow down and move her work into more conceptual territory by creating

sculptural knitted works that didn't fit into the confines of the fashion industry, Isabel had to come up with an alternative to runway shows and fashion fairs. "I have always done things in my own way," she declares.

Isabel joined a cutting-edge group of independent Danish designers named Könrøg, who promoted themselves as a collective instead of individuals competing against each other. The designers each presented their own lines, which fit the group's concept of unique and excellent Danish design, and Isabel was the only knitwear designer among them. Könrøg had a shop and a showroom in the center of Copenhagen, where everyone involved could hold fashion shows, present designs, and sell work. They all pushed each other to create, and they each benefited from the publicity the group got for such an unusual program. The group lasted for five years.

During the time that she was involved with Könrøg, Isabel had the freedom she needed to explore what might happen if her knitwear became so voluminous that it threatened to take over its wearers. "I had an urge to completely exaggerate the knit," she says, and in 2003, she did so by creating an entire knitted room. Knit garments from past collections were knit into the walls so that observers could actually slip into them,

City of Stitches, installed at the Charlottenborg Exhibition Hall in Copenhagen, Denmark, 2003.

and a giant knitted tree, inspired by Paul Auster's novel *City of Glass,* sprouted toward the ceiling. Isabel describes a scene in that book in which the novel's protagonist is talking to a friend: "He wonders if he saw the city as his friend did, what would it look like—if he saw this tree, what would the tree look like to his friend? This made me wonder: If I saw the tree as knitted, maybe someone else wouldn't." She named the installation City of Stitches.

The room took fourteen people almost two months to make. Each knitter used size 17 (12.75mm) needles and twenty strands of cotton yarn to make each stitch. The walls alone weigh 506 pounds. "It was a conceptual idea," Isabel says. "Instead of simply making a nice-looking garment, I wanted people to disappear into knitwear. Fashion is so serious; I wanted to do something with a bit of humor, something that was absurd. I was asking, how do you place yourself between clothes and a room?" Visitors help complete the work by donning the clothes waiting on the walls; the room sucks human bodies into its form and muffles voices like snow. Isabel appreciates this interactive element more than having people buy her free-standing knit designs. She's been able to witness people climbing around the installation three times: The piece has shown at the Charlottenborg Exhibition Hall—a contemporary art space—as well as in two fine art galleries in Copenhagen. It's due to travel to the National Museum of Norway next.

"Am I a knitwear designer or an artist? I don't know," Isabel says, but she's found a balance dividing her time between the two. "What I'm aware of now is what I make for art, and what I make to sell," she says. "I know when I make a mad piece it won't sell, but I also make more classic designs that will bring me money." In the meantime, late at night, she draws secret sketches for future installations that bring concept to homecraft, pushing the boundaries between art and life, knitted dream space and domestic interiors.

Jump in the Wall Jumper

This is one panel of my entire knitted room. You can knit this wall and hang it in your living room for the occasional guest to try on! You can also continue by knitting a whole room with any kind of garment you like.

— **Isabel Berglund**

FINISHED MEASUREMENTS
Panel: 24" wide x 114" tall
Jumper: 24" chest, front piece

YARN
Hjertegarn Soft Cotton (100% cotton; 92 yards / 50 grams):
140 balls, white.
*Note: You may use any worsted-weight 100% cotton yarn with
a gauge of 18 sts and 25 rows = 4" (10 cm).*

NEEDLES
One 32" (82 cm) circular (circ) needle size US 19 (15 mm)
One pair straight needles size US 11 (8 mm)
Change needle size if necessary to obtain correct gauge.

NOTIONS
One crochet hook size US L/11 (8 mm); extra-large
tapestry needle

GAUGE
5 sts and 7 rows = 4" (10 cm) in Reverse Stockinette stitch
(Rev St st) using larger needles and 20 strands of yarn
held together

NOTES
The Wall Panel is worked back and forth on a circular needle to
accommodate the large number of sts worked.

To hang the Wall in your home, fold the top end of the knitted
Panel over a round metal pole (¾" wide and 78" long), sewing
tightly around it. The pole can be hung from two hooks in the
ceiling with heavy thread or yarn attached at each end of the
Panel. Adjust the length of the thread so that you can hang the
wall as low or high as you like.

WALL PANEL (make 3)
Using larger needle and 20 strands of yarn held together, CO
30 sts. Begin Rev St st; work even for 200 rows. BO all sts.

JUMPER
Body
Using larger needle and 20 strands of yarn held together, CO
30 sts. Begin Rev St st; work even for 16 rows.

Split for Neck (RS): Work 15 sts, join a second ball of yarn and
work to end. Working both sides at once, work even for 15 rows.

Shape Shoulders (RS): BO 5 sts at beginning of next 2 rows,
then decrease 1 st each armhole edge every 3 rows 5 times–5
sts remain each side for shoulders. BO all sts.

Sleeves (make 2)
Using smaller needles and 20 strands of yarn held together,
CO 15 sts. Begin Rev St st; work even for 3 rows.
(WS) Change to larger needle. *K1-f/b; rep from * across–30
sts. Work even for 14 rows.
(WS) Change to smaller needles. *P2tog; rep from * across–15
sts rem. Work even for 2 rows. BO all sts.

FINISHING
Using 4 strands of yarn held together, sew Wall Panels together
along long sides. Sew Jumper to center Panel, approximately
68 rows from top of Panel (adjust to fit the person to be "wearing" the Jumper). *Note: The BO sts at either top edge of the Neck
Slit form the shoulders. Sew these sts to the Panel wide enough
apart to fit the shoulders of the person to be "wearing" the
Jumper.* Make sure to leave adequate room so that a person
can slip into the Jumper from below. Sew the long edge of the
Sleeve to the armhole of the Jumper (see photo).

Ribbon Tie: (make 2)
Cut 10 strands of yarn each 3' long. Holding strands together,
fold in half. With RS of piece facing, insert crochet hook into st
along neck edge, approximately 2" below shoulder, from back
to front; catch the folded strands of yarn with the hook and pull
through work to form a loop, insert ends of yarn through loop
and pull to tighten.
Weave in all loose ends.

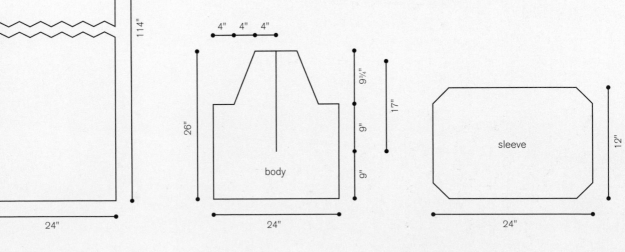

Risto
Bimbiloski

Risto Bimbiloski is a men's knitwear designer at
Louis Vuitton, and the designer of his own women's
knitwear collection, sold in high-end department and
specialty stores around the world. He alternates his time
between the bright, bustling Parisian offices of Louis
Vuitton, where he oversees a team of other designers
and an industrial production system, and the cozy, one-
bedroom apartment where he keeps one wall filled with
a changing selection of images that inspire his own collections. Twice a year, he heads to his small hometown
in Macedonia, where a studio of hand knitters works
with him to create his designs. At the young age of
thirty-two, and after working as a fashion designer for
only eight years, Risto has developed a sophisticated
aesthetic he calls "naïve elegance," consisting of simple-
shaped garments in exaggerated proportions with typical
couture details. The unique construction techniques and
childlike sense of wonder found in his designs may be
attributed to his innate artistic talent, his enterprising
drive, and the fact that he doesn't know how to knit.

Risto Bimbiloski's memories of growing up in Ohrid, a
small lakeside town in southwest Macedonia, are illus-
trated by descriptions of clothing: He recalls wearing a
required uniform of white shirt, black pants, red scarf,
and triangular hat when he recited his communist vows
in school at age six. "Mine was the last generation of
communism," he explains, noting that fashion at the
time was about following convention. During the chaotic
years after Macedonia seceded from the Socialist
Federal Republic of Yugoslavia in 1991, Ohrid was
filled with mixed religions, cultures, and fashion. Risto
remembers that the women living there at the time tried
to achieve a style he describes as "average elegance."
This idea of everyday stylishness is what led to his aesthetic of naïve elegance. "All people are authentic," he
says, "it wasn't the stereotypical Paris fashion. I try to
apply this sense of average elegance to my work."

Risto left Macedonia for Paris when he was eighteen.
Enrolling in l'Ecole des Arts Appliqués Duperre, he
worked toward a bachelor's degree in fashion design,
learning the basics of sketching, draping, and creating
a collection. He had no interest in knitwear at the
time, and he hated his class in machine knitting.

Facing page
**Risto sits in a friend's
apartment in Paris.**

This page
**A knitted garment from
Risto's fall/winter 2000
collection.**

When he graduated in 1995, Risto completely stopped making clothes for three years and worked for the graphic design firm Tdm Studio, where he directed design projects like *Iceberg* and *Harvey Nichols* magazines. His first clothing collection, all wovens, was presented at the 1998 International Festival of Art in Hyères, France, a prestigious European event. Immediate success at the festival inspired him to continue with fashion design. As his collections grew, Risto started to design garments with embroidery, which he had produced in his hometown. When he discovered that his embroiderers were also avid knitters, he started to collaborate with them on knitwear designs, falling for the sense of uniqueness in each knitted garment. Slowly, his work evolved into entirely hand-knit collections "that are translated through a prism of elegance," he describes.

In an unusual design process that he describes as a visual brainstorm, Risto begins his eponymous collection by selecting a group of images from his gigantic image archive, which includes photocopies from old newspapers, stills from Fassbinder and Cassavetes

movies, and cutouts from vintage magazines. "I collect photographs all the time," Risto explains. "When I do a collection, I edit down the photos that interest me and then do more research." Once he finalizes an image group, Risto scans and then composites the different images into one look using Photoshop. He'll print out the composites and put them up on a wall in his apartment. He first looks for shapes or attitudes, and then matches ideas with fabrics, corresponding the vision to certain yarns, usually using natural fibers like cashmere, silk, and cotton. While he worked with asymmetrical shaping for several years, placing swatches onto a dress form made him think more about the impact of knitwear on a body. "Since I started using a dress form to design, I became more interested in volume," he explains in somewhat halting English. "Working on a dress form, it is much easier to work on shapes that are either close to or far from the shape of the body."

Risto goes to an atelier—the entire top floor of an apartment building—in Macedonia each December and July or August to work on the prototypes for his designs. There, his knitters, about fifty women aged

twenty-two to sixty, hand-knit his garments year-round. Risto found the knitters through word of mouth, and then placed an advertisement on local television when he needed to expand production. "They're happy because they love to knit modern designs, and I'm happy because I get to work with an ancient technique," he says. Having assisted him for more than seven years, the knitters understand Risto's aesthetic and process, and they often help him come up with design solutions during the two- to three-week period he is there. They fuss around dress forms draped with swatches while Risto describes shapes using one hand, his other hand gripping a cigarette. In a frenzied fury, Risto always finishes the final designs just as he has to head back home to Paris. "My best ideas always come at the very end of my time there. There isn't time to finish, but I just save my ideas for the next season," he says.

The finished Risto Bimbiloski collections have been presented as runway shows during some seasons, but Risto prefers more informal exhibitions to showcase his interpretations of "average elegance." One year his collection was shown on models standing in the windows of a laundry, a bookshop, and a bakery on a single street in Paris's ninth arrondissement. "The audience was catwalking from window to window!" Risto recounts.

Describing himself as a workaholic who thrives while pursuing several different projects at once, Risto has been designing his own collections and Louis Vuitton collections simultaneously since 2006. His work at Vuitton provides Risto with exposure to a completely different knitwear production and presentation system, one that is industrial "and quite far from artisanal handmade," Risto says. "Vuitton is the peak of international luxury and it provides another creative direction for me," he explains. At Vuitton, Risto directs a design team in creating men's clothing, including sweaters, vests, and tank tops. "It is exciting for me to work as a team," he says, "and I have learned a lot of new technical terms. Working at Vuitton has really pushed my technical education." His next technical challenge, he admits, is learning to knit during an upcoming work session in Macedonia.

Paris Jacket

The idea of this knit was to try to do an elegant, kind of couture-like piece in a most simple, naive way. I proposed to work with simple, un-decorative stitches and to put an accent on the volume and the drapery.
— **Risto Bimbiloski**

FINISHED MEASUREMENTS
To fit 32-36" (36-40)" bust

YARN
Bulky weight mohair bouclé yarn: cream (MC),
250 (275) yards (such as Ironstone Yarns Big Loop Mohair)
Worsted-weight wool/nylon blend yarn: brown (A),
100 (125) yards (such as Valley Yarns Florence)

NEEDLES
One pair straight needles size US 10½ (6.5 mm)
One pair straight needles size US 8 (5 mm)
Change needle size if necessary to obtain correct gauge.

NOTIONS
Removable markers; two ⅝" snaps; matching sewing thread and sewing needle

GAUGE
13 sts and 17 rows = 4" (10 cm) in Stockinette stitch (St st) using larger needles and MC
17½ sts and 30 rows = 4" (10 cm) in Stockinette stitch (St st) using smaller needles and A

NOTES
This Jacket is worked as 3 simple Panels which are then sewn together.

STITCH PATTERN
1x1 Rib (Multiple of 2 sts)
All Rows: * K1, p1; repeat from * to end of row.

JACKET
Panel A
Using larger needles and MC, CO 33 (35) sts. Begin St st; work even until piece measures 86½ (96½)" from the beginning. BO all sts.

Panel B
Using smaller needles and A, CO 8 sts. Begin 1x1 Rib; work even until piece measures 45 (46)" from the beginning. BO all sts.

Panel C
Using smaller needles and A, CO 120 (124) sts. Begin 1x1 Rib (K1, p1; repeat from * to end of row). Work even for ½".

Short Row Shaping (see Special Techniques, page 172)
Row 1: Continuing in 1x1 Rib, work to last 2 sts, wrp-t.
Row 2: Repeat Row 1.
Row 3: Work to 2 sts before last wrapped st, wrp-t.
Repeat Row 3 eleven (seven) times.
Row 15 (11): Work to 3 sts before last wrapped st, wrp-t.
Repeat Row 15 (11) twenty-seven (thirty-one) times, then work
to end of row, working wraps with wrapped sts.
Work across all sts, working remaining wraps with wrapped sts.
BO all sts.

FINISHING
Note: Refer to Assembly Diagram.
Lightly block pieces if desired. Fold Panel A in half lengthwise.
Place markers 7" to either side of fold along one edge (for Step
2), and 1 marker at fold on opposite edge (for Step 5).

Step 1: Sew CO and BO ends of Panel A together; this
becomes center back seam. Place markers 7" to either side of
seam along same edge as other markers (for Step 2).

Step 2: Lay piece flat, with center back seam in center of
bottom piece, so that markers line up. With matching sewing
thread and needle, sew edges together for 14" between
markers. Place markers 4" to either side of seam on opposite
edge of Panel. Fold marked edge to WS so that center back
seam is folded back on itself.

Step 3: Sew marked edge, between markers, for 8".

Step 4: Fold last 2½" of Panel B to WS and sew to itself,
gathering edges in so piece is ½" wide at seam, and so that
end forms one loop of a bow. Repeat for opposite end of
Panel. Place marker 9 (9½)" from either side of Panel C, along
CO edge.

Place marker 9" in from seam on either end of Panel B. Pin
seams of Panel B to ends of CO edge of Panel C; pin Panels
together at markers. With matching sewing thread and needle,
sew Panel B to Panel C, gathering center 22" of Panel B to fit
between markers on Panel C.

Step 5: Fold B/C in half widthwise, and place marker at fold on
shaped edge of Panel C. Pin to Panel A at marker along edge
of opposite seam. Pin ends of Panel C along this edge, being
careful not to stretch or gather either piece. With matching
sewing thread and needle, sew Panel C to Panel A. Sew one
side of each snap to Panel A, ½" in from Panel C at either neck
edge, and the other side of each snap to WS of bow on end of
Panel B.

Assembly Diagram

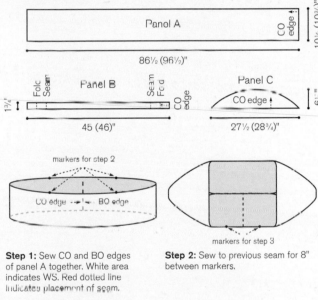

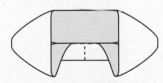

Step 1: Sew CO and BO edges
of panel A together. White area
indicates WS. Red dotted line
indicates placement of seam.

Step 2: Sew to previous seam for 8"
between markers.

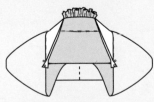

Step 3: Sew to previous seam for 8"
between markers.

Step 4: Sew Panel B to CO edge
of Panel C, gathering center section
between markers.

Step 5: Sew shaped edge of Panel C
to side edge of Panel A.

Wenlan Chia

What started as a small collection of hand-knit clothes in Wenlan Chia's closet has grown, in just six years, to fill an 1,800-square-foot studio in New York's fashion district that might be too small for all of her new designs. Racks of clothing neatly arranged by color are pushed up against piles of pillows, rugs, and bedding. Fabric swatches spill off a table, forming a puddle on the floor at the feet of two knitters who furiously make sample sweaters as they chat. An intern sits cross-legged on a mound of yarn, sewing a belt onto a dress while ignoring Milan, the yapping French bulldog that Wenlan's husband is trying to leash. This scene of happy chaos is also a measure of Wenlan's success: What started so small—and not so long ago—has broadened into a dreamy, brightly colored, and acclaimed clothing line, plus jewelry, home furnishings, and even yarn collections.

Born in Taipei, Taiwan, Wenlan left her hometown for the first time in 1991 to do graduate work at New York University (NYU). But after earning a degree in contemporary art and taking a job at an art gallery, Wenlan felt that something was missing creatively. Her mother had worked as a patternmaker when Wenlan was a child, and Wenlan had always been curious about fashion, so she signed up for night classes at New York's Fashion Institute of Technology (FIT). A turning point came when a classmate showed up in a hand-knitted hot pink, funnel-neck, sleeveless mohair sweater. "It was very tight, and she had crazy hair. It made a big impression!" Wenlan remembers. "I was so inspired. I said, 'I want to be able to do that!'" Her classmate gave her a few lessons, and Wenlan learned the rest from books.

With the kind of sweeping enthusiasm that best illustrates Wenlan's personality, in her early days as a knitter she would often knit through the night instead of sleeping, and in 1999, when she spotted an announcement for an international competition being judged by a committee that included Jean Paul Gaultier on an FIT bulletin board, she decided to enter even though the deadline was the next day. Wenlan stayed up all night sketching her submission, including a bright gold-yellow knitted tunic worn with a long taupe fishtail skirt and hat, and when she won the US candidacy for her designs, she was required to send the finished pieces to Japan for the international finals. "That knitted tunic was complicated," she remembers. "My knitting skills really had to improve to be able to knit what I had drawn." For her efforts, she won fourth prize, after which she entered and won more competitions.

Infused with confidence from those awards and from being stopped on the street whenever she wore her creations, Wenlan organized her closet into a section of all hand-knitted garments, and realized she might have a collection. She began selling her pieces to boutiques in New York City, San Francisco, and Tokyo, and launched Twinkle, a complete line of knitwear, separates, coats, dresses, and accessories, in 2001. Today the Twinkle fashion line is shown on the runway at New York's Fashion Week, and sold in over three hundred boutiques throughout the world.

While the business has expanded quickly to include jewelry, housewares, and yarn, the core of what Wenlan does remains hand-knitting, her trademark being vibrant, mischievous, and chunky knits. "I design handknits first, then machine-knits, and then incorporate intarsia," she explains. "Next, I do my own printed fabrics that incorporate intarsia design, then the jewelry I design references my prints," she continues. "In high fashion, sweaters seldom play a lead role in a collection, but I don't mind letting my sweaters do that." Wenlan's clothing collections are streetwise but delicate, often layered, mixing bulky or long hand-knit sweaters with striped leggings, camisoles, soft silk dresses, and graceful chiffon skirts. She consistently conjures a magical world through motifs like cherry blossoms, forests, and castles.

Looking around her bustling studio, Wenlan has reason to stop to consider her progress. "I have gone from working out of my one-bedroom apartment and paying my first production costs with my credit card to having ten employees and sixteen freelancers today," Wenlan says. "On the business side, Twinkle has had very healthy growth. Some people maybe see me as successful. But I know there is more to accomplish. In those terms, I say my dream has yet to come true."

Facing page
Wenlan in her Manhattan studio.

Wenlan's rug, Formosa, was inspired by one of her drawings.

Above
A young Wenlan wearing a dress her mother made for her

Convertible Cardigan

For this garment, I was thinking of the woman who goes out of town. This is a sweater to be worn when relaxing. You can have it open with just a bikini underneath—it's perfect for strolling on the beach. Or it can be buttoned up, very crisp.

— **Wenlan Chia**

SIZES
X-Small (Small, Medium, Large)

FINISHED MEASUREMENTS
34½ (37¾, 39¼, 41)" chest, including Button Bands

YARN
Twinkle Cruise (70% silk / 30% cotton; 120 yards / 50 grams): 18 (19, 20, 21) balls #31 tea rose

NEEDLES
One 32" (82 cm) circular (circ) needle size US 15 (10 mm)
Change needle size if necessary to obtain correct gauge.

NOTIONS
Cable needle (cn); stitch markers; stitch holders; ten 1⅛" buttons

GAUGE
10 sts and 14 rows = 4" (10 cm) in Reverse Stockinette stitch (Rev St st) using 4 strands of yarn held together

NOTES
The Cardigan is worked back and forth in one piece to the armholes, where the Sleeves are joined for the Yoke.

ABBREVIATIONS
T2L: Slip 1 st to cn and hold to front, k2, k1 from cn.
T2R: Slip 2 sts to cn and hold to back, k1, k2 from cn.
MB: [K1, yo, k1, yo, k1] in same st–5 sts, turn, p5, turn, k5, turn, p2tog, p1, p2tog, turn, sk2p.

STITCH PATTERNS
2x2 Rib
(multiple of 4 sts + 2; 2-row repeat)
Row 1 (WS): P2, *k2, p2; repeat from * across.
Row 2: K2, *p2, k2; repeat from * across.
Repeat Rows 1 and 2 for 2x2 Rib.

Cable Pattern
(panel of 6 sts; 10-row repeat)
Rows 1 and 9 (RS): K6.
Row 2 and all WS rows: P6.
Row 3: T2L, T2R.
Row 5: K1, MB, k2, MB, k1.
Row 7: T2R, T2L.
Row 10: P6.
Repeat Rows 1–10 for Cable Pattern.

CARDIGAN
Pocket Linings (make 2)
Using 4 strands of yarn held together, CO 14 sts. (RS) Begin St st. Work even for 13 rows. Place sts on holder for Pocket.

Body
Using 4 strands of yarn held together, CO 19 (21, 22, 23) sts, place marker (pm) for Right Front, CO 42 (46, 48, 50) sts, pm for Back, CO 19 (21, 22, 23) sts–80 (88, 92, 96) sts.

Begin 2x2 Rib:
Row 1 (WS): P1 (edge st, keep in St st), work in 2x2 Rib to last st, p1 (edge st, keep in St st).
Row 2: K1 (edge st, keep in St st), work in 2x2 Rib to last st, k1 (edge st, keep in St st). Work even for 10 rows.

Establish Pattern:
Row 1 (RS): K1 (edge st, keep in St st), p5 (6, 6, 7), work 6 sts in Cable Pattern, purl to last 12 (13, 13, 14) sts, work 6 sts in Cable Pattern, p5 (6, 6, 7), k1 (edge st, keep in St st).
Row 2: P1 (edge st, keep in St st), k5 (6, 6, 7), work 6 sts in Cable Pattern, knit to last 12 (13, 13, 14) sts, work 6 sts in Cable Pattern, k5 (6, 6, 7), p1 (edge st, keep in St st). Work even for 2 rows.

Shape Waist (RS): Decrease 4 sts this row, then every 4 rows once, as follows: *Work to 3 sts before marker, p2tog-tbl, p1, sm, p1, p2tog; repeat from * once, work to end–72 (80, 84, 88) sts remain. Work even for 3 rows.

Establish Pocket:
Row 1 (RS): K1 (edge st), p1 (2, 2, 3), [k, p2] 3 times, k2, *purl to 1 st before marker, m1p, p1, sm, p1, m1p-L; repeat from * once, purl to last 16 (17, 17, 18) sts, [k2, p2] 3 times, k2, p1 (2, 2, 3), k1 (edge st)–76 (84, 88, 92) sts.
Row 2: P1 (edge st), k1 (2, 2, 3), [p2, k2] 3 times, p2, knit to last 16 (17, 17, 18) sts, [p2, k2] 3 times, p2, k1 (2, 2, 3), p1 (edge st). Work even for 2 rows.
Row 3: K1, p1 (2, 2, 3), BO next 14 sts, work to last 16 (17, 17, 18) sts, BO 14 sts, p1 (2, 2, 3), k1.

Join Pocket Lining:
Row 1 (WS): P1, k1 (2, 2, 3); working across sts from first holder, k4, p6, k4; work to next BO sts; working across sts from second holder, k4, p6, k4, k1 (2, 2, 3), p1.
Row 2: K1, p5 (6, 6, 7), work 6 sts in Cable Pattern, *purl to 1 st before marker, m1p, p1, sm, p1, m1p-L; repeat from * once, purl to last 12 (13, 13, 14) sts, work 6 sts in Cable Pattern, p5 (6, 6, 7), k1—80 (88, 92, 96) sts. Work even until piece measures 10½" from the beginning, ending with a RS row.

Shape Armholes (WS): *Work to 2 sts before marker, BO 4 sts, removing marker; repeat from * once, work to end—72 (80, 84, 88) sts remain.
Set aside, but do not break yarn.

Sleeves (make 2)
Using 4 strands of yarn held together, CO 16 (16, 20, 20) sts.

Begin 2x2 Rib:
Row 1 (WS): P1 (edge st, keep in St st), work in 2x2 Rib to last st, p1 (edge st, keep in St st).
Row 2: K1 (edge st, keep in St st), work in 2x2 Rib to last st, k1 (edge st, keep in St st). Work even for 10 rows.
Change to Rev St st, increase 3 sts across first row—19 (19, 23, 23) sts. Work even for 1 row.

Shape Sleeve (RS): Increase 1 st each side this row, then every 8 (6, 8, 6) rows 4 (6, 5, 6) times—29 (33, 35, 37) sts. Work even until piece measures 17½" from the beginning, ending with a RS row.

Shape Cap (WS): BO 2 sts at beginning of next 2 rows—25 (29, 31, 33) sts remain. Break yarn and set aside.

Yoke
Using yarn attached to Body, and continuing pattern as established, work across 17 (19, 20, 21) sts for Right Front, pm, 25 (29, 31, 33) sts for right Sleeve, pm, 38 (42, 44, 46) sts for Back, pm, 25 (29, 31, 33) sts for Left Sleeve, pm, and 17 (19, 20, 21) sts for Left Front—122 (138, 146, 154) sts. Work even for 3 rows.

Shape Yoke (RS): Decrease 8 sts this row, then every other row 6 (8, 8, 9) times, as follows: *Work to 3 sts before marker, p2tog-tbl, p1, sm, p1, p2tog; repeat from * 3 times, work to end—66 (66, 74, 74) sts remain. Work even for 1 row.

Next Row (RS): Decrease 4 sts this row, then every other row 0 (0, 1, 1) time, as follows: *Work to second marker, p1, p2tog, work to 3 sts before third marker, p2tog-tbl, work to end—62 (62, 66, 66) sts remain. Work even for 1 row.

Begin Collar (RS): Change to 2x2 Rib, as follows: K2, *p2, k2; repeat from * across. Work even until Collar measures 10", ending with a WS row. BO all sts in pattern.

FINISHING
Button Band: RS facing, pick up and knit 66 (70, 70, 74) sts along Left Front. Begin 2x2 Rib: Work even for 7 rows. BO all sts in pattern. Place markers for 10 buttons, the first and last ½" from the bottom and top, and the remaining 8 evenly spaced between.

Buttonhole Band: Work as for Button Band, working buttonholes on Row 5 (RS) opposite button markers, as follows: Yo, work 2 sts together (k2tog if second st is a knit st; p2tog if second st is a purl st).
Sew Pocket Linings to WS, being careful not to let sts show on RS. Sew side, underarm and Sleeve seams. Weave in all loose ends. Block to finished measurements. Sew on buttons at markers.

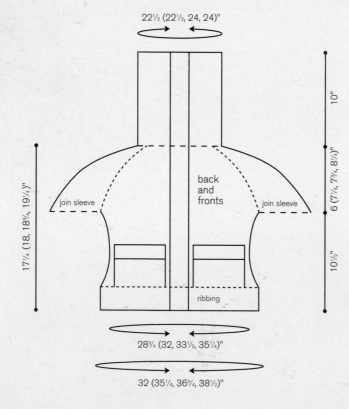

22½ (22½, 24, 24)"

17¼ (18, 18¾, 19¼)"

join sleeve   back and fronts   join sleeve

10"

6 (7¼, 7¾, 8¼)"

10½"

28¾ (32, 33½, 35¼)"

32 (35¼, 36¾, 38½)"

ribbing

11½ (13¼, 14, 14¾)"

sleeve

17½"

6½ (6½, 8, 8)"

ribbing

Wenlan's drawing later inspired dress prints and rug patterns.

Dave
Cole

On the second floor of the twelve-hundred-square-foot Providence studio where he works full-time and sometimes sleeps, Dave Cole keeps a small baby blanket inside a glass display case. Because he knit the piece with spun porcelain, which is carcinogenic, yellow signs that read "Warning: Cancer and Lung Disease Hazard," and "Do Not Open Without Approved Respirator" are placed around the object. Across the room, Dave stores an abundant collection of knitting needles, including custom needles made from found Beaver skulls and white pine. Nearby he keeps a group of special tools that he uses to custom-make yarn, like a plate cutter that can cut license plates into knittable ribbon, and an orthopedic device, which consists of a four-legged geriatric cane with a jewelers vice clamped to the top and a hand drill locked in the vice. A wooden spindle chucked into the drill allows Dave to spin steel wool into yarn. Scattered throughout his studio are remnants of other materials Dave has knit with, like lead, Kevlar, filter media (normally used to clean pools), shredded dollar bills, and rubber, but there is no cotton, wool, or mohair yarn anywhere in his space.

There are myriad difficulties to overcome when knitting with heavy, toxic, industrial, or otherwise unusual materials, but those difficulties are what make Dave's finished projects into what he calls "conceptually driven sculpture." To knit a piece titled "Money Gown," for example, Dave first made yarn from one thousand dollar bills by stapling eight stacked dollar bills together and then cutting a long, thin spiral ending at the center of the bills. He repeated this action over one hundred times before he could even start knitting the pattern, a Vera Wang evening gown. Though knitting projects often require countless repetitive motions, Dave's sculptures are such time-consuming and laboriously difficult tests of his own perseverance that they border

on the obsessive. He seeks to provoke a response that progresses from intrigue over his unusual material choices to a sense of wonder at the labor involved. Dave's early forays into knitting were linked to productivity. Diagnosed with Attention Deficit Hyperactivity Disorder when he was young, Dave had an extremely difficult time being productive in school. After learning and applying studying methods that helped him become a better student, Dave completed two successful years at Landmark College, the premier school for students with learning disabilities. The summer after his second year at Landmark, Dave led workshops for teachers on how to educate students with disabilities. Vicki Dim Williams, a Minnesotan Hebrew teacher in the summer workshop taught him how to knit, remarking, "If I can teach hyperactive four-year-old boys how to knit, I can teach you." Dave used the craft as a way to stay focused during lecture classes when he started

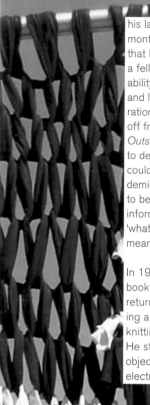

his last two years of college at Brown University a few months later. It was during his first semester at Brown that Dave formed a close bond with Jonathan Mooney, a fellow college transfer who also had a learning disability. An independent study they created on schools and learning disabilities developed into a larger exploration of the topic; they ended up taking a semester off from school to co-write a book called *Learning Outside the Lines*. A primary objective of the book was to demonstrate how people with learning disabilities could succeed in school. Writing about his early academic failures forced Dave to articulate what it meant to be focused and dedicated to a task, and that later informed his ideas for art projects. "I had to ask myself, 'what does it mean to be productive?' 'What does it mean to be creative?'" Dave explains.

In 1998, immediately after Dave finished writing the book (which was published by Fireside in 2000), he returned to Brown. Knitting hats in classes after writing a book about productivity led Dave to think about knitting more abstractly, as a metaphor for production. He started knitting ridiculously impractical familiar objects through obsessive efforts, like a queen-sized electric blanket knit from contractor's cord, a sweater

made of Kevlar (commonly used in bulletproof vests), and a bowl knit out of cut license plates. Dave was able to thwart the objects' usefulness while expressing a kind of thoughtful gloom about what it means to work towards an absurd goal. Dave says that knitting reflects the obsessive drudgery he remembers from school, and the inefficacy of his toils. He has also said that all of his knitting goes back to the special ed room. Dave's own personality, intense and willful, is reflected in the work, as well as his skill: The work is impeccably made.

Though many of his pieces have required spectacular or theatrical feats of labor, Dave insists that his sculpture is not about performance or about subverting associations of knitting as women's work. "It's about the creation of an object rather than the carrying out of an action," he explains. "It's about presenting contradictory ideas in a single form, and co-opting the craft to move into bigger, louder, more toxic and heavy-duty materials." For the knitted teddy bear he made in 2003, Dave first unrolled a sixteen foot length of paperbacked fiberglass, which he cut in half lengthwise with a utility knife attached to a mop handle. He then turned both halves of the fiberglass over, spread contact cement on them, and joined the two pieces to make double-sided yarn. He had to do this one hundred and seventy five times to have enough yarn to knit a fourteen foot tall, twelve hundred pound sculpture. Though his bear is cute, pink, and soft-looking, it's also oversized and untouchable: installers had to wear respirators, gloves, and goggles when they put the figure together from eight separate pieces. The Knitting Machine, a project he undertook the summer of 2005 for Mass MoCA, a contemporary art museum in North Adams, Massachusetts, offered an eight hundred stitch, thirty-five-by-twenty foot American flag made from acrylic felt. While one viewer might have seen his flag as a commentary on aggressive U.S. foreign policy, another could have interpreted it as a patriotic, Fourth of July gesture. As Dave says, "The flag is a promise and a threat." Digging deeper, one could read the piece as a commentary on how work and production relate to the machine, and how the machine relates to national identity.

Dave estimates that the project, which required two John Deere excavators, a cherry picker, two twenty-five-foot aluminum poles, over a mile of red, white, and blue acrylic felt, and a crochet hook made from an upside-down bike storage hook attached to a pole, utilized three quarters of a million dollars worth of equipment. Construction of the piece was done by two friends who manned the excavators while Dave directed their stitches from inside a cherry picker thirty feet above the ground. He explains that he purled the entire piece: "I was purling ambidextrously in both directions because I didn't want to have to move the machines to do the next row." If a stitch was dropped or knit incorrectly, Dave used his homemade crochet hook to fix the problem. The completed flag was left on its needles for a few days, then bound off into the back of a pickup truck, folded into a traditional triangle, and kept in a five-by-ten-foot display case at the museum.

Dave's next big project is a gigantic mobile taller than the Statue of Liberty and made from eight antique pickup trucks. Dave says that it helps him to work through smaller studio pieces by having an enormous challenge looming in the future, and this project may take decades to fundraise. A permanent sculpture resting on a yet-to-be-determined hilltop, the piece will require a team of structural engineers and architects, and millions of dollars to execute.

Both pages:
The Knitting Machine installation at Mass MoCa in North Adams, Massachusetts, 2005.

Fiberglass Teddy Bear

This is the pattern I used to knit the giant fiberglass teddy bear that I installed as a part of the Decordova Museum's 2003 Annual. The final assembled piece was fourteen feet tall and covered 256 square feet. It was made out of 175 (16-foot) rolls of fiberglass. The bear was knit flat in eight pieces and then stuffed and assembled in the space. Due to the extreme gauge of the stitches (four linear feet of material per stitch) needles were not needed to hold the stitches open. Instead, I knit kneeling on the floor, using my arms to make the stitches.

The body was assembled around an armature to support the four-hundred-pound head, which had to be dragged into place up an improvised ramp. Since the pieces together weighed more than half a ton, they were wrapped individually in tarps, and loaded onto cargo trucks with a crane before being driven to the museum.

As appealingly pink and apparently soft as fiberglass is, working with it is difficult, hazardous, and extremely unpleasant. All of the dozen or so people who helped install this piece spent the entire time in Tyvek Coveralls and wearing respirators, gloves, and goggles.

This installation was made possible by the generosity of Dr. Armand Versaci and Mr. John Carter, and also could not have happened without the support of Mr. Clayton Anderson Rockefeller and The Steelyard.

— **Dave Cole**

MATERIALS

362 rolls Owens Corning R13 PINK Fiber Glass
 Insulation, kraft-faced (23" wide x 93" long x 3½" thick)
350' kraft paper, 2' wide
9 gallons neoprene rubber contact adhesive, water-based
2 gallons urethane sealant, water-based
NOSH-approved respirator equipped with organic vapor/
 acid gas cartridges specifically approved for use with
 formaldehyde; P98 particulate pre-filters for same
Lead wool, for stuffing
Utility knife lashed to broom handle, plus extra blades

GAUGE

1 st = 2' wide x 2½' high in Stockinette stitch (St st)

BEAR

Preparing the Materials

It is the kraft paper backing on the rolls of insulation that provides the tensile strength of the yarn; the fiberglass alone is so
fragile as to be unworkable. In order to create yarn, each roll of
insulation must be cut in half along its entire length and glued
paper-side to paper-side. The lengths of insulation also need to
be spliced end-to-end with each other.

1. Unroll insulation.
2. Using a utility knife lashed firmly to a broom
   handle, cut through fiberglass lengthwise. Blade
   will most likely need to be changed after every roll.
3. Flip roll, exposing kraft paper backing.
4. Apply contact adhesive to entire kraft paper
   backside of insulation.
5. Spread adhesive on scrap pieces of kraft paper
   approximately 2' square, 1 piece per roll of
   insulation. These will be the splices that connect
   one roll to the next.
6. When adhesive has dried completely, adhere splice
   paper to one end of the insulation roll, leaving half
   of the paper overhanging the end of the roll to
   connect to the next roll. Fold roll in half lengthwise,
   gluing backing to backing, resulting in a fiberglass
   rope 93" long with a cross section approximately
   7½" thick, and with a core of two layers of paper
   and glue.

Repeat Steps 1-6 361 times.

*Note: Dave built two giant corrugated cardboard structural cubes
to serve as an internal armature, which supported the 400-pound
head. After the armature was in place, he wrapped the body piece
around the armature and stuffed the belly, then attached the previously stuffed legs and arms to the body. He then assembled the
head with the ears in place and slid it up a 16' ramp onto the body
with the assistance of eight fully outfitted workers.*

Body

CO 8 sts.
Row 1 (WS): Purl.
Row 2: K1, *m1, k1; repeat from * to end—15 sts.
Rows 3-9: Work even in St st.

Shape Neck

Row 10: K1, [k2tog] twice, k5, [k2tog] twice, k1—11 sts remain.
Row 11: P1, [p2tog] twice, p1, [p2tog] twice, p1—7 sts remain.
Break yarn, thread through remaining sts, pull tight and fasten
off. Sew sides together (this will become the back seam), stuffing the piece as you sew.

Head

CO 6 sts.
Row 1 (WS): Purl.
Row 2: K2, [m1, k2] twice—8 sts.
Rows 3, 5, and 7: Purl.
Row 4: K3, m1, k2, m1, k3—10 sts.
Row 6: K2, m1, k1, m1, k4, m1, k1, m1, k2—14 sts.
Rows 7-9: Work even in St st.
Row 10: [K1, k2tog] twice, k2tog, [k2tog, k1] twice—9 sts remain.
Row 11: P1, *p2tog; repeat from * across—5 sts remain.
Break yarn, thread through remaining sts, pull tight and
fasten off. Sew sides together, stuffing the piece as you sew.

Ears (make 2)

CO 3 sts.
Row 1 (WS): Purl.
Row 2: Knit.
Row 3: Purl.
BO all sts purlwise. Sew CO sts to BO sts. Sew sides closed.

Right Leg

CO 8 sts.
Row 1 (WS): Purl.
Row 2: Knit.
Row 3: Purl.
Shape Foot
Row 4: K2, sk2p, k3—6 sts remain.
Rows 5-10: Work even in St st. Break yarn, thread through
remaining sts, pull tight and fasten off. Sew sides together,
stuffing the piece as you sew.

Left Leg

Work as for Right Leg to beginning of shaping.
Row 4 (RS): K3, sk2p, k2—6 sts remain. Complete as for
Right Leg.

Arms (make 2)

CO 5 sts. (WS) Begin St st; work even for 9 rows.
Break yarn, thread through remaining sts, pull tight and
fasten off. Sew sides together, stuffing the piece as you sew.

FINISHING

Sew Ears to top of Head. Sew Head to top of Body. Sew Arms
to top sides of Body, below Head. Sew Legs to bottom sides of
Body, towards the Back.

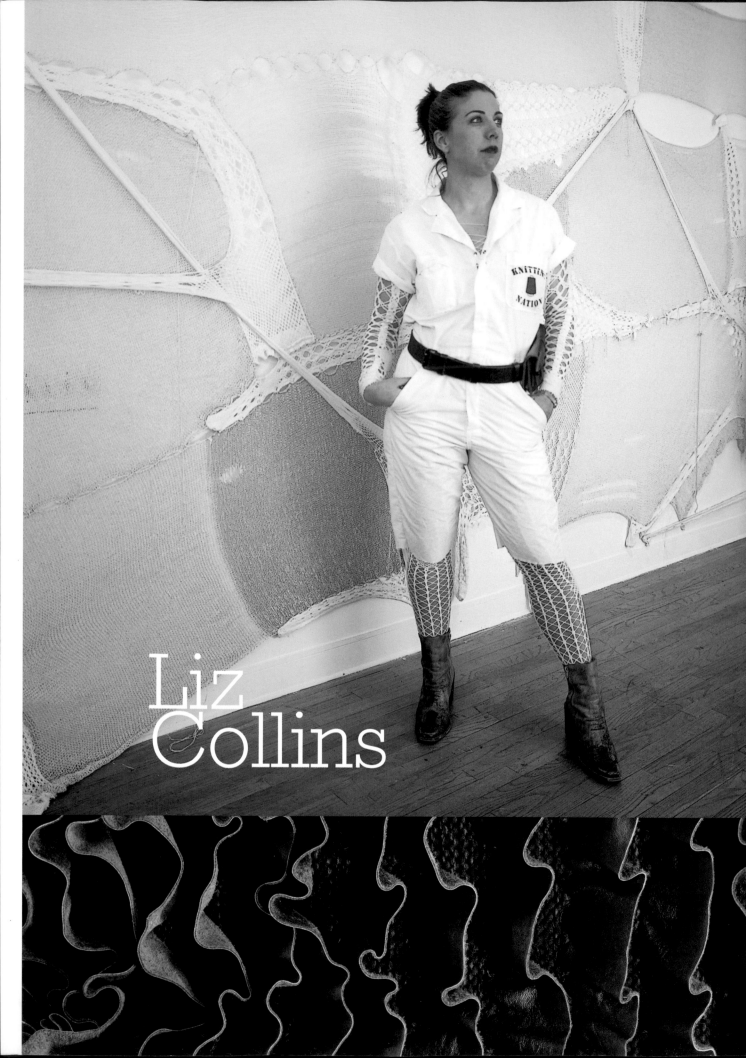

Liz
Collins

One sunny May day in 2005, on Governors Island, the former national military post in New York Harbor, Liz Collins, her colleague Elyse Allen, and her current and former students from the Rhode Island School of Design (RISD) knit as an army under a tent encampment made of cream-colored knitted fabric. Next to them, an art critic and historian, Julia Bryon Wilson, wearing an extravagantly deconstructed American flag, sat on a stool reading knitting chants from the Civil War era, as well as articles from the *New York Times* and *Women's Wear Daily* on textile and apparel manufacturing and trade. The performance, called *Knitting During Wartime,* unified Liz's roles as a fashion designer, fine artist, and textile educator. Dressed in the stylish uniform she designed for herself and her knitters—white knitted tights on her arms and legs, and white cut-off coveralls with an insignia of knitting needles and a yarn cone silk-screened onto the back—Liz worked for most of the day in a trancelike state at a manually operated knitting machine, clearly enjoying its rhythmic clanging. Occasionally, she would pause to chat amiably with her crew or to inspect the emerging lengths of red, white, and blue knitted fabric that grew to spread across the grassy lawn into what loosely resembled an American flag.

After she received her BFA in textiles from RISD in 1991, Liz moved to New York City to work as a hand weaver for the fashion industry, where she made what are called handlooms: swatches of machine-woven yardage that are shown to potential customers. Two years later, she returned to Providence. "I didn't like my path," she explains. "I wanted more freedom. I didn't know if I wanted to be an artist or a designer, and I thought I had to decide one way or another." Liz had learned to knit from her New York City loftmate Olivia Eaton a year before, and she turned to it again during her first Providence winter in 1993, when she started knitting with her friends. "Knitting felt like a missing piece of me and my creativity, and I felt a rush of possibilities," she says. In 1994, Liz and a friend opened a boutique in Providence, Planet 7, where they sold a line of clothing they designed and made together under the same name. They also sold Liz's own knitwear, then called Warp. Liz sold her hand-knit clothes to a boutique in New York City, too, and received an invitation from Patricia Field, a Hollywood stylist and boutique owner, for a retail opportunity. But Liz wasn't ready to manufacture clothing then, and she had to turn it down.

In 1997, a year after Planet 7 closed, Liz went back to RISD for a graduate degree in textiles. "I was doing all hand-knitting, and I realized that I had to learn knitting machines," Liz explains. "I also thought that I could use those two years at school as research and development for a business, as well as for personal and creative development. It totally transformed me." Working on manually operated knitting machines, Liz found that she could attach fabrics to each other during knitting, fusing one layer to another for the purpose of seaming, creating layers, building forms, and embellishing in a process she calls knit grafting. "It was a form of alchemy—turning simple cones of yarn into three-dimensional, multilayered, and wearable pieces in a very short time frame," she writes in an artist statement. During her time in graduate school, Liz created an extensive sample library of machine-knit fabrics and experimental garments that fueled the development of knitwear collections for the high fashion market, which is where she took her work immediately upon receiving her degree in 1999. Her first step was Manhattan's East Village boutique, Horn, owned by designer Miguel Adrover, where pieces by Tess Giberson, As Four, and Alexander McQueen were sold.

During the next four years, Liz presented highly acclaimed runway shows, developing knitwear with sensual qualities, clever constructions, and nostalgic silhouettes. Her collections featured machine-knit items such as sock monkeys sewn into a stole, cashmere baseball sweaters, and single-sleeved white dresses reminiscent of Greek tunics. Her experimentation with strategic shrinking methods and materials like reflective safety yarn, digitally imaged fabrics, crocheted lace, leather, and fur inspired some reviewers to describe her work as neo-punk, organic, and gothic. She built a reputation as an inventive designer of knits that could be worn upside down or backward, allowing the wearer some control over how the piece looked on his or her own body. Liz herself describes that clothing as transformative—it could make the wearer into someone else. "I'm interested in the human as a creature, and I believe that certain clothing allows people to experience creature-like transformations," she explains. "To this end, I build fabrics and pieces that have gill-like insets, thorny spines, and armadillo-like protective leather shells, with breathable, flexible knit cores close to the skin."

After five years of fashion industry success, during which Liz's designs were featured in a range of international publications and sold in boutiques around the world, she decided to make a change. She found that running an independent clothing business was taking too much time away from the actual act of creating. Liz

accepted a job as an assistant professor in the textile department at her alma mater in 2003, and since then she has focused on teaching textiles, designing garments, and developing fine art projects and performances. She teaches a range of classes and initiates projects in which her students are able to interact with the fashion industry. In 2005 and 2006, for example, her students redesigned the DKNY Cozy, a hybrid sweater/shawl and one of that company's most successful garments.

As a freelance designer, Liz creates knit prototypes and collections for other fashion designers. "It's so exciting to me," Liz says. "I don't have to worry about production as much. I can concentrate on the pure design aspect." Simultaneously, Liz designs her own small collections, which she sells at a few select boutiques, trunk sales, and art exhibitions.

The idea for knitting performances began to emerge in 2002 during a series of conversations with friend and fellow independent fashion designer Gary Graham. "We felt we needed to create an outlet for our aggressions and a platform to reveal the raw, creative energy and the labor-intensive processes that were part of our work," Liz recalls. When artist Allison Smith announced her public art project, The Muster (supported by the Public Art Fund, a nonprofit organization that presents contemporary art in public spaces), which was a one-day, open-air public event in which over seventy volunteers created campsites on Governors Island dedicated to their personal causes, Liz decided it was the perfect platform to launch a series of knitting machine performances she calls Knitting Nation. "This particular context inspired me to explore the history of knitting

and to use the piece to comment on the Iraq war," Liz explains. "I was inspired by the military aspects of The Muster and the request to present something I was fighting for. I wanted people to think about the flag; I wanted to deface it in my own way by creating it in a mutated state with human hands and then allowing it to drag across the ground. I wanted people to see how the fabric is made, to think about the people who work in this very physically taxing manner to produce textiles and clothing for our backs and for our soldiers' backs. Another piece of the story was the challenge of our global economy—the supply-and-demand market of excess that drives factories to open and close depending on the whims of the marketplace and the drive for cheaper goods." Added to the multifaceted political messages were Liz's interests in humans' relationships to machines, and in exposing the public to the process of machine-knitting, which she calls "beautiful and noisy alchemy."

After the success of her knitting machine performance at Governors Island in 2005, Liz decided to try it again in another forum: as a residency, installation, and trunk show at the Felissimo Design House in Midtown Manhattan during fashion's fall 2006 runway season. For one week, she and a team of uniformed knitters created garments in the space that were exhibited and sold on site. In 2005, Liz presented a solo show of garments at the Knoxville Museum of Art, and exhibited a large machine-knitted wall piece at the Deutsche Bank's Manhattan building gallery, in a group show called Woven. Liz has plans to continue Knitting Nation as an ongoing and collaborative project, laying bare the process of knitting and continuing to explore the meanings associated with building knitted fabric structures.

Facing page
Vein Bustier, 1999. Hand-painted cotton sheeting with machine-knit wool, plastic, rayon, and silk.

This page
Liz's performance piece, Knitting Nation, created for The Muster (A Project of the Public Art Fund by Allison Smith, 2005) on Governors Island in New York City.

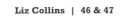

Stretchy Stocking Top/Dress

How many stockings, tights, and hose do you throw away every year? And what about those wacky hot pink, leopard-print tights that you keep in your drawer because you love the idea of them, but you never wear them? Instead of tossing those trashed or tired tights, put them in a special box and save them until you have several pairs for this wild, hand-knit, super-stretchy wearable. The colors and textures of your piece will be determined by the stockings you have on hand. If you do not have enough stockings to get started, supplement by buying more at the dollar or thrift store, or asking friends for their rejects.

— Liz Collins

SIZES
To fit 32-34 (36-38)" chest

FINISHED MEASUREMENTS
Approximately 30 (34)" chest, unstretched

YARN
Approximately 20 (25) pairs of stockings, hose, and/or tights. *Note: Knee-highs will work, too, but yield shorter lengths of yarn. The piece shown is made primarily with panty hose, with a few pairs of colored stockings and fishnets thrown in for color and texture.*

NEEDLES
One pair straight needles size US 35 (19 mm)
Change needle size if necessary to obtain correct gauge.

NOTIONS
Sharp scissors, crochet hook size US S (19 mm); extra-large tapestry needle (optional)

GAUGE
3¾ sts and 6 rows = 4" (10 cm) in Reverse Stockinette stitch (Rev St st)

STITCH PATTERN
2x2 Rib
(multiple of 4 sts + 2; 2-row repeat)
Row 1 (WS): K2, *p2, k2; repeat from * across.
Row 2: Knit the knit sts, and purl the purl sts as they face you.
Repeat Row 2 for 2x2 Rib.

DRESS
Preparing the Yarn
Cut out the crotch of the stocking, hose, and/or tights. Cut open the toes. Cut 1 continuous strip of material at least 1" wide, as follows: Beginning at the center seam of the waistband, *cut lengthwise to 1" from the toe (do not cut all the way through the toe), turn and, beginning at the toe, 1" to the left of the first cut, cut another strip to 1" from the waistband (do not cut all the way through the waistband), turn; repeat from * for as long as you can. Try to keep strips at least 1" wide. Narrower strips might break or be too thin for the project. If you cut narrower widths, be sure to use smaller needles.

Tie sections together with a simple knot and wind into a ball as you go. The knots can be very clean and small, or you can make bigger knots with more ends. If you like the fringy, wild look, you can keep longer ends to the knots. You may also go back and trim too-long ends later, when the piece is finished.

Front Panel
CO 14 (16) sts. Begin 2x2 Rib; work even for 20 (22) rows.

Next Row (WS): Change to Rev St st, beg with a knit row. Work even for 14 rows.

Shape Armholes (WS): Decrease 1 st each side this row, then every other row once, as follows: K2tog, knit to last 2 sts, k2tog–10 (12) sts remain.

Shape Neck (RS): Decrease 1 st each neck edge this row, then every other row once, as follows: P3, p2tog, join a second ball of yarn, p2tog, purl to end–3 (4) sts remain each side. Work even for 4 rows. BO all sts.

Back Panel
Work as for Front Panel through Armhole Shaping, ending with a WS row–10 (12) sts remain. Work even for 4 (6) rows.

Shape Neck (WS): K3 (4), BO 4 sts, k3 (4)–3 (4) sts remain each side for shoulders.
Working each side separately, work even for 2 rows. BO all sts.

FINISHING
Sew shoulder seams. Sew side seams.

Armhole Edging: Using crochet hook, work 1 rnd single crochet around armhole edges.

Neck Edging: Using crochet hook, work 1 rnd single crochet around neck edge.

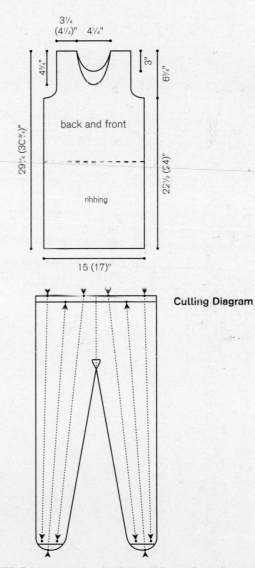

Culling Diagram

NOTE: Beginning and ending points will vary, depending on the size of the stockings used. Always begin each cut at the edge, and end each cut approximately 1" from the edge as shown.

In 2000, two years after he received his BFA in sculpture from the Rhode Island School of Design (RISD), Jim Drain moved back into Fort Thunder, the 9,000-square-foot warehouse in Providence where he had lived from 1996 to 1998. At Fort Thunder, each of the about twenty-five resident artists had a dedicated skill set they practiced tenaciously in hand-crafted spaces adorned with layers of found trash staple-gunned and plastered to the walls—Jim's specialty became machine-knitting. "After I moved in, I wanted to learn a technique and get really good at it so that I could contribute in some way," says Jim, now well-known for his raw, gaudy, machine-knitted sculptures. "Also, I was just out of school, and I was all over the place. I wanted focus."

During his first year back at Fort Thunder, Jim got two artists who had made drawings and music together under the name Forcefield to start up new projects. Jim and another Fort Thunder resident joined the duo, and the foursome expanded into other media including video and performance art. In keeping with Fort Thunder's predominant aesthetic, Forcefield created artwork out of refuse found around town as well as from the sorts of dark, psychedelic, and disorienting stuff they imagined might come from some unknown place very far away. Their artwork was alternately frightening, silly, hallucinogenic, and cryptic—take, for example, *Warm Up,* a 2002 video in which three Forcefield members wearing full-bodied knit suits are animated by repeated zoom cuts and a thronging electronic soundtrack. During music performances, the four members of Forcefield wore face-obscuring outfits made from handmade afghans purchased at local thrift stores. When the group found themselves depleted of afghans, Jim decided that he could knit new fabric. Knitting would be his dedicated skill; something he could contribute to Fort Thunder. Because Providence had once been a booming textile mill town, places to find inexpensize yarn were plentiful. As Jim puts it, "Knitting was salvaging."

Jim turned to his friend and fellow RISD graduate Elyse Allen for knitting lessons. She taught him some of the things she had learned as a textile major, like how to make a knitted swatch with a manually operated knitting machine. She also tutored him in different yarn qualities and let him practice on her knitting machine while she worked at a rug repair company. Jim took his swatches to Liz Collins (see page 44), a knitwear designer and artist who lived nearby, and asked her how to make them into garments. She outlined the options. "I had no idea what she was talking about," Jim says. Because Jim wanted to make things as quickly as possible for Forcefield's one-night shows and video shoots, "getting techie seemed like a waste of time," he says. He found that when he cut his knitted fabric, it would fray and unravel, so he hand-sewed and hot-glued seams together.

In one prolific year, Jim and the other members of Forcefield created four elaborate sets of machine-knit "costumes"—a provisional term with which Jim is not totally comfortable. "It's not like Forcefield set out to make costumes," he said in an interview published in *KnitKnit's* premiere issue, "it just sort of came out of what we were doing, [which was creating] a painful excitement." The first set of outfits was knit with dizzying patterns in bright colors meant to saturate the videos in which the members starred. The second set was for a series of work they referred to as their "darkly shrouded assassin period," in which the knit clothing was dark and gothic. The third marked a depletion of "neon" yarn; through being forced to figure out how to create fluorescent colors, they came up with autumnal combinations. The fourth and final set of costumes could be called the "black rainbow group." Though Jim was the main creator of the clothing, fellow members of Forcefield made individual adjustments, and with Forcefield, it was always hard to discern who was responsible for what artwork.

In 2001, Fort Thunder inhabitants started a long eviction process—their building was going to be torn down for the creation of a shopping center—and Jim moved into a nearby apartment with his friend Elyse. They started collaborating under the name Happy Banana to machine-knit armbands, hats, tops, banana warmers, and other garments first for friends, then for *Nylon* magazine, and finally for the annual RISD alumni art sale. The same year, Jim taught himself the basics of

Facing page
Jim in his Miami art studio.

Above
A machine-knitted Forcefield costume, 2002.

hand-knitting during a two-week trip to China. "I think I got treated a whole lot better because I was hand-knitting." he says. "I would go to yarn shops in Beijing, and everyone was so nice and helpful. There were places all over where you could get a custom sweater made. I was only in China for two weeks, but I'm still talking about it. Being there made me realize that knitting is a living tradition—it's physical knowledge of a culture. Knowledge as language dies so quickly. It's awesome to find a sweater and look at the language of it—to see how it's made, what yarn is used, and how problems were solved. A sweater is a form of consciousness."

When Jim returned from China, Forcefield was invited to participate in the 2002 Whitney Biennial, generally regarded as one of the leading shows in the contemporary art world. Their installation, titled Third Annual Roggabogga, was a room filled with elaborately constructed knit costumes, nomadic-looking sculptures, overstimulating silkscreened wallpaper, a psychedelic projected video, and electronic audio works, all encountered in dim light. It became one of the signature pieces of the exhibition.

After the show, Forcefield disbanded, and Jim took a break from knitting for about a year. "I needed to separate from the Forcefield stuff," he says. From 2003 to 2005, Jim made large-scale, psychedelic sculptures in collaboration with artist Eamon Brown and with fellow ex-Forcefield member Ara Peterson. He also made artwork on his own and knitted a few outfits for the band Erase Errata. "It was a tough few years," Jim says. "Bush got reelected, my aunt died, an uncle close to me died, and Forcefield died too." He was shocked when what he describes as his mourning sculptures—large machine-knit sculptures made in a gray palette—won the prestigious Baloise Art Prize at the 2005 Basel Art Fair. The juried prize came with abundant press, prestige, and money.

Jim moved from Providence to Miami in early 2006, where he set up a studio with three other artists in a space donated by a Miami art collector. Located on the second floor of a building inside the heart of Miami's high-end furniture district, the studio space is about 2,000 square feet and divided into three sections with a small exhibition area in the front.

When he works, Jim wears noise-canceling head phones so that he can "zone out," but when his headphones are off, Jim talks to his studio mates or to his RISD grad assistants in halting, poetic sentences. He has a sly sense of humor and dresses in eye-popping patterns so conflicting they actually match. Though Jim sort of looks like some of his knit sculptures, he stresses that he does not want to be known just as a "knit sculptor." He spends a lot of time drawing, painting, and working with appliqué and embroidery, among other mediums, and is learning more advanced hand-knitting techniques. "Knitting has been helpful and informative in how I approach all of my materials, so I don't see it moving out of my practice any time soon," says Jim. "But I'm interested in the differences between machine- and hand-knitting, and want to utilize both in new sculpture projects. With machine-knitting, you're making decisions row by row, but with hand-knitting, you make decisions stitch by stitch. Machine-knit stitches are so uniform, but I like that you can get inconsistencies with hand-knitting, and want to exploit that in future projects."

Sweatshirt Kimono

Here was a chance to combine the best of three worlds: hand-made world with sweatshirt world and kimono world. What came out is maybe the weird offspring of these three. It is a bit knightly. It brings the conquistador blood out of Genaro, the model. I tried using the ribbon that Liz Collins gave to me a few years ago. It was knit loosely to keep the garment breathable. The ribbon is fantastic: elastic, soft, strong, and with the most perfect blend of beige and red. Everything to like about Italians rolled up in a ribbon. Combined with this is a glittery viscose fiber, an unnecessary thing and a pain to hand-knit with (according to Emily Drury, who knit this piece for me), but it adds the magic (or at least the novelty of "novelty yarn"). One suggestion in hindsight: It might be better to get a yarn with a glitter already within the yarn. That way, the glitter won't get in the needles' way. The linen was used to add a bit of structure to the garment. I knew it would also create a flat plane where the ribbon would be more voluminous. Plus, linen is such a great material. It's so soft and durable. I plan to wear this Sweatshirt Kimono every day.

— **Jim Drain**

FINISHED MEASUREMENTS
40½" chest

YARN
1300 yards ³⁄₁₆" wide ribbon yarn with a horizontal binder in red/beige (MC) (see sample on page 57)
1300 yards metallic thread in pink (A)
Valley Yarns ¹⁰⁄₂ Dyed Linen (100% linen; 825 yards / 8.8 oz): #2635 red (B), #2628 bright purple (C), and dark natural (D), 1 tube each
Note: As an alternative to combining a ribbon yarn with a metallic thread, you may want to substitute a ribbon yarn with a metallic thread already running through it (such as Louisa Harding Glisten or Gerifil Scarabeo). The ribbon used in Jim's sample came from Lineapiù but is no longer available.

NEEDLES
One pair straight needles size US 11 (8 mm)
One pair straight needles size US 7 (4.5 mm)
Change needle size if necessary to obtain correct gauge.

NOTIONS
Crochet hook size US H/8 (5 mm); stitch holders; stitch markers

GAUGE
12 sts and 23 rows = 4" (10 cm) in Garter stitch (knit every row) using larger needles and 1 strand each of MC and A held together
16 sts and 32 rows = 4" (10 cm) in Garter stitch using smaller needles and B

NOTES
This Sweatshirt Kimono is worked entirely in Garter Stitch. Body is made up of three pieces, the Back/Front Placket, the Bottom Front, and the Hood, which is picked up and worked up from the Back. The Back/Front Placket and Bottom Front are sewn together in the center front. Side Panels are picked up and worked out from these two pieces, and the Sleeves are then worked down from the Side Panels (see schematic).

SWEATSHIRT
Back/Front Placket
Using larger needles and 1 strand each of MC and A held together, CO 46 sts. Begin Garter st (knit every row); work even until piece measures 30" from the beginning.

Shape Neck (RS): K9, place next 28 sts on holder for hood, join a second ball of yarn, knit to end–9 sts remain each side. Working both sides at same time, work even for 2½", ending with a RS row.

Establish Front Placket (WS): K9, CO 28 sts for Front Placket, k9, breaking second ball of yarn–46 sts. Work even for 2½", ending with a WS row. Place markers each side for finishing.

Shape Front Placket (RS): Decrease 1 st at beginning of next 44 rows–2 sts remain.
K2tog–1 st remains. Break yarn, thread through remaining st, pull tight and fasten off.

Hood
RS facing, using larger needles and 1 strand each of MC and A held together, pick up and knit 9 sts along right neck edge, work across 28 sts from holder, pick up and knit 9 sts along left neck edge–46 sts. Work even until piece measures 10" from pick-up row, ending with a WS row. Place marker each side for finishing.

Shape Hood (RS): Decrease 2 sts each side this row, then next 5 rows, as follows: K3tog, work to last 3 sts, k3tog–22 sts remain. BO all sts.

Bottom Front
Using larger needles and 1 strand each of MC and A held together, CO 46 sts. Begin Garter st; work even until piece measures 11" from the beginning.

Shape Front Vee (RS): K23, join a second ball of yarn and knit to end. Working both sides at same time, work even for 1 row.

Decrease Row (RS): Decrease 1 st each neck edge this row, then every 3 rows 21 times–1 st remains each side. Break yarn, thread through remaining st, pull tight and fasten off.

Establish Stripes (RS): RS facing, using smaller needles and 1 strand of B, beginning at left point of Vee, pick up and knit 42 sts along left inside edge of Vee, 1 st in center, then 42 sts along right inside edge of Vee–85 sts. *Knit 1 row.
Next Row (RS): K1, m1, k40, sk2p, k40, m1, k1. Knit 1 row. Repeat last 2 rows twice.*
Change to C. Repeat from * to *.
Change to D. Repeat from * to *. BO all sts.
Sew Front Placket to Bottom Front, matching markers on Front Placket to points of Vee (see Assembly Diagram).

Side Panels (make 2)
RS of Back and Front facing, using smaller needles and 1 strand of C, pick up and knit 210 sts along entire side edge. Begin Garter st; work even until piece measures 2½" from pick-up row. BO 75 sts, work across 60 sts and place on holder for Sleeve, BO remaining 75 sts.

Sleeves (make 2)
Using larger needles and 1 strand each of MC and A held together, CO 15 sts, work across 60 sts from holder, CO 15 sts–90 sts. Begin Garter st. Work even for 5", ending on a WS row.

Establish Stripes (RS): Change to smaller needles and D; **work even for 6 rows.
Change to larger needles and 1 strand each of MC and A held together; work even for 5", ending on a WS row.**
Next Row (RS): Change to C. Repeat from ** to **.
Next Row (RS): Change to B. Repeat from ** to **. BO all sts.

FINISHING
Using 1 strand of C, sew side seams from Sleeve to 5" from bottom edge of Sweater, leaving last 5" unsewn for vent. Using 1 strand of MC, sew Sleeve seams.

Hood: Fold Hood in half so that markers are together. Sew from markers to back of Hood.

Hood Trim: Using crochet hook and 1 strand of B, beginning at right bottom of Hood, work 1 row single crochet around front edge of Hood.

Sweater Trim: Using crochet hook and 1 strand of B, beginning and ending at left Side Panel, work 1 rnd single crochet along lower edge of Sweater.

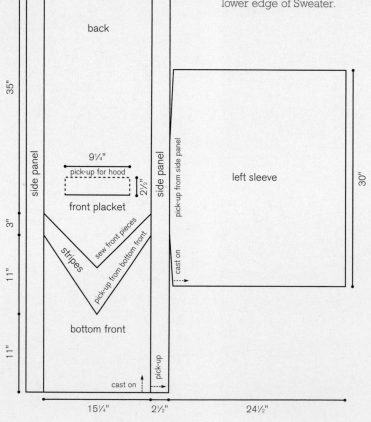

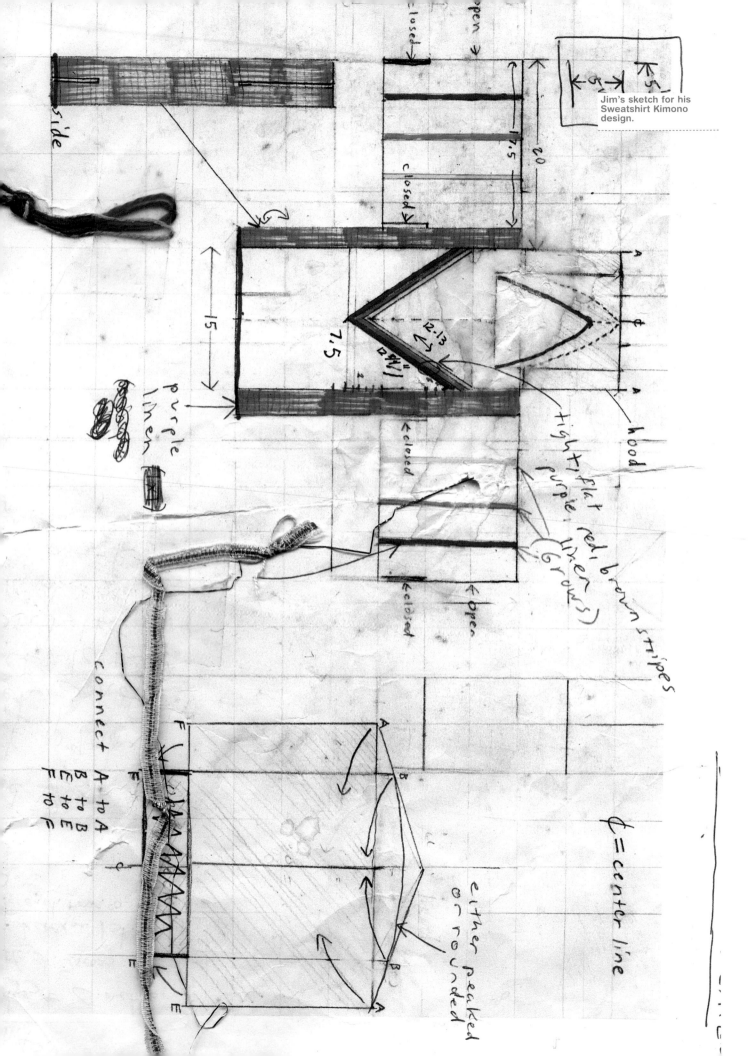

Jim's sketch for his Sweatshirt Kimono design.

Teva
Durham

Each floor of Teva Durham's small duplex apartment in midtown Manhattan houses a drawing that speaks to her artistic development. Framed in her second-floor office, a drawing she did of her father when she was young exhibits an early focus on clothing: The jacket collar and the width of his tie are given more attention than his facial features. On a wall above the couch in her first-floor living room is an inconographic white chalk drawing done on black subway paper. It's an early Keith Haring, who was a friend of Teva's mother. "When I first saw a Keith Haring, it was a revelation, with the energy bars coming from the cookie-cutter-like bodies and the bold lines all contributing to the expression. I hope that my work has a similar effect," Teva says, drawing the connection between Haring's art and her own: knitting. "Energy, spirit, whatever you want to call it, when you transmit it into your knitting, it is there to see." After first trying acting, and then writing, Teva finally settled on knitting as a humble, expressive medium outside the world inhabited by her artist parents. It's a medium that she imbues with confident, expressive textures and an idiosyncratic, dramatic sense of character.

Teva credits the energy of New York City as a primary influence. She spent her early years in St. Louis, where her father headed a community college art department, but she left to study theater at La Guardia High School of Performing Arts in New York City, where she lived with her mother after her parents split up. Her mother's life revolved around a group of former beatniks, artists, and writers who had been part of Black Mountain College, the fabled North Carolina art school that launched a remarkable number of artists involved in the 1960s avant-garde art movement. Teva hung around with artists like Keith Haring, Jean-Michel Basquiat,

Charlotte Moorman, and Laurie Anderson, and she found the scene demanding. "I felt I was supposed to be a great artist too—I could not just be a child, I had to do important things," she explains. She tunneled her creative expectations into acting and collecting clothing that she wore for scene study and performance; the drama department at her high school required students to come up with their own costumes. "I think I might have had nearly a hundred sweaters that I had bought at thrift shops and flea markets for about one or two dollars," Teva recalls. Her mother made a soft sculpture for Teva's gigantic sweater collection by sewing large pockets onto a long piece of canvas she then hung from a dowel in their living room. Each pocket contained about ten sweaters, some of which were knit by Teva's grandmother, who also taught Teva to knit when she was in first grade. "No one else in the family cared to wear them because they were outlandishly oversized and in bright colors that reflected my grandmother's manic personality," Teva says.

After high school, Teva briefly attended Swarthmore College before dropping out to study acting with the American Stanislavski Theatre and La MaMa Experimental Theatre Club, both in downtown Manhattan. A series of misadventures and odd jobs ensued, including proofreading, babysitting, boutique sales, modeling, and, at a low point, selling her wardrobe on the street. During a brief stint in London, studying Shakespeare with faculty from the Royal Academy of Dramatic Arts, Teva spotted elaborate hand-knit sweaters on display in the store window of a Patricia Roberts shop and was inspired to revisit knitting. As her passion for acting began to wane, Teva's interest in knitting intensified.

Facing page
Teva sitting in her egg chair (see page 62) in her New York City apartment. Behind her are two projects from her book *Loop-d-Loop Crochet*.

Above
Teva's childhood drawings of her mother and father.

After returning to New York and completing a degree in English at Marymount Manhattan College, Teva started writing about fashion for a newsletter that forecasted jewelry and accessory trends. "I wrote fluffy copy about shoes and handbags," she says. "I had a knack for fluffy." Covering runway shows, Teva began to appreciate fashion as a medium that can "embody social messages and evoke emotion like the theatre; which, though wordless, can almost have a narrative, can set a scene and be poetic; or which can display a purity of form and color like a painting," she describes in an artist's statement. By then she was passionate about knitting and knitwear design. *Vogue Knitting* was her favorite magazine; she had taught herself every knitting technique from its pages, so she was thrilled when she was offered a job as associate editor there in 1997.

"It took me a long time to figure out my place; it only really happened once I relaxed," Teva reflects. She left *Vogue Knitting* in 1999 to become a full-time knitwear designer, and shortly thereafter, she founded her own company, called Loop-d-Loop. She offered patterns and kits as well as ready-to-wear knits with one of the first knitting websites to feature edgy photography.

Initially, like many knit designers, the bulk of her income came from creating samples for lines that were produced inexpensively in developing countries, but Teva decided to pay local knitters a decent wage to produce her own designs. She also sought out knitters who could imbue her designs with a quality she describes as "knitterly." "The primary thing about my approach to knitting is the process, the actual making, the energy of the hands," she explains. "My knits should be knitterly in the way a painting can be painterly or a story writerly. This is the magic. Tight, mechanical-looking stitches are a no-go with me. Give me expressive texture. I create designs to bring out this expressive quality, but in reproducing them, not every knitter has the touch. There are two levels," she continues, "the design and the implementation or interpretation—like a Chopin nocturne needs a feeling pianist." Teva's work, in a similar vein, seeks to inspire "feeling" knitters through design techniques such as exaggerated stitches and patterns, with thick yarns and huge cables that emphasize the hand-wrought quality of the pieces.

This page
This Fair Isle Short-Row Pullover crosses two traditional pattern bands around the body.

Facing page left to right
Teva's Zip-Off Color-Block Yoke Sweater.

Three designs on a dress form: Cowl with Optional Drawstring, Ballet T-Shirt, and Slip-Stitch Intarsia Kilt. *Taming the Tiger*, a **print by artist Phillip Evergood, hangs in the background. Teva's mother gave her the print because it reminded her of Teva's drawings.**

Note: All garments on these pages from *Loop-d-Loop*.

Teva sometimes begins her design process with a naive idea, like a scarf inspired by the kinds of chain-link garlands kindergartners make with construction paper. She then develops and resolves the idea through the knitting process. The result is pared-down and romantic but always with some degree of dramatic flair. Her designs for a midriff sweater inspired by a toreador's costume and a holiday sweater with large, reflective paillettes are flashy, while a tunic with keyhole openings at the neck, cuffs, and hem has a more subtle theatricality. Teva's interpretations of simple, classic garments are like actors themselves, changing character—take, for example, a scarf that's also a stole, and a tricolored tube that can be worn as a hood, shawl, or poncho.

But just as Teva was breaking into a few stores in Soho and looking forward to a trunk show at Henri Bendel, September 11 altered her path. "The retail and manufacturing side of fashion takes a lot of energy, pavement pounding, and an aggressive sales personality," Teva says. "I was five months pregnant with my daughter at the time, and [September 11 made me realize that] I wanted to manage my business from home and do a little nesting." A timely invitation to create a book allowed her to further develop her designs while taking care of her daughter, and it ended up pushing Teva's work to a new level. "I love to work on books because they combine writing and knitting," Teva says. "In a way I was a frustrated writer; somehow I put all that into my hands." Teva's book *Loop-d-Loop*, named after her company, pairs her innovative designs with explanations of her inspirations and process. Touching on philosophy, other knit designers, fine art, and popular culture, Teva's text describes her own creative world, one she calls comfortably domestic and humble. "Knitting is considered domestic so it's not thought of as an egotistical art," she explains. "I'm able to be an artist with it. I can do it without feeling stuck … it frees me to take big risks." Those risks have paid off, leading to an increased sense of fulfillment. With a much-anticipated second book—*Loop-d-Loop Crochet*—completed and a yarn line in development, Teva feels that her circuitous route, finally, has put her in the place she is meant to be.

Slip Cover for Egg Chair

I love that the form of this slipcover is so sculptural. It's like some futuristic satellite, yet also looks organic like a pod or mushroom. The cables mimic petals or seeds, but the surface is so blatantly yarn that has been worked by human hands. And it actually is functional, and makes the otherwise lightweight slippery chair underneath into a cozy retreat.

— **Teva Durham**

FINISHED MEASUREMENTS
To fit chair approximately 38" tall at back, 14½" tall at front, legs spaced 26" apart at bottom

YARN
Reynolds Yarns Bulky Lopi (100% Icelandic wool; 67 yards / 100 grams): 27 hanks, #600

NEEDLES
One pair straight needles size US 11 (8 mm)
One pair straight needles size US 19 (15 mm)
Change needle size if necessary to obtain correct gauge.

NOTIONS
Cable needle (cn); stitch markers; aluminum framed folding chair with lycra seat cover
Note: Chair used here is Spandex Egg Chair from Bed, Bath and Beyond; similar chair available from Target.

GAUGE
16 sts and 15 rows = 5" (12.5 cm) in Braided Cable Pattern using smaller needles and 1 strand of yarn
5 sts and 7 rows = 4" (10 cm) in Stockinette stitch (St st) using larger needles and 2 strands of yarn held together

ABBREVIATIONS
C4B: Slip next 2 sts to cn, hold to back, k2, k2 from cn.
C4F: Slip next 2 sts to cn, hold to front, k2, k2 from cn.
C6B: Slip next 3 sts to cn, hold to back, k3, k3 from cn.
C6F: Slip next 3 sts to cn, hold to front, k3, k3 from cn.

STITCH PATTERNS
Braided Cable Pattern (multiple of 6 sts + 3; 4-row repeat)
Row 1 (RS): *C6F; repeat from * to last 3 sts, k3.
Row 2: Purl.
Row 3: K3, *C6B; repeat from * across.
Row 4: Purl.
Repeat Rows 1-4 for Braided Cable Pattern.

Hem Pattern (variable multiple; 8-row repeat)
Row 1 and all WS rows: Purl.
Rows 2 and 6: Knit.
Row 4: Work to last 6 sts, C4F, k2.
Row 8: Work to last 4 sts, C4B.
Repeat Rows 1-8 for Hem Pattern.

NOTE
The Slip Cover is composed of six pieces, three of which form the Seat: Bottom Arch, Top Arch, and Keyhole Center.

SLIP COVER

Seat Bottom Arch

Using smaller needles and one strand of yarn, CO 69 sts. Purl 1 row.

Establish Braided Cable Short Row Pattern:

Row 1 (RS): *C6F; repeat from * to last 3 sts, k3.

Row 2: Purl.

Rows 3-4: K51, wrp-t, purl to end, turn.

Rows 5-6: K33, wrp-t, purl to end, turn.

Rows 7-8: K15, wrp-t, purl to end, turn.

Row 9: Working wraps together with wrapped sts, k3, *C6B; repeat from * across.

Row 10: Purl.

Rows 11-16: Repeat Rows 3-8.

Repeat Rows 1-16 until outer edge of piece measures approximately 32" from the beginning, ending with Row 16. BO all sts.

Seat Top Arch

Using smaller needles and one strand of yarn, CO 69 sts. Work as for Bottom Arch until outer edge of piece measures approximately 74" from the beginning (or until, when placed on chair with Bottom Arch, the circumference of the chair is completely covered, leaving only center oval open), ending with Row 16. BO all sts.

Seat Keyhole Center

Using smaller needles and one strand of yarn, CO 33 sts. Purl 1 row.

Next Row (RS): Begin Braided Cable Pattern; work even until piece measures 7" from the beginning, ending with Row 4. BO all sts.

Bottom Hem

Using larger needles and 2 strands of yarn held together, CO 33 sts. Begin Hem Pattern; work even for 3 rows.

Shape Hem (RS): Decrease 1 st this row, then every 4 rows 9 times, as follows: Ssk, work to end–23 sts remain. Work even until piece measures approximately 26" from the beginning, ending with a WS row. Place marker for left front leg. Work even for 8 rows.

Next Row (RS): Decrease 1 st this row, then every 4 rows once, as follows: Ssk, work to end–21 sts remain. Work even for 10 rows, omitting decreases.

Next Row (RS): Increase 1 st this row, then every 4 rows once, as follows: K1, m1, work to end–23 sts. Work even until piece measures approximately 26" from first marker, ending with a WS row; pm for right front leg. Work even for 4 rows.

Next Row (RS): Increase 1 st this row, then every 4 rows 9 times, as follows: K1, m1, work to end–33 sts. Work even until piece measures approximately 26" from second marker, ending with a WS row; pm for right back leg. Work even until piece measures 26" from third marker, ending with Row 3 or 7. BO all sts.

Seat Back

Using larger needles and 2 strands of yarn held together, pick up and knit 34 sts along shaped edge of Bottom Hem (not cabled edge), between marker for right back leg and BO edge of Bottom Hem (skipping approximately every third row). (WS) Begin St st.

Next Row (RS): Decrease 1 st each side this row, then every other row 8 times, as follows: Ssk, work to last 2 sts, k2tog–16 sts remain. Work even until piece measures 12" from pick-up row. BO all sts.

Seat Front Underside

Using larger needles and 2 strands of yarn held together, pick up and knit 34 sts along shaped edge of Bottom Hem (not cabled edge), between markers for left front leg and right front leg (skipping approximately every third row). (WS) Begin St st.

Next Row (RS): Decrease 1 st each side this row, then every other row 6 times, as follows: Ssk, work to last 2 sts, k2tog–20 sts remain. Work even until piece measures 8" from pick-up row. BO all sts.

FINISHING

NOTE: Assembling and sewing is easier when pieces are draped over the chair (also see Assembly Diagram).

Using Kitchener Stitch with Bound-Off Stitches (see Special Techniques, page 172), graft Seat Bottom Arch and Top Arch together. Insert Keyhole Center into center of Seat, sewing piece neatly to edges of Top and Bottom Arches, hiding some of the edges of the piece behind the Top and Bottom Arches as needed to keep center oval (see photo). Graft CO and BO rows of Bottom Hem (this seam will be at left back leg). Sew shaped edge (not cabled edge) of Bottom Hem/Seat Back/Seat Front Underside around Seat piece, using markers to align with chair legs.

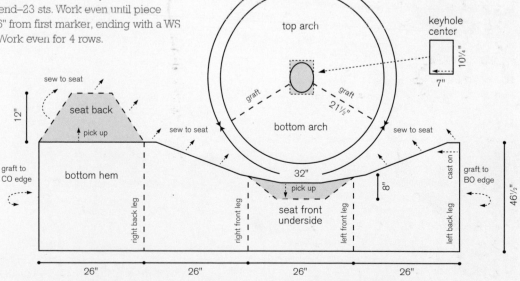

Norah
Gaughan

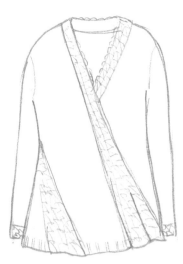

A few months after her book *Knitting Nature* **was published,** Norah Gaughan picked a piece of seaweed off a fishing pole and thought, "Look at the fractal branching!" She was excited by the sighting, having used fractals—structures in nature that branch out in similar shapes of increasing or decreasing size—as inspiration to design seven garments in her book. Norah revels in the process of noting biological phenomena and translating it into knitwear that is chic, wearable, and not too hard to make; knitters find her designs simultaneously accessible and groundbreaking in their basis on a deep understanding of scientific principles. Aware of her talents but not overly impressed by them, Norah is the kind of person who is happiest when she can hole up in her studio to work through design challenges, whether it be innovating a new construction, perfecting a novel stitch pattern, or figuring out the perfect rate of decrease to finesse a neckline.

Norah grew up in a creative household in Rifton, New York. Both of her parents were commercial illustrators, and her maternal grandmother, who lived with the family, was an avid needlewoman. Norah learned embroidery from her grandmother, then picked up machine-sewing and tailoring skills from her mother, all at a young age. When she was eight, Norah joined a 4-H group that met after school and over summer vacations, and during her ten-year tenure there, she presented increasingly complicated garments at the annual 4-H clothing and dress reviews, in which young sewers would model their handmade garments and be judged on the quality of their construction. She describes herself as a competitive sewer who strove to create well-made, wearable, and innovative designs, like an ensemble of corduroy jeans, flannel shirt, and down vest, and a

tweed skirt and vest with a turtleneck knit in fingering-weight wool, which she made after she became a knitter.

Norah learned how to knit when she was fourteen years old, from her friend Grace Judson, who went on to earn the title of World's Fastest Knitter at the 2002 National Needlework Association conference. Norah took to knitting instantly, but she really had to study knitting patterns to understand how to read them. When Norah decided to make a fisherman's gansey from a set of instructions that made her cry with frustration, her mother bought her a copy of Elizabeth Zimmermann's classic book *Knitting Without Tears*. "I was trying to follow every instruction perfectly," Norah says, "but [Zimmermann's] book encouraged me to knit according to my own proportions." Three years later, Norah's mother introduced her to an industry contact at *Ladies Home Journal Needle and Craft,* and at the age of seventeen, Norah published her first knit pattern. "It was based on a Zimmermann-inspired technique of decreasing yoke proportions," she explains.

Norah quit 4-H and sewing when she moved to Providence to attend Brown University at age eighteen. In college, she was encouraged to pursue fields that had long been male-dominated, and Norah was good at math and had always enjoyed science. She kept up with knitting as a hobby, making things for herself and for her friends. Norah gave herself over to biology as a main field of study, yet was always torn by a simultaneous desire to study art and science. During her senior year, Norah took her second painting class, and added studio art as a minor to her biology major. She presented a series of oil paintings of vegetables at her senior show in 1983.

Facing page top to bottom
Norah in her New Hampshire home with her cat Jake.

The shape of the hem on Norah's Coastline Skirt is based on a fractal called the Koch Snowflake, discovered by Helge von Koch in 1904.

Above left to right
Some preliminary sketches for *Knitting Nature.*

Norah crocheting in her dad's studio.

"After Brown I floated," she says. When asked why she drifted toward knitting as a career rather than science or art, Norah, a pragmatist, says, "I wanted to do what I do best." Norah knit for designers Margery Winter and Deborah Newton, and she credits working with them as a sort of graduate school that prepared her to become a knitwear designer. "It was an intense period of design study with Margery, who was my mentor," she says. During that time, Norah resolved her anxieties that knitting wasn't a serious enough profession and abandoned thoughts of pursuing biology professionally. From 1987 to 1995, Norah lived in Providence and made a living by designing knitwear for publications and companies like *Vogue Knitting, Knitter's* magazines, and Classic Elite Yarns. Norah describes her work during this period as committed and creative fulfillment of her clients' design needs. She was so prolific, and her designs were so recognizable, that she soon became one of America's best-known hand-knit designers. Although admirers of Norah's work have always remarked that there is a mathematical logic to her pieces, Norah doesn't think that math or science were direct factors in her creative process at the beginning of her career.

In 1995, Norah moved to Hastings-on-Hudson, New York, commuting distance to Manhattan, to do free-lance design work for the sportswear department of Adrienne Vittadini. Concurrently, she made stitch patterns for other design houses on Seventh Avenue. Norah enjoyed the design challenge of making up new stitches, and often found inspiration in the abstract forms of nature. "Because of my degree in biology, natural forms were sometimes the forms I was attracted to. But I wouldn't bend over backward to make something look so much like nature that it looks unknitterly," she says. With one knit swatch inspiring the next, Norah was able to create and sell a copious quantity—more than two hundred in just eighteen months.

When the owner of Reynolds/JCA hired her as design director in 1997, Norah moved to New England to work for the Massachusetts-based company. While at JCA, Norah experimented with nontraditional construction techniques. She created designs for sweaters with circle insertions and made garments that were knit with a side-to-side construction. "My many years of experience gave me the skills and confidence to explore uncharted territory," she writes in her introduction to *Knitting Nature*. "So I was ready when I tripped across the idea for [my] book."

Browsing through the popular science section of her local bookstore, Norah stumbled across *The Self-Made Tapestry: Pattern Formation in Nature* by Philip Ball. The book describes how constants in physics are responsible for all the patterns in nature, and covers a wide range of examples, including pattern formation on the

hides of zebras, giraffes, and leopards, as well as in bee's honeycombs. The book was filled with patterns that Norah knew would relate to the shapes she wanted to use in knitting.

"I felt like I had been saving up all the things I could do to write the book," Norah explains. "I wanted to break some of the rules I had learned, but still create shapes that were wearable." Norah left JCA in 2004 to spend a year and a half relating the physical principles found in nature to the construction of knit garments. She rented a studio a quarter mile from her Greek revival house in Peterborough, New Hampshire, to create patterns and write explanations of the scientific principles that inspired her designs. Her process involved reading *The Self-Made Tapestry,* looking at images of microscopic creatures, staring at diagrams of fractals, and then making sketches for garments without working out the details of how they would come together. After that, Norah would pull out her knitting needles and start to create what she had drawn. Norah let the idea that physical constants are repeated over and over in nature lead the fabrication of her garments. "Like in nature, beautiful and seemingly complex designs can be made by the repetition of a few simple steps," she explains.

The resulting book is divided into six chapters, each focused on a different category of patterns found in

nature: hexagons, pentagons, spirals, phyllotaxis, fractals, and waves. Each chapter begins with an introduction in which Norah conveys a sense of deep appreciation for the underlying scientific principles that inspired her designs. After explaining the efficiency of nature's hexagons, for example, Norah presents the Snapping Turtle Skirt, in which hexagons are knitted from top down in increasing increments to create an A line skirt. The cables in her Turbulence U-Neck Pullover illustrate the swirl of fluid flowing into a funnel. Her Target Wave Mitten pattern is based on the spiraling waves caused by chemical reactions, and the Serpentine Coat includes a fractal motif as a visual design that drapes over the shoulders and across the chest. The repeated visual patterns on the coat can be appreciated as both a geometric representation of simple, repeating equations and as elegant adornment. Even when using the mathematical structure of certain natural phenomena to determine the structure of a garment, Norah designed garments that were both flattering and wearable.

After Norah finished her book in early 2006, she was hired as the design director for Berocco Yarns, working with the company's creative director and her early mentor, Margery Winter. She's circled back in a way, as though her pattern of growth evolved according to the physical phenomenon of the spiral she incorporated into her knit designs.

Missing Piece Hobo Bag

As I worked on *Knitting Nature,* I became increasingly fascinated with the idea of knitting polygons—that is, multisided figures—and combining them to create functional forms, such as garments, or as shown here, a bag. In this case, I worked triangular shapes to create a pentagon, except the fifth wedge is "missing," forming a V-shaped opening. The body of the bag is worked in two identical pieces. Each piece is then sewn to a long strip of knitting that becomes both the bottom band and shoulder strap.

— **Norah Gaughan**

FINISHED MEASUREMENTS
20" long x 6" wide x 10" high, at shallowest point

YARN
Berroco Suede (100% nylon; 120 yards / 50 grams): 12 balls # 3718 holster

NEEDLES
One pair straight needles size US 10 (6 mm)
Change needle size if necessary to obtain correct gauge.

NOTIONS
Cable needle (CN)

GAUGE
14 sts and 21 rows = 4" (10 cm) in Stockinette st (St st), using 2 strands of yarn held together

BAG
Back and Front (both alike)
Using 2 strands of yarn held together, CO 199 sts.

Begin Chart (WS): *Work across Chart, repeating sts as indicated on Chart. Work even until Chart is complete (37 rows), working decreases as indicated–55 sts remain.
Row 38: K2, *p2tog, k1, yo, ssk, p2tog, k1, k2tog, k1; repeat from * 3 times, p2tog, k1, yo, ssk, p2tog, k2–41 sts remain.
Row 39: P2, *k1, p1, yo, p2tog, k1, p1, p2tog; repeat from * 3 times, k1, p1, yo, p2tog, k1, p2–37 sts remain.
Row 40: K2tog, *p1, k1, yo, ssk, p1, k2tog; repeat from * 3 times, p1, k1, yo, ssk, p1, k2tog–31 sts remain.
Row 41: P1, k1, *p1, yo, p2tog, p3tog; repeat from * 3 times, p1, yo, p2tog, k1, p1–23 sts remain.
Row 42: K1, *k2tog; repeat from * across–12 sts remain.
Break yarn, leaving a 6" tail; thread through remaining loops, pull tight and fasten off.

Norah's original sketch for the Missing Piece Hobo Bag design.

Shoulder Strap/Bottom Band

Using 2 strands of yarn held together, CO 40 sts.

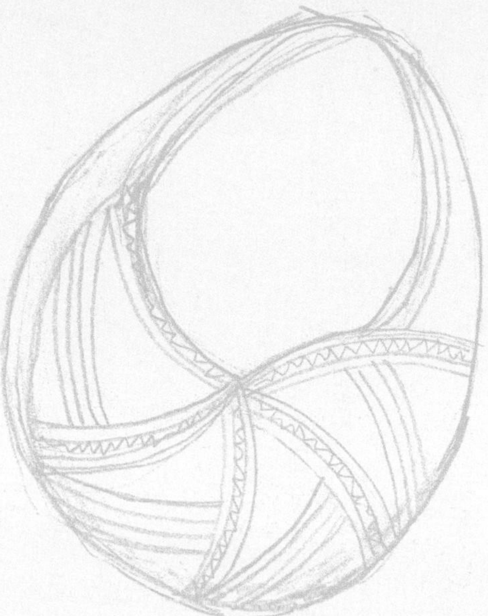

Begin Pattern (WS): [P2, k2] twice, p1, k1, p20, k1, p1, [k2, p2] twice.

Decrease Row: [K2, p2] twice, k1, p2tog, knit to last 11 sts, p2tog, k1, [p2, k2] twice–38 sts remain. Work even for 1 row. Repeat Decrease Row every other row 5 times, then every 4 rows twice–24 sts remain. Work even until piece measures 75" from the beginning. BO all sts in pattern.

FINISHING

Sew one long side of Shoulder Strap/Bottom Band (beginning at BO end of Band) to CO edge of Front, beginning at left end of CO edge, and leaving 20" of Shoulder Strap/Bottom Band free for Strap. Sew remaining long side to CO edge of Back. Sew CO end of Shoulder Strap/Bottom Band to BO end and top of Bag (see photo).

Key

- Knit on RS, purl on WS.
- Purl on RS, knit on WS.
- Yo
- No stitch
- or K2tog on RS, p2tog on WS.
- Ssk
- Slip 2 sts to cn, hold to front, p2, k2 from cn.

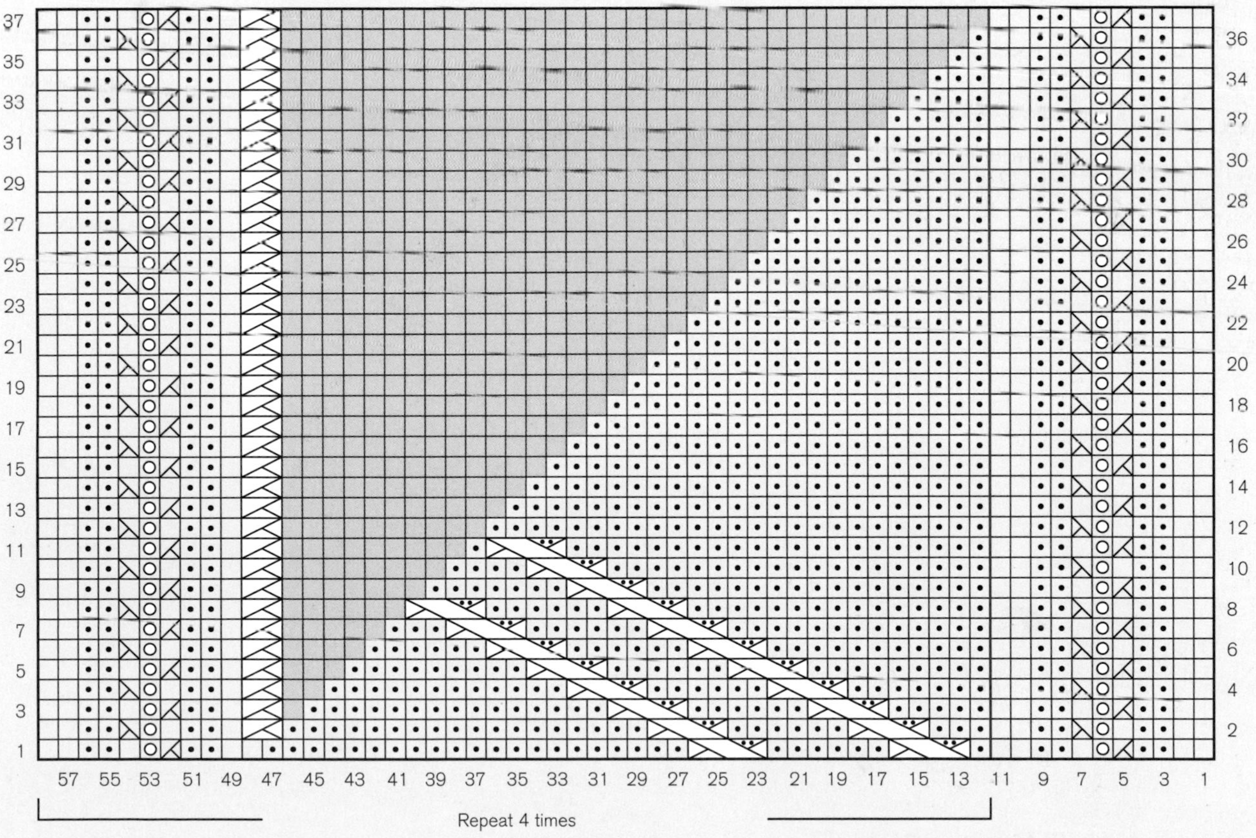

David
Gentzsch

In 1980 David Gentzsch and his wife bought a twenty-five-acre farm in the Missouri Ozarks that happened to come with two stray ewes. Inspired to make a business out of the sheep's wool—and with no experience as a farmer, knitter, or fiber artist—David, who had studied horticulture in college, began making his own yarn. He taught himself every aspect of the business—from tending the sheep, to managing the books, to spinning and dyeing the fiber. He also packed the yarn, shipped it, and took calls from customers, all by himself. The experience turned out to be more stressful than satisfying. Six years into it, he decided to pursue a different path, moving with his wife and daughter into town. David took a job at the *Jefferson City News Tribune* bindery, bought several rental buildings, and became a landlord. In 1998, while his daughter was in college, David and his wife divorced.

David married his second wife, Terri, in 2003, and they honeymooned in San Francisco. Wandering into a yarn store there, David was blown away. "I hadn't been in a yarn shop in fifteen years," he explains. "I hadn't seen all the new yarns, and I was amazed. I told Terri, 'I can do this—and even better.'" She said, 'Well, honey, prove it.'" And that's what David began doing immediately upon their return home. He pulled his spinning and dyeing equipment out of storage and named the new yarn he was going to make Ozark Handspun. He then set about creating the riotously colorful, wildly textured handspun yarn now sold in yarn shops across the United States, Canada, and England.

David and Terri run their company out of the same two-story, red brick home in Jefferson City that David purchased after he sold the sheep farm. With Terri's management assistance, as well as supplemental income from tenants, David can completely devote himself to the creative process. "If I don't sell any yarn this month, I'm fine. So I can play with my art and with my yarn," he says in a slow Missouri drawl. "That's an important aspect of being an artist. Before, I didn't have that, and it just wore me out."

David's process begins after he's cleaned his wool and mohair fleeces, which he purchases from a select group of domestic and foreign shepherds. Then he puts the fibers into an assortment of dye pots in his basement to heat and absorb color for about forty-five minutes. Next he rinses the fibers and carefully places them on drying racks, where they will sit for one to two days. Once dry, David sorts the fibers into containers according to color. He then mixes and matches them to create intricate, multicolored combinations, sometimes tailoring his choices to certain distributors. "In New York they love hot pink," he divulges, appending six months later that "now it's turquoise." No two combinations are alike. After David makes his color choices, he takes the

fibers—what Terri fondly calls "the clouds"—upstairs to his spinning studio. Once the master bedroom, the studio is a wide, open space, its purple walls sponged with lavender and white. David's spinning wheel stands directly in front of a large window that overlooks a busy city street and, in the distance, the surrounding hills. Periodically peering out of the window to enjoy the impressive view, David listens to the Beatles, the Who, Johnny Cash, and the Rolling Stones while he spins, leaving a fine dust of colored fiber on his jeans.

"There's only so much you can do at the spinning wheel," he says. "You can control the size of the yarn and a little of the texture, but much of the art is in the blending of the colors." When David is at his wheel, he works very quickly. "I think the faster you spin, the more texture you let go through, and that's what I want," he explains. "I want my yarn to look like hand-spun yarn. I can make a real fine yarn, but that's what the machines are doing." His yarn is alternately thick, then thin; uneven, with loose curls sticking out in unpredictable places. Strands of various colors spiral, coil, and intertwine. Finished skeins look like dread-locks, driftwood, and finger coral. When David picks up a handful of skeins that are ready for shipping, tiny twigs, a few pieces of straw, and a smell like freshly washed T-shirts tumble out.

A skein of Ozark Handspun, with all of its texture, shape, and color is almost like an object that's already been knitted. With it, David hopes to inspire a whole new crop of knitters and all new types of knitted objects: "I think it's important to bring new blood into the knitting world, and to have new people working with their hands. They can sit down and knit one evening, and come up with a great piece of art."

Mind Fire Bag

Have you ever sat and looked at a fire and noticed how it will flash as it gets hotter and hotter and hotter? It's as if the flames themselves cannot contain the power held within the heat. My mind works a lot like that. As I held this wonderful pink, orange, and brown Ozark Handspun, my brain took off like wildfire, flashing here and there with ideas and visions of new and unusual creations that were just burning to be made.

The main body of the bag represents downed wood that fuels the fire and the wild, unpredictable, passionate, and expressive rim around the top of the bag evokes flames of creativity shooting out and about my mind. The handles help you to maintain your own fire without getting burned.

Go ahead, see for yourself! I'll bet you can set your own mind aflame.

— Sarah Kohl for David Gentzsch

FINISHED MEASUREMENTS
Approximately 12½" long x 3" wide x 20" tall, before blocking
Approximately 10" long x 2" wide x 16" tall, after blocking

YARN
Brown Sheep Lamb's Pride Bulky (85% wool / 15% mohair; 125 yards / 100 grams): 2 skeins #M89 roasted coffee (A)
Ozark Handspun (50% wool / 50% mohair; 34 yards / 100 grams): 1 skein San Diego (B)

NEEDLES
One 24" (60 cm) circular needle (circ) size US 13 (9 mm)
One 24" (60 cm) circular needle size US 15 (10 mm)
One pair double pointed needles (dpn) size US 10½ (6.5 mm), for I-cord
Change needle size if necessary to obtain correct gauge.

NOTIONS
Stitch marker

GAUGE
8 sts and 12 rows = 4" (10 cm) in Stockinette st (St st), using size US 13 needles and 1 strand of A, before felting

BAG
Base
Using size US 13 circ needle and 2 strands of A held together, CO 25 sts. Working back and forth, begin Garter St (knit every row). Work even for 12 rows. Break 1 strand of yarn.

Body
Continuing with 1 strand of A, pick up and knit 6 sts along one short side of Base, 25 sts along CO edge, 6 sts along remaining edge of Base, then 25 sts along BO edge–62 sts. Join for working in the rnd; pm for beg of rnd. Begin St st (knit every rnd); work even until Body measures 10" from pick-up rnd. Change to size US 15 circ needle and 1 strand each of A and B held together.

Decrease Rnd: *K2, k2tog; repeat from * to last 2 sts, k2—47 sts remain. Work even for 9 rnds. Break B.

Increase Rnd: Change to size US 13 circ needle. *K3, m1; repeat from * to last 2 sts, k2—62 sts. Work even for 5 rnds. BO all sts.

Handles (make 2)
Using dpn and 1 strand of A, CO 5 sts. Work I-Cord (see Special Techniques, page 172) for 55 rows. BO all sts.

FINISHING
Lay Bag flat. Sew Handles to inside top edge of Bag. Weave in all loose ends.

Felting
Place bag in a 100% cotton pillowcase and pin closed with safety pins, leaving ample room in the pillowcase for the purse to move around. Fill your washing machine with the hottest water possible. Add a tiny amount of detergent (less than ⅛ tsp liquid or a pinch powder). Place pillowcase in washer along with an old pair of blue jeans, for friction. Wash at fastest agitation setting possible. Open pillowcase and check felting progress every 5 minutes until you reach desired size. Drain washing machine. Rinse purse (still in pillowcase) in hot water, then let it complete spin cycle. Remove purse from pillowcase. Shape bag over solid box (a puzzle box or a cereal box works great) and let it air dry on the box for 24 hours.

A friend of the Gentzsch's since 1993 **Sarah Kohl** began designing unique creations using Ozark Handspun in 2005. She joined David in spinning Ozark Handspun months later. Sarah's designs can be seen at Kohleidoscope: One of a Kind Creations at Every Turn at www.knit-pics.blogspot.com.

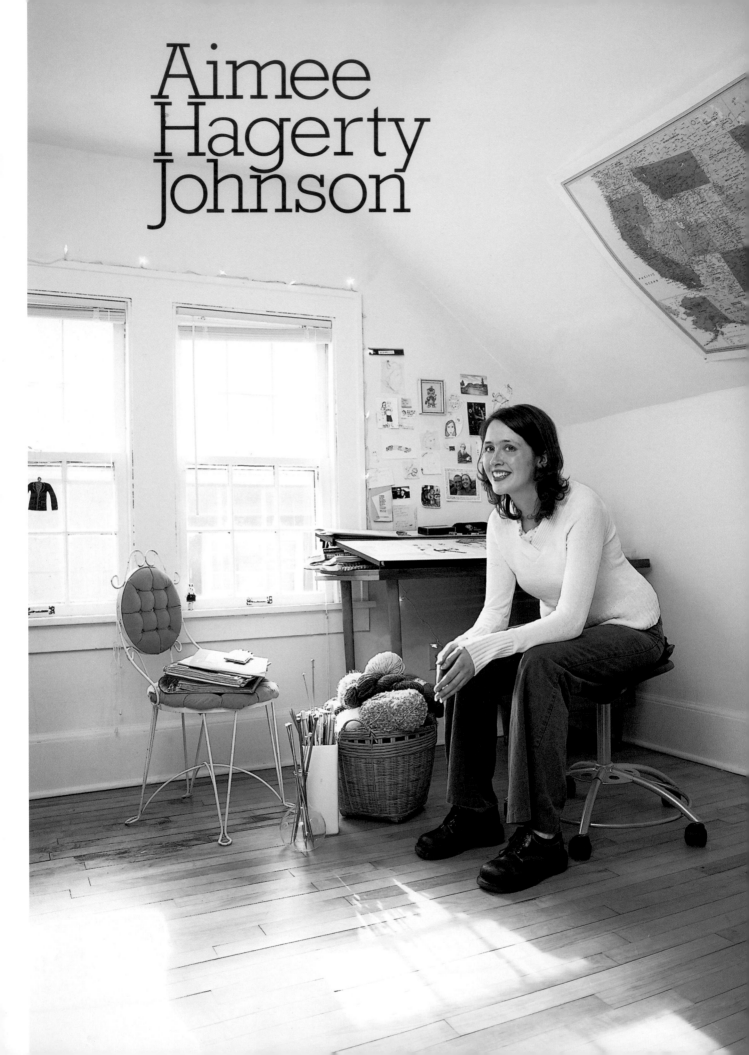

Aimee
Hagerty
Johnson

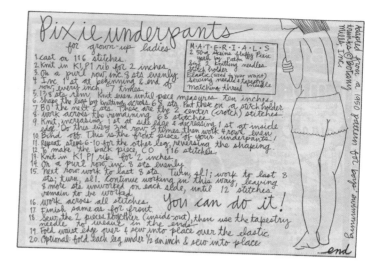

Aimee Hagerty Johnson is an artist, activist, and knitter who combines all three interests in a charming zine of underground fame called *Slave to the Needles*. Her forty-page, randomly published digest is an outlet for comics relating to her personal life and knitting escapades, as well as interviews with indie rockers who knit, reviews of knitting books and other zines, original knit patterns, and general enthusiasm for the craft. It's somewhat surprising that Aimee doesn't mention food more often in her zine, as she's a committed vegan who dreams about the vegan soup bar at Rainbow Grocery in Seattle. She's taken to cooking and baking at home ever since 2004, when she and her husband, Ben, moved from Seattle to Madison, Wisconsin, so that he could start graduate school. Before they moved, Aimee worked Mondays through Thursdays, which left Fridays, Saturdays, and Sundays for eating out and going to rock shows. In Wisconsin she lives a quieter life, working as the fundraising director for a nonprofit organization that produces a radio show about workers' rights, volunteering at a domestic violence shelter on the occasional weekend, and drawing in the attic space on the top floor of her house. The room has slanted ceilings, shiny hardwood floors, and walls covered with maps and sketches. It's furnished with a big desk, a bright lamp, and a drafting table that Aimee traded for her old painting easel to a woman on Craigslist. Aimee makes time every day to draw and plot out future issues of *Slave to the Needles* in her studio while listening to NPR.

Aimee's academic background is in applied linguistics, but after she got her master's degree from Penn State University in 2000, she moved to Seattle and sought out a non-academic life. "I guess I was a little burnt out on academics after grad school," Aimee explains. "I just wanted to live in a cool city, have an interesting job, and go to rock shows." Just a few weeks after graduation, Aimee convinced someone at a women's shelter in Seattle to hire her. "I didn't have a lick of social work experience, but had done all of this women's studies stuff in school and was really fervent and excited about doing feminist work," she says. "I ended up working at that women's shelter, in various capacities, for close to five years. I have this motto—if I have to work, I might as well work for social justice." In early 2002, Aimee started a full-time job at the AIDS Alliance, finding homeless people places to live, and learning how to knit during her lunch breaks.

"The best thing about working for Seattle's big HIV/AIDS foundation—besides meeting my future husband—was that the HR director taught me how to knit," she describes in *Slave to the Needles* issue #2. The human resources director was, according to Aimee's sketches in the zine, an elegant woman of about fifty with pouffy hair and a stern expression. "Johnnie was a Mormon who had been knitting since the Patty Duke era," Aimee's comic reads. "She could knit anything!" Johnnie taught Aimee all the fundamentals of knitting, from casting on to purling and reading patterns. "Her political views creeped me out, but she was a remarkable knitter," Aimee says. "Johnnie was a very devoted Mormon, and the Church of Latter-Day Saints doesn't look kindly upon gay and bisexual men, which were most of the AIDS foundation's clients. I don't know how she reconciled her religious beliefs with her work, but she doesn't work there anymore."

Facing page
Aimee in the attic room she uses to knit and draw comics.

This page
Cover and interior from Aimee's zine *Slave to the Needle*, issue #2.

Aimee started working on her knitting zine when she had only been knitting for a few months. "If you read the patterns I was writing back then, you can see that I was definitely a beginning knitter. I didn't know how to knit in the round or do any kind of decrease besides k2tog, for example, so I had to figure out how to make a good-looking mitten using straight needles and a decrease that slants to the right. Even ribbing was a hurdle back then. But lots of people all over the country were learning to knit at that time, so plenty of people liked my very uncomplicated patterns." Aimee also didn't have much experience drawing, but she combined learning how to knit, draw, and develop comic narratives at night and over weekends.

Almost exactly a year after she started knitting, Aimee made a thousand staple-bound photocopies of the first issue of *Slave to the Needles.* She immediately submitted it to Pander, a high-quality zine distributor run by riot grrrl Ericka Bailie, who closed down the punk, woman-friendly, decade-old business two years later. Pander distributed the first two issues of *Slave to the Needles,* then Aimee sent the third issue out to independent bookstores all across the United States. She's received an array of accolades: from a hearty endorsement on *Air America* by Janeane Garofalo to an interview in *Punk Planet* magazine.

On the surface, *Slave to the Needles* is basically a love letter to music and handcraft, written in a peppy tone and neat cursive script. "Learn new knitting moves! Create naughty cozies!" Aimee proclaims. Her neat, pared-down sketches illustrate a selection of completed knit projects, original patterns for items like a vibrator cozy or a sweet-looking bonnet, and even random depictions of her own intestines. Though Aimee is fond of retelling incidents from her own life (like falling in love with her husband, going to an intimidating meeting of the Seattle Knitters' Guild, or sending a care package to a friend), she also takes submissions from other writers—she's published "Primal and Sophisticated," an Iranian woman's account of how she realized that knitting, which she was forced to learn in a home economics class in grade school, could be a subversive act, and "Knitting a Force Field," an artist's statement written by Mark Newport, who has knit elaborate superhero costumes. Yet, "it's the rock star knitter interviews that are turning out to be my claim to (extremely low-grade) fame," Aimee says. Her interviews with indie-rock knitters and seamsters from bands like Fugazi, the Magnetic Fields, Tortoise, Tracey and the Plastics, Bikini Kill, Rainer Maria, the Polyphonic Spree, the Gossip, Cursive, Tegan and Sara, and the Aislers Set are succinct but revealing. "Who taught you to knit?" or "How did you learn to knit?" are usually her opening queries, which

often elicit personal stories about grandmothers or close friends. "The interviews are the most fun part," she says. "It's easy to get in touch with people involved in independent music, and these are people who pay attention to what they listen to, make, and consume." When Aimee first started *Slave to the Needles,* she asked the publicity people at various independent labels to find out if they had any knitters on their roster. Occasionally, she e-mails musicians to see if she can interview them, but often she just asks them directly at shows. Sometimes musicians she interviews tip her off to other knitters. "When I talked to Kori Hammel from Mates of State, she told me to call Ben Gibbard from Death Cab for Cutie, who's a knitter," Aimee says. "Knitting has experienced such a revival among the hip that it's pretty safe to assume most indie rock and DIY types at least know a little bit of knitting or crochet, even if they don't identify as full-fledged knitters."

Fundamentally, Aimee's zine is about how her interests in music and knitting are related to her activist stance, and it proposes that these hobbies can be means of social change. "There's more going on in a music underground than just music, which is why you hear so many people say that punk rock changed their lives," Aimee says. "About twelve years ago when I started tagging along with friends—and boyfriends—who went

to shows, I discovered that there were tons of bands I'd never heard on the radio who were breaking new ground with powerful, incredibly original music. Then I found out that there were girls making punk rock, and that was it for me—I really think the direction of my life changed the first time I heard a Kathleen Hanna record. I realized that music isn't just music; it's political and it's unalterably linked to a subculture. Politics, grassroots activism, and art (like zines, stenciling, posters, and knitting) are all tied up together."

Straight Edge Mittens

The hardcore band Minor Threat inspired the straight edge movement in a 1980 song that made an alcohol- and drug-free lifestyle seem really, really cool:

I'm a person just like you / But I've got better things to do
Than sit around and smoke dope / 'Cause I know I can cope…
Always gonna keep in touch / Never want to use a crutch
I've got the straight edge.

When I started going to rock and punk shows in college, the guy taking money at the door would draw either an O or an X on your hand with a permanent marker, indicating that you were either over-age (O) or too young to drink at the bar (X). As a symbol of their beliefs that drugs and drinking should be rejected, the straight edge kids—punks who didn't smoke, drink alcohol, or do drugs—started showing up at the clubs with X's already on their hands. I designed these mittens—which are convertible so that you can effortlessly get your hand marked at the door to the club—with reverence to the straight edge lifestyle. I love the way the intarsia X's look like they were drawn on with a Sharpie marker. Punk rock!

— Aimee Hagerty Johnson

FINISHED MEASUREMENTS
8" circumference x 10" long, to fit an average woman's hand

YARN
Nashua Handknits Creative Focus Chunky (75% wool / 25% alpaca; 220 yards / 100 grams): 2 skeins #1837 soft pink (MC); 1 skein #500 ebony (A)

NEEDLES
One set of five double-pointed needles (dpn) size US 9 (5.5 mm)
Change needle size if necessary to obtain correct gauge.

NOTIONS
Stitch marker; small amount of waste yarn

GAUGE
16 sts and 22 rows = 4" (10 cm) in Stockinette stitch (St st)

STITCH PATTERN
1x1 Rib
(multiple of 2 sts; 1-rnd repeat)
All Rnds: *K1, p1; repeat from * around.

MITTENS
Left Mitten
Cuff
Using two dpns held together, CO 26 sts. Divide sts among 4 needles as follows: 6 sts each on Needles 1, 2, and 3, and 8 sts on Needle 4. Join for working in the rnd, being careful not to twist sts; place marker (pm) for beginning of rnd (center front of Mitten). Begin 1x1 Rib. Work even until Cuff measures 2¾" from the beginning.

Mitten Body
Increase Rnd 1: K6, m1, knit to last 6 sts, m1, knit to end–28 sts. Continue in St st (knit every rnd), work even until piece measures 4¾" from the beginning.
Increase Rnd 2: *K3, m1, k4; repeat from * to end–32 sts Redistribute sts so that there are 8 sts on each needle.
Begin Chart: Continuing in St st, k11, work across 10 sts from Chart, knit to end. Work even for 1 rnd.

Thumb Opening
On Needle 1, k3, change to waste yarn, k5; slip last 5 sts worked back to left-hand needle, change to A, k5, work to end of rnd. Work even until entire Chart is complete, ending with Needle 3.
Next Rnd: K2, place these sts on Needle 3, work in 1x1 Rib over next 12 sts. Place last 12 sts worked on Needle 4; pm for new beginning of rnd. Work even as established for 2 rnds.

Finger Opening
Work even over Needles 1, 2, and 3, BO 12 sts on Needle 4. Work even for 1 rnd, CO 12 sts over BO sts.
Next Rnd: Knit to last 12 sts, work in 1x1 Rib to end. Work even for 2 rnds.
Next Rnd: Change to St st and redistribute sts on Needles 1, 3, and 4 so that there are 8 sts on each needle, as follows: Transfer last 6 sts on Needle 4 to Needle 1, and last 2 sts on Needle 3 to

Needle 4. Pm for beginning of rnd at end of Needle 4. Work even until piece measures 5¾" or to desired length from end of Cuff.

Mitten Top
Decrease Rnd:
*Needle 1: Knit to last 3 sts, k2tog, k1.
Needle 2: K1, ssk, knit to end.
Needle 3: Knit to last 3 sts, k2tog, k1.
Needle 4: K1, ssk, knit to end–28 sts remain.
Work even for 2 rnds.
Repeat from * once–24 sts remain.
Repeat Decrease Rnd every rnd 4 times–8 sts remain.
Transfer sts from Needle 4 to Needle 1 and sts from Needle 3 to Needle 2.
Using Kitchener St (see Special Techniques, page 172), graft sts together.

Thumb
Carefully remove waste yarn from Thumb sts, and place 9 live sts on 3 dpns as follows: First 3 bottom sts on Needle 1, next 2 bottom sts and 1 top st on Needle 2, and last 3 top sts on Needle 3. Join for working in the rnd; pm for beginning of rnd. Rejoin yarn and begin St st as follows: Pick up 1 st from Body, work 5 sts, pick up 1 st, work 4 sts–11 sts. Work even until piece measures ¾". Transfer last 4 sts to one needle.

Establish Thumb Flap: *Work to last 4 sts, [k1, p1] twice. Work even for 2 rnds.*
Next Rnd: Work to last 4 sts, BO 4 sts.
Work even for one rnd, CO 4 sts over BO sts.
Repeat from * to * once.
Next Rnd: [K2tog] 6 times, removing end of rnd marker–5 sts remain.
Break yarn, thread through remaining loops, pull tight and fasten off.

Right Mitten
Work as for Left Mitten to Thumb Opening, ending with Needle 3.

Thumb Opening
On Needle 4, change to waste yarn, k5; slip last 5 sts worked back to left-hand needle, change to A, k5, work to end of rnd. Complete as for Right Mitten.

FINISHING
Block Mittens if desired. Weave in all loose ends.

Key
☐ Knit using MC
■ Knit using A

Joelle Hoverson

Facing page
Joelle at Purl, her yarn shop in New York City's Soho neighborhood.

This page
Joelle's Chevron Scarf from *Last-Minute Knitted Gifts* is made with contrasting colors of multicolored merino.

Joelle Hoverson's yarn shop, Purl Soho, in New York City, is both a knitter's bliss and a place that draws in passersby who may never knit anything. It's a small space with mosaic floor tiles, a white tin ceiling, sliding screens made from patterned vintage fabric, a copious selection of natural fibers arranged in deference to the color wheel, and the name Purl spelled out in embroidered letters on four tiny hand-knit sweaters hanging on the shop door. The shop has a palpable, inviting, and affectionate personality, thoroughly consistent with that of its owner. Dressed in simple, modern clothing made from beautiful, natural fabrics, Joelle always greets her customers as they enter, knowing many of them by name. In a sweet, attentive voice, she helps them find patterns, fix dropped stitches, or choose yarns. Many knitters come to her just for her color advice. Her lively yarn shop has generated a book of her own knit designs, consulting roles with artisan yarn producers, and a second store down the block dedicated to making things with fabric. Her staff believes she might be the next Martha Stewart.

After she received an MFA in painting from Yale University in 1996, Joelle moved to New York City "to become a famous artist," she says, laughing. Though she had never heard of Martha Stewart, Joelle got a job working at the Martha Stewart Living Omnimedia company through a grad school friend. Her position as an assistant stylist—painting frames and ironing—slowly grew into a role as a senior style editor for *Martha Stewart Living* magazine. "It was eye-opening to see so many amazing handcrafted things for the home," Joelle says. "I had never really been exposed to early American objects." She recalls a turning moment: "When I worked with collections editor Fritz Karch on a story about homespun linen, I discovered the beauty of utilitarian things." Another *Martha Stewart Living* magazine story about knitting also stuck in her mind: "I realized that you can get really serious about lovely, natural materials, and handcraft," she says.

Despite an increasingly fulfilling job, Joelle was drawn back to her oil paints. She quit Martha Stewart and freelanced as a photo stylist for clients like Crate & Barrel, *Gourmet,* and *O, The Oprah Magazine,* so that she could have more time in her studio, where she worked on abstract paintings. She also started knitting during her travels for photo shoots. Joelle had learned the basics of knitting from a friend in college, picked up more working at Martha Stewart, and even recalled a few lessons from her grandmother—whom she says "made awful acrylic things"—and was now turning to it for complex color explorations. She got so into knitting that when she wasn't traveling and had time to paint in her studio, she still prioritized handcraft over fine art. "I sat in my studio, and all I could think about were my knitting projects at home," she says. "I realized then that it's really about making things. I like working with color and working with my hands."

Joelle closed down her studio and gave her paints, canvass, and stretchers to artist friends. "I also got rid of a huge expense," she says of abandoning her painting. One day soon thereafter, while walking down Soho's Sullivan Street looking for props for a photo shoot and in need of some yarn for a knitting project, Joelle thought to herself, I wish there was a yarn store here. She started shop research that evening, and spent the next six months working on a business plan. "Closing the studio meant less rent, and freelancing more meant more income," she says. "I saved my freelance income to do something. The something ended up being Purl."

When Joelle opened Purl in August 2002 on the same street where she had wished to find a yarn store, she envisioned herself standing in the shop quietly knitting alone while customers periodically dropped in. Instead, she had to hire staff members right away to keep up with the traffic. She had opened Purl at the peak of knitting's resurgence, and its location provided both local neighborhood charm and easy access to tourists visiting Soho. She now employs six people, and co-owns the business with her sister Jennifer, who manages the company website with two employees out of Costa Mesa, California. Joelle and Jennifer go to trade shows together each spring and fall to buy yarns in natural fibers, which they prefer. Joelle chooses to work with smaller companies because their yarn tends to have a more artisan quality, and she's noticed that her customers have become more sensitive to high-quality fibers. One of the store's most popular yarns is Manos del Uruguay, a merino wool that's kettle-dyed and handspun by craftswomen throughout isolated areas of Uruguay. Other yarns sold at Purl include handspun wool from Bolivia, alpaca from Peru, and Californian hand-dyed silk. Her artist's eye informs her choices as well. Describing Ozark Handspun yarn (see page 70), which she also sells, Joelle says: "When I first saw David's orange yarn, I said to him, 'Oh my God, it's like a Bonnard painting.'"

Joelle has developed such trusting relationships with her vendors that they often call her for color advice. A dialogue with the owner of the yarn company Blue Sky Alpacas resulted in a series of pure cotton yarns labeled "color palette inspired by Joelle Hoverson." Lorna's Laces, another yarn company, created a series of custom-dyed sock yarns that knit up in charming stripes in colors that are exclusively distrib-

uted at Purl. Also deferring to her color sensitivity, customers seek Joelle's yarn advice or approval before starting their projects.

Joelle's first book, *Last-Minute Knitted Gifts,* was a natural outgrowth of her experiences at the store. Though she found the writing process daunting, pattern ideas came easily. "People would come into the store and ask, 'Do you have a basic hat pattern?'" she explains. "Every time ten people asked me for something, I knew I had to make it and put it in the book." Her knit projects display unusual focus on color depth, saturation, and hue, but a special chapter called "Exploring Color" makes the book an invaluable resource. Like a private art class from the former painter, the chapter elucidates basic color concepts and illustrates them in yarn and finished projects.

Dedicated to making beautiful, utilitarian things, Joelle took a quilting class a few years ago and started making an increasing number of sewing projects at home. "Quilting is a lot like painting—making relationships with color on a two-dimensional surface," she says. "But I love the usefulness of quilts. They seem like art that you live with." In 2006, she opened a fabric shop a few doors down from Purl Soho filled with vintage-style prints, historical reproductions, and multihued solid colors. The fabric shop is like a second studio that allows Joelle to work with her hands and with color, and to share her love of the materials with which she is inspired to craft utilitarian beauty. "I feel like I'm in the perfect place," she says. "All of my interests are being fulfilled by my work and my environment, and I get to meet really interesting and creative people all the time. I'm not sure where all of this is taking me," she admits. "I'm just thrilled to be doing what I'm doing."

Spread left to right
"I have put together a color wheel of yarn samples that follows this arrangement," Joelle explains in her book *Last-Minute Knitted Gifts,* "but you can see that in many places the samples don't necessarily flow perfectly from one color to the next. This is because in practice both pigments and fibers have irregularities and impurities in them that give us colors that are more complex than simple red, orange, yellow, green, blue, and violet, and these complex colors are often more beautiful as well."

A window display at Purl.

Joelle's Favorite Yoke Sweater

This cap-sleeve yoke sweater is shaped at the waist with a rib stitch. Short rows at the back of the neck make it sit nicely on your shoulders, and the wide neckline is both flattering and quick to finish. The yarn—Koigu Premium Merino—is one of my favorites. The color and texture are wonderful and it is the perfect weight for creating wearable garments.

— **Joelle Hoverson**

SIZES
X-Small (Small, Medium, Large, X-Large)

FINISHED MEASUREMENTS
33¼ (36, 39½, 42¼, 45¾)" chest

YARN
Koigu Premium Merino (KPM) (100% merino; 170 yards / 50 grams): 6 (7, 8, 9, 10) hanks #2220

NEEDLES
One 24" (60 cm) circular (circ) needle size US 3 (3.25 mm)
One 16" (40 cm) circular needle size US 3 (3.25 mm)
One set of five double pointed needles (dpn) size US 3 (3.25 mm)
Change needle size if necessary to obtain correct gauge.

NOTIONS
Stitch markers (including 1 different color marker); stitch holders

GAUGE
28 sts and 40 rows = 4" (10 cm) in Stockinette st (St st)

STITCH PATTERN
2x2 Rib
(multiple of 4 sts; 1-rnd repeat)
All Rnds: *K2, p2; repeat from * around.

SWEATER
Body
Using circ needle, CO 116 (126, 138, 148, 160) sts, place marker (pm) for Back, CO 116 (126, 138, 148, 160) more sts, pm for beginning of rnd-232 (252, 276, 296, 320) sts. Join for working in the rnd, being careful not to twist sts. Purl 1 rnd. Knit 1 rnd. Purl 1 rnd.

Change to 2x2 Rib; work even for 9 rnds. Purl 1 rnd. Knit 1 rnd. Purl 1 rnd.

Change to St st (knit every rnd); work even until piece measures 5" from the beginning.

Change to 2x2 Rib; work even until piece measures 9½" from the beginning.

Change to St st.

Sizes X-Small, Medium, and X-Large
Working in St st, decrease 2 sts on first rnd as follows: K2tog, work to next marker, slip marker (sm), k2tog, work to end—230 (274, 318) sts remain.

All Sizes
Continuing in St st, work even until piece measures 14½ (14½, 15, 15, 15½)" from the beginning, ending 6 (7, 8, 9, 10) sts after beginning of rnd marker (removing marker).
Next Rnd: Place previous 12 (14, 16, 18, 20) sts on holder for armhole; work to 6 (7, 8, 9, 10) sts after next marker (removing marker), place previous 12 (14, 16, 18, 20) sts on holder for armhole, work to end—206 (224, 242, 260, 278) sts remain. Set aside, leaving sts on needle.

Sleeves (make 2)
Using dpn, CO 16 (18, 20, 22, 24) sts on each of 4 needles—64 (72, 80, 88, 96) sts. Join for working in the rnd, being careful not to twist sts; pm for beginning of rnd. Work as for Body for 15 rnds.
Next Rnd: Work to 6 (7, 8, 9, 10) sts after marker (removing marker), place previous 12 (14, 16, 18, 20) sts on holder for armhole—52 (58, 64, 70, 76) sts rem. Break yarn and set aside.

Yoke
Note: Change to 16" circ needle when necessary for number of sts remaining.
Using yarn attached to Body, pm for beginning of rnd (use different color marker), work across 52 (58, 64, 70, 76) sts for right Sleeve, pm, 103 (112, 121, 130, 139) sts for Back, pm, 52 (58, 64, 70, 76) sts for left Sleeve, pm, 103 (112, 121, 130, 139) sts for Front-310 (340, 370, 400, 430) sts. Continuing in St st, work even for 10 (12, 14, 16, 18) rnds.
Decrease Rnd 1: *K3, k2tog; repeat from * around—248 (272, 296, 320, 344) sts remain. Work even for 10 (12, 14, 16, 18) rnds.
Decrease Rnd 2: *K2, k2tog; repeat from * around—186 (204, 222, 240, 258) sts remain. Work even for 10 (12, 14, 16, 18) rnds.
Decrease Rnd 3: *K1, k2tog; repeat from * around—124 (136, 148, 160, 172) sts remain. Work even for 2 rnds.

Begin Short Rows: Work to 1 st before second marker, wrp-t, work to 1 st before next marker, wrp-t, work to 7 sts before previous wrapped st, wrp-t, work to 7 sts before previous wrapped st, wrp-t, work to end of rnd, working wraps together with wrapped sts. Work even for 3 rnds. Purl 1 rnd. Knit 1 rnd. Purl 1 rnd.
Change to 2x2 Rib; work even for 9 rnds. Purl 1 rnd. Knit 1 rnd. Purl 1 rnd. BO all sts loosely.

FINISHING
Using Kitchener Stitch (see Special Techniques, page 172), graft underarm sts from holders. Block piece to measurements. Weave in all loose ends.

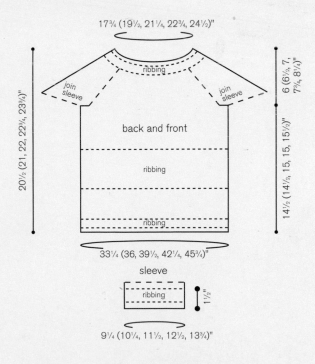

17¾ (19½, 21¼, 22¾, 24½)"

6 (6½, 7, 7¾, 8¼)"

20½ (21, 22, 22¾, 23¾)"

join sleeve

join sleeve

ribbing

back and front

ribbing

14½ (14½, 15, 15, 15½)"

ribbing

33¼ (36, 39½, 42¼, 45¾)"

sleeve

ribbing

1½"

9¼ (10¼, 11½, 12½, 13¾)"

Erika
Knight

Erika Knight does some of her design work inside a black-and-white studio at the top of her house, among the seagulls and rooftops of other Victorian homes in Brighton, England. She does the rest on trains or airplanes, lugging yarn, twine, and notebooks inside a large handbag while travelling to meet with her corporate clients. Although she describes herself as a knit designer "first and foremost," and most knitters identify her as the author of books brimming with simple, elegant, and classic patterns, Erika has other, simultaneous occupations, such as corporate brand consultant and trend spotter. Dynamic and impassioned, Erika takes very broad ideas about why people make and buy things and distils them into artistic, tactile handcrafts.

Erika's grandmother taught her to knit when she was six years old, after Erika had asked how she could make a yellow tweed scarf for Pussy Cat Willum, the star of a popular British children's television program called *Small Time,* broadcast in the early 1960s. "I received a paw-print-signed postcard for my efforts, and of course I never looked back!" she says. Her career in textiles began while she was still in college, studying painting at the Brighton School of Art. When she wasn't painting, Erika knitted pieces for fashion collections and printed fabric for designers, including Vivienne Westwood. A few years after earning her bachelor's degree in fine art, Erika broke into the early 1980s new romantic fashion scene by cofounding a clothing company called Molto—Italian for "very." New romanticism emerged in the United Kingdom as a backlash against the punk movement and celebrated glamorous clothes and hedonism; in keeping with this style, Molto's collection consisted entirely of hand-knit garments, like unstructured, raw-edged sweaters Erika calls "a little bit underground club." Producing garments abroad wasn't as commonplace as it is now, so Erika created her own "factory" along the English south coast, and learned to design with the skills of those thousand outworkers in mind. "The knitters who made the clothing I designed were not just outworkers, but a new-found family who grew with us, helped make the company grow, cared about what they did, and got involved," Erika says. "I believe in a certain integrity, especially with handcrafts."

The fashion line lasted successfully for ten years, until the partnership split. "But I never have done just one thing," Erika maintains. Even as she designed for Molto, Erika was creating garments for leading Italian and British designers and fashion enterprises, and she began consulting for companies like Marks & Spencer and Country Road, advising them on all aspects of brand identity and maintenance, from concept through manufacture to marketing.

Her current work involves broad consumer strategizing for large fashion companies; in other words, looking at trends in a wide sense, not only in terms of color, textile, and style, but also forecasting how people will shop, and how they will spend their leisure time and money. Additionally, Erika runs workshops for H&M buyers on the etiquette of visiting knitting factories and advises Rowan Yarns on the development of new yarns and colors.

This type of corporate work has given Erika a keen appreciation for consumers' urges to make by hand instead of buy, which she responds to in her publishing endeavors. "There is a desire for something a little different," Erika says, "a look inward, to the home, the homespun, the handcrafted as our personal security is threatened." Her book *Simple Knits for Cherished Babies* responds to the crafter's desire to make something unique for relatives' or friends' children. *Simple Knits with a Twist, New Knits,* and *Simple Knits for Easy Living* all encourage knitters to expand their repertoire by working with uncommon materials, everything from wire and ribbon to leather, string, and leftover plastic bags.

"I love finding the unexpected, which often creates new possibilities and ways of working," she explains. "I like to put opposites together; the juxtaposition creates a disturbance, a visual parody, or merely surprise. I go for a combination of hard and soft, natural and manmade, fine and thick—any opposite!" she says, laughing. She'll take a bag filled with mohair, twine, raffia, and hand-painted strips of felt along with her when she rides the train from her Brighton home to London, where she is a visiting lecturer at the Royal College of Art, or to Scotland, Italy, Spain, Australia, and China, all countries she visits regularly. "I spend a fair amount of time on trains and planes, where I adore putting new concepts together," she says.

One of Erika's most passionate beliefs is that today's knitters are ready to tackle issues of garment worker exploitation and ecologically damaging yarn production. From her corporate work, she knows that consumers are now using their ethical buying power when shopping for food, and she wants to encourage knitters to do the same with yarn. She also hopes to encourage her corporate contacts to focus on the traceability of natural fibers, ensuring they are produced in a sustainable way, and to educate knitters about alternative yarns such as organic cotton, hemp, and bamboo, which are chemical-free. "Knitting gives people a wonderful feeling of both personal and social responsibility," Erika says, and in describing these knitters, she is also describing herself.

Facing page
Erika at the Waterloo train station in London. "This is so me," she said of the photo. "Running to catch a train, with yarn spilling out of my bag."

Above
Erika's design process can include pairing fabrics with knitted swatches.

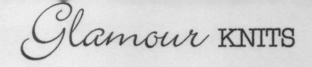

Glamour KNITS

Working boards showing color, swatch, and design for *Glamour Knits.*

02. Lace knit shrug
Yarn – 4 ply
Yeoman Q: Cotton Cannele col: Lag
Technique focus– Simple lace

01. Sequin & bead cable sweater
Yarn – Chunky
Rowan Q: Big wool col: Swish no: 22
Technique focus – Simple cables

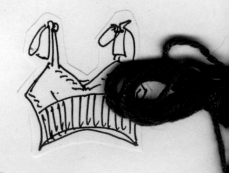

04. Appliqué cardigan
Yarn – 4 ply RYC Q: Cashcotton *col; ecru*
Technique focus – Simple embroidery

Chevron sweater
Yarn – 4plys Q: Yeoman Cotton Cannele 100% merc
cotton & Rowan shimmer col: various

05. Bra top
Yarn – 4 ply Jaeger Q: Silk [double] col: Royal p
Technique focus – Simple short rows

Metal and Mohair Belt

I am constantly intrigued by the juxtaposition of materials and process to create and control the unexpected. For this belt, whisper-fine and refined silk mohair is bound with ordinary fuse wire to create a textile of fragility, force, and flexibility. Found, collected, and collated bits and buttons satisfy my need for thrift and recycling and provide an intrinsic element of personalization and yet preciousness to this pedestrian piece.

— **Erika Knight**

FINISHED MEASUREMENTS
39" long x 5" wide, at widest point

YARN
Rowan Kidsilk Night (67% super kid mohair / 18% silk / 10% polyester / 5% nylon; 227 yards / 25 grams): 1 ball #610 starry night (A)
34-gauge wire (24 yards): 4 reels silver (B)

NEEDLES
One pair straight needles size US 9 (5.5 mm)
Change needle size if necessary to obtain correct gauge.

NOTIONS
Assorted buttons and beads of various sizes, textures, and colors; 6" of ¾" Wide Velcro to match

GAUGE
17½" sts and 20 rows = 4" (10 cm) in Stockinette st (St st), using 1 strand each of A and B held together

BELT
Using 1 strand each of A and B held together, CO 15 sts. Begin St st; work even for 24 rows.
*Increase Row: (RS) Work to last st, m1, k1–16 sts. Work even for 25 rows.
Repeat from * 6 times–22 sts. Work even until piece measures 41" from the beginning, ending with a WS row. *Note: Adjust the length here as desired, so Belt will ride low on hip.*
Decrease Row 1: (RS) Work to last 3 sts, k3tog–20 sts remain.
Decrease Row 2: P3tog, work to end–18 sts remain.
Repeat Decrease Rows 1 and 2 three times–6 sts remain.
Repeat Decrease Row 1 once–4 sts remain.
(WS) P2tog, work to end–3 sts remain.
(RS) K3tog. Fasten off.

FINISHING
Weave in all loose ends. Gently stretch Belt into desired shape (flat, scrunched, or twisted). Place marker 4" in from BO edge. Using A or B, sew buttons to Belt randomly, between marker and BO edge. Thread lengths of beads and sew through holes of buttons. Sew Velcro 1" in from end on back of BO end, and 1" in from end on CO end.

Knitta

Knitta is a Houston-based graffiti crew of eleven knitters aged twenty three to seventy-one. Working together under knitting related aliases—PolyCotN, AKrylik, Purl Nekklas 14kt, SonOfaStitch, LoopDogg, MascuKnitity, The Knotorious N.I.T., P-Knitty, Knidiot, and GrannySQ—the crew combine the idea of a knitted tea cozy, which covers a teapot to keep it warm, with the seditious gesture of street graffiti. They tag street lamps, public statues, handrails, gates, and other public and private property with impractical hand-knit cozies late at night, then return home to kiss their sleeping children and take out the trash. Knitta advocates knitting as an adventurous experience, and hopes to instigate other knit graffiti groups around the world.

Knitta started in 2005, the inspiration of two decade-long friends, both mothers in their thirties, who couldn't manage to finish their knitting projects. Feeling restless, uninspired, and frustrated by the swatches, half-scarves, and sweater sleeves piling up in their living rooms, they tried to come up with more thrilling projects, things they would actually want to complete. One hot August afternoon, they knit a pink and blue acrylic "cozy" and then, later that evening, they crocheted it onto an industrial-looking doorknob on a boutique in Houston's Montrose neighborhood. One of the women, PolyCotN, was able to see the cozy through her office window at work the next day, and encouraged by the pleasure, confusion, and surprise she saw on peoples' faces, she convinced her friend, AKrylik, that they should tag the stop sign across the street next. PolyCotN and AKrylik invited another friend to help them with their second tag, and Knitta had begun.

Through word of mouth, in just a month, AKrylik and PolyCotN's partnership grew into a large and stable crew. "It was something we stumbled into that turned into something amazing," PolyCotN says. The Knittas now count among themselves two graduate students, two undergraduates, a biophysics researcher, a retiree and grandmother, a working mom, two artists, a nuclear physicist, and a writer. "We decided to be anonymous early on, because we thought what we were doing was more in the realm of graffiti than art," one of the Knittas explains. "Our group is composed of people who don't do illegal things, and we were worried about how people would react to what we were doing." Each member brings a special skill to the collaborative: One has an excellent eye for color, one can knit letters, one has enterprising ideas about using magnets and fishing poles to tag hard-to-reach objects, and one can recite the measurements of Houston area stop-sign posts without pause (seven inches in circumference and up to six feet tall). The Knittas meet for up to three hours every Tuesday night in rotating homes to eat, drink, pool their yarn stashes, knit, and scheme—and to commit, by the end of the evening, to tags they will carry out a few days later.

In furtive fashion, the Knittas set out on Friday night expeditions to cover Houston with site-specific knit projects—stair railings, car antennas, park benches, bike racks, moped rearview mirrors, and tree trunks have all earned original cozies. A beautiful clash emerges with daybreak: Something personal, handmade, and irreverent covers their dispassionate, metropolitan, and familiar landscape. The Knittas add tags to their tags, tying a small piece of paper that announces their motto—"Knitta, please"—to their work. They have also learned that fastening their knits to objects using knots or knit stitches takes far too long, so now they sew buttons onto their graffiti before heading out. They judge one of their most successful undertakings as a series of light pole cozies on the three bridges over

Facing page
A portrait of one of the Knittas—MascuKnitity—during a Knitta working session.

Clockwise from top left
A tag on the Great Wall of China.

A stoplight tag on Manhattan's Lower East Side.

The Knitta's first tag, a door handle.

Route 59 in the Montrose neighborhood. "That was a local favorite," PolyCotN says. "The modern-looking bridge is nice, but the antique light poles are awkward, and everyone loves the splash of pink we added to the scene." Locals have come to appreciate how, at a bar, they can turn back to their beers to find that a Knitta has swapped the usual cardboard coaster with a knitted one.

Largely, their work is publicly sanctioned. "It's covering, not defacing," says PolyCotN. "It's considerate to the victim. If they don't like it, they can just unbutton it." A police officer, speaking to a small neighborhood newspaper called the *West University Examiner,* said their work was illegal in some sense, but that it was easy to take down. Juxtaposing craft and vandalism, their work questions the nonthreatening nature of knitting by aligning itself with a tougher, male-dominated art medium. "We go beyond simply wanting attention. We prove that disobedience can be beautiful and that knitting can be outlaw," reads their newly penned artist statement. Detractors have told them their work isn't useful, and that they should make scarves for the homeless. Joy, however, is the primary response to Knitta, and admirers focus on the knit graffiti's workmanship, beauty, and social commentary. Knitta members believe that as their work becomes more visible, they might want to start taking credit for what they've done. "It seems like what we are doing is inspirational," PolyCotN says. "We might not have to keep our identities a secret anymore."

Knitta has realized both local and international exposure through an inviting website, an enduringly popular MySpace page, and the tags themselves. A local Houston photographer named Deborah Smail usually accompanies them on tag missions to take high-resolution documentation that they post to their sites or e-mail. Individuals outside the group also photograph Knitta tags and post them on various websites and blogs. Fanning out beyond Houston, the Knittas have

tagged Las Vegas, Denver, San Francisco, Seattle, Beijing, San Miguel, and Manhattan, among other cities. Tina Fey mentioned their New York handiwork during an edition of *Saturday Night Live's* "Weekend Update." Yarn donations have poured in. Three different individuals have sent the group their deceased grandmothers' unfinished knit projects.

Because their tags are promptly removed in Houston—sometimes by authorities, but mostly by fans—the Knittas also focus their efforts elsewhere. They tagged more than thirty items in New York City one spring, and when one of them returned for a business trip seven weeks later, the work was still up. They're actively looking for unusual, large-scale objects to tag, "like Big Ben in London," PolyCotN says, and they're increasingly appreciative of places that have objects unfamiliar to them, like taxicab handles in New York City and tourist binoculars in Marfa, Texas. They have even received invitations for new tag sites through public art funding. Bumbershoot, Seattle's yearly music and arts festival, sponsored cozies for seventeen trees, three forty-foot poles in the Seattle Center, and several columns that hold up the city's monorail. The success of the show prompted tagging invitations from a few nonprofit art institutions and art galleries.

Because Knitta receives so many e-mails from knitters wanting to get involved, they've decided to encourage people to start their own Knitta chapters. "They could create their own identity, and we could collaborate and keep in touch," PolyCotN explains. Sympathetic groups are already brewing in Los Angeles and New York. As Knitta collectively writes by e-mail: "We have all entered into this project not knowing what the response would be. [It] has been overwhelmingly positive and greatly satisfying on many different levels. So for now, we will continue letting the dirty laundry sit so we can knit."

The Preppy Car Antenna Cozy

Each member of the Knitta crew has his/her own unique style, therefore our customary pile of antenna cozies is a veritable melting pot of tubular design. The next time you're planning a knit graffiti tagging raid at a law office, you might want to think about whipping up a briefcase full of Preppies to distribute across the sea of Benzo's you're sure to encounter. Knitta, please!

— Knitta

FINISHED MEASUREMENTS
Approximately 32" long

YARN
Red Heart Super Saver (100% acrylic; 364 yards / 7 oz):
1 skein each of #065796 soft white (MC), #304113 spring green (A), #064943 paddy green (B), and #067311 gold (C)

NEEDLES
One pair straight needles size US 8 (5 mm)
Change needle size if necessary to obtain correct gauge.

GAUGE
20 sts and 20 rows = 4" (10 cm) in Stockinette st (St st)

ANTENNA COZY
Using MC, CO 10 sts. Purl 1 row.
(RS) Begin Chart, using Intarsia Colorwork Method (see Special Techniques, page 172). Work even until entire Chart is complete. BO all sts. *Note: Experiment with the color and length of the shapes in the chart to add your own unique style.*

FINISHING
Using MC, sew back seam. Weave in all loose ends.
Attach tag. Insert over the antenna belonging to the intended target. Run away.

Key

☐ Knit on RS, purl on WS   ☐ MC   ▨ A   ▩ B   ☐ C   start here

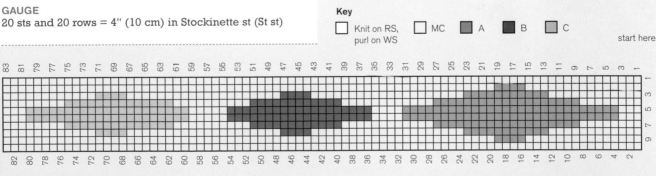

Catherine Lowe

A typical knitting pattern written by Catherine Lowe is about thirty-five pages long; it can be as many as seventy. Her designs are not extravagant; the patterns are just written out in extraordinarily precise detail. Because creating and blocking a swatch of at least ten inches is a necessary first step, and finishing procedures can take up to fifteen pages of description, knitting one of Catherine's patterns requires commitment that contradicts the notion of knitting as mere hobby. In her workshops, Catherine treats her students as though they have signed up for a graduate seminar, handing out thick packets comparable to academic syllabi before introducing herself and her theories on couture knitting. Artfully, Catherine then awes her students by pulling out her samples and explaining her designs. Diagonally shaped shoulders flatter the body, vertical lines mesmerize the eye, and luxurious materials give off a becoming sheen. By this point, students are audibly sighing over the garments, which Catherine has sent around the room. She assures her knitters that once they have mastered her techniques, they too will be able to make knitted clothes worthy of the title couture.

From the time she was born, Catherine was draped in clothing made exclusively for her. Her mother and grandmother were both dressmakers who created their family's clothes during spare hours. "They were what is called today home sewers," Catherine says, "but the term does no justice to their skill." As she grew up, first in Bangkok, Thailand, and then in various towns on the East Coast, depending on where her father's military job took the family, Catherine became an avid sewer. When Catherine was ten, she asked her mother to show her how to knit. The lessons mostly consisted of watching her mother make stitches and occasionally trying out a stitch or two on her own. Catherine quickly announced that she wanted to knit a sweater and chose a Bavarian pullover worked in the round using ten colors. While completing it was a challenge, she did such a good job that it is still impressive to look at today.

Catherine wore that sweater all through college in the late 1960s, but she did not knit. "Knitting was not considered a serious pursuit," Catherine explains. During graduate school at Yale, and later, while teaching French, Italian, and comparative literature at Williams and Wesleyan colleges, and at the University of California, San Diego, Catherine knit only in private. More publicly, Catherine put her energy into writing academic papers that compared figuration in visual and verbal languages, among other scholarly discourses.

In 1992, after seventeen years of teaching, Catherine left academia and settled in the Washington, D.C., area, spending her free time at a yarn store where she eventually became the in-house designer. Three years later, Catherine moved to the Berkshires, where she worked

as a designer for another shop. By 2002 she had set out on her own and procured a business license for what she calls the Couture Knitting Workshop.

"It's not subway knitting," she says of her approach. "I have no illusions about it having a popular appeal." Catherine's couture knitting techniques translate principles of haute couture—elegance of design, flawless fit, and refined detail—into an approach to hand-knitting that re-imagines its traditional design and technical vocabularies. Her form of knitting places primary emphasis on preparation, construction, and finishing, so that the knitter can create a long-lasting garment well-suited to his or her body.

Catherine looks at the technical aspects of flat pattern dressmaking and applies them to a knitted garment. But there is no sewing: Catherine has developed ways to knit and shape in one gesture, wherein separate pieces of knitting are joined on the needles. Sometimes pieces are joined on the bias of a garment, which makes a beautiful drape. She has also created her own methods for casting on, increasing, and decreasing that serve to maintain the integrity of her designs.

Catherine teaches at her studio in upstate New York and at yarn stores across the United States. She also distributes her designs in kits, such as a vest that can also be worn upside down as a shrug with a collar, and a baby blanket and hat set. In 2006, Catherine developed her own line of yarns that include royal baby alpaca, silk, extra-fine merino, and silk-mohair. She is able to customize her kits according to each knitter's preference, not just for color, but for fiber content and weight, as well. "The Hippari Jacket for this book, for example, can be made in a blend of fibers as she did it or in all merino, silk, or alpaca," she explains. "It's a commitment, but making Catherine's jacket, like all her patterns, offers knitters a chance to rethink how a knit garment is produced and how it looks on the body as well as their own dedication to the knitting process.

Hippari Jacket

Inspired by the elegance and ease of traditional Japanese design—the hippari coat in particular—this jacket is minimal in its construction and detail, yet infinitely protean as a wardrobe element. It derives its versatility from the knitted fabric—silk and merino with a bit of mohair—which behaves more like a woven textile than a handknit, and from the myriad draping and wrapping possibilities afforded by the oversize shaping. Designed intentionally without buttons or closures to interfere, it becomes both canvas and inspiration for accessorizing.

— Catherine Lowe

SIZES
One size

FINISHED MEASUREMENTS
54" chest, blocked

YARN
Catherine Lowe Couture Yarns #5 (40% merino / 40% silk / 20% silk/mohair blend): 1900 yards peacock (MC)
Catherine Lowe Couture Yarns #4 (100% silk): 200 yards peacock (A)
Note: A kit for the Hippari Jacket is available directly from Catherine Lowe. The kit includes the yarn as well as a 60-page pattern that includes the information presented here as well as instructions for all of Catherine's couture techniques. This is the first full garment Catherine has designed using all of her own yarns.

NEEDLES
One 32" (82 cm) circular (circ) needle size US 6 (4 mm)
One 32" circular needle size US 5 (3.75 mm)
One pair straight needles size US 3 (3.25 mm), for finishing
One pair straight needles size US 2 (2.75 mm), for finishing
One 32" circular needle size US 1 (2.25 mm), for finishing
Two 32" circular needles size US 0 (2 mm), for finishing
Change needle size if necessary to obtain correct gauge.

NOTIONS
Stitch markers; row counter (optional)

GAUGE
24¾ sts and 32¾ rows = 4" (10 cm) in Moss st using size US 6 needle, before blocking
24 sts and 32 rows = 4" (10 cm) in Moss st using size US 6 needle, after blocking
34 sts and 42 rows = 4" (10 cm) in Reverse Stockinette stitch (Rev St st) using size US 1 needle, before and after blocking

STITCH PATTERN
Moss Stitch
(multiple of 2 sts + 1; 4-row repeat)
Row 1 (RS): K1, *p1, k1; repeat from * across.
Row 2: P1, *k1, p1; repeat from * across.
Row 3: Repeat Row 2.
Row 4: Repeat Row 1.
Repeat Rows 1-4 for Moss Stitch.

ABBREVIATIONS
Sskp: Slip next 2 sts to right-hand needle one at a time as if to knit; return them back to left-hand needle one at a time in their new orientation; knit them together through the back loops; transfer this st back to left-hand needle, pass second st on left-hand needle over first st; transfer st back to right-hand needle.
Ksp: K1, transfer st back to left-hand needle, then pass second st on left-hand needle over st just worked, transfer st back to right-hand needle.
Spp: Slip next st purlwise to right-hand needle; p1, pass slipped st over purl st.
Psp: P1, transfer st back to left-hand needle, then pass second st on left-hand needle over st just worked, transfer st back to right-hand needle.

NOTES

All sts are slipped purlwise unless otherwise noted.

Each piece will be worked with 1 or more selvage sts at the beginning and end of each row.

When working the Long-Tail CO, make sure sts are cast-on firmly.

Reverse Joinery BO: Hold the pieces to be joined with the wrong sides facing each other and the needles parallel, both pointing to the right. *Note: Text will indicate which needle is to be held in front.* Holding both needles in your left hand, using working yarn and a third needle of specified size, insert third needle into first st on front needle, then into first st on back needle; knit these two sts together; *knit next st from each needle together (two sts on right-hand needle); pass first st over second st to BO one st. Repeat from * until one st remains on third needle; break yarn, leaving 6" tail and fasten off yarn through final st.

JACKET

Back

Using size US 6 circ needle, Long-Tail CO (see Special Techniques, page 172) and MC, CO 165 sts.

Establish Pattern

Row 1 (RS): Change to size US 5 needle. P1 (selvage st), work in Moss st to last st, p1 (selvage st).

Row 2: Slip 1 knitwise (selvage st), work in Moss st to last st, k1 (selvage st).

Row 3: Slip 1 purlwise tbl (selvage st), work in Moss st to last st, p1 (selvage st).

Row 4: Slip 1 knitwise (selvage st), work in Moss st to last st, k1 (selvage st).

Repeat Rows 3 and 4 twice.

Row 9 (RS): Change to size US 6 needle. Work even for 136 rows (piece should measure approximately 17¾" from the beginning).

Shape Armhole

Row 145 (RS): K1 (selvage st), sk2p, work to last 4 sts, sskp, k1 (selvage st)–161 sts remain.

Row 146: K1 (selvage st), p1, work to last 2 sts, p1, k1 (selvage sts).

Rows 147-156: Repeat Rows 145 and 146–141 sts remain.

Row 157: K1 (selvage st), skp, work to last 3 sts, ksp, k1 (selvage st)–139 sts remain.

Row 158: K1 (selvage st), p1, work to last 2 sts, p1, k1 (selvage st).

Rows 159-168: Repeat Rows 157 and 158–129 sts remain.

Row 169: Slip 1 purlwise tbl (selvage st), k1, work to last 2 sts, k1, k1 (selvage st).

Row 170: Slip 1 knitwise (selvage st), p1, work to last 2 sts, p1, p1 (selvage st). Work even for 53 rows (piece should measure approximately 27¼" from the beginning).

Short Row Shoulder Shaping (see Special Techniques, page 172).

Note: Stitch counts that follow are for all sts on the needle, including those that are left out of work while working short rows.

Row 224 (WS): Work to last 5 sts, wrp-t.

Row 225: Slip 1, work to last 5 sts, wrp-t.

Row 226: Slip 1, work to last 10 sts, wrp-t.

Row 227: Repeat Row 226.

Row 228: Slip 1, work to last 15 sts, wrp-t.

Row 229: Repeat Row 228.

Row 230: Slip 1, work to last 21 sts, wrp-t.

Row 231: Repeat Row 230.

Row 232: Slip 1, work to last 27 sts, wrp-t.

Shape Neck

Row 233: Slip 1, work 23 sts, join a second ball of yarn and BO next 27 sts for Back neck, work 24 sts, wrp-t–51 sts remain each side for shoulders.

Row 234: Working both sides at once, on left side of neck, slip 1, work to last 2 sts, p1, k1 (selvage st); on right side of neck, k1, p1, work to last 33 sts, wrp-t.

Row 235: On right side of neck, slip 1, work to last 4 sts, sskp, k1 (selvage st); on left side of neck, k1 (selvage st), sk2p, work to last 33 sts, wrp-t–49 sts remain each side.

Row 236: On left side of neck, slip 1, work to last 2 sts, p1, k1 (selvage st); on right side of neck, k1 (selvage st), p1, work to last 39 sts, wrp-t.

Row 237: On right side of neck, slip 1, work to last 4 sts, sskp, k1 (selvage st); on left side of neck, k1 (selvage st), sk2p, work to last 39 sts, wrp-t–47 sts remain each side.

Row 238: On left side of neck, slip 1, work to last 2 sts, p1, k1 (selvage st); on right side of neck, k1 (selvage st), p1, work to last 2 sts, working wraps together with wrapped sts as you come to them, p1, p1 (selvage st).

Row 239: On right side of neck, p1-tbl, BO 42 sts (beginning with first st worked), sskp, BO st last worked, k1, BO st last worked, fasten off last st; on left side of neck, k1 (selvage st), sk2p, work to last 2 sts, working wraps together with wrapped sts as you come to them, k1, k1 (selvage st).

BO all sts purlwise, except first and last sts, which should be worked knitwise.

Right Front

Using size US 6 circ needle, Long-Tail CO and MC, CO 91 sts.

Establish Pattern

Row 1 (RS): Change to size US 5 needle. K3 (selvage sts), work in Moss st to last st, p1 (selvage st).

Row 2: Slip 1 knitwise (selvage st), work in Moss st to last 3 sts, [slip 1, p1-tbl, p1] (selvage sts).

Row 3: [Slip 2 knitwise one at a time, k1] (selvage sts), work in Moss st to last st, p1 (selvage st).

Row 4: Slip 1 knitwise (selvage st), work in Moss st to last 3 sts, [slip 1, p1-tbl, p1] (selvage sts).

Repeat Rows 3 and 4 twice.

Row 9 (RS): Change to size US 6 needle. Work even for 136 rows (piece should measure approximately 17¾" from the beginning).

Shape Armhole

Row 145 (RS): [Slip 2 knitwise one at a time, k1] (selvage sts), work to last 4 sts, sskp, k1 (selvage st)–89 sts remain.

Row 146: K1 (selvage st), p1, work to last 3 sts, [slip 1, p1-tbl, p1] (selvage sts).

Rows 147-148: Repeat Rows 145 and 146–87 sts remain.

Shape Neck

Row 149: K2tog (selvage st), skp, work to last 4 sts, sskp, k1 (selvage st)–83 sts remain.

Row 150: K1 (selvage st), p1, work to last 2 sts, p1, k1 (selvage st).

Row 151: K1 (selvage st), k1, work to last 4 sts, sskp, k1 (selvage st)–81 sts remain.

Rows 152, 154, 156, 158, 160, 162, 164, 166, and 168: Repeat Row 150.

Row 153: K1 (selvage st), skp, work to last 4 sts, sskp, k1 (selvage st)–78 sts remain.

Row 155: Repeat Row 151–76 sts remain.

Row 157: K1 (selvage st), skp, work to last 3 sts, ksp, k1 (selvage st)–74 sts remain.

Row 159: K1 (selvage st), k1, work to last 3 sts, ksp, k1 (selvage st)–73 sts remain.

Row 161: K1 (selvage st), sk2p, work to last 3 sts, ksp, k1 (selvage st)–70 sts remain.

Row 163: Repeat Row 159–69 sts remain.

Row 165: Repeat Row 157–67 sts remain.

Row 167: Repeat Row 159–66 sts remain.

Row 169: K1 (selvage st), skp, work to last 2 sts, k1, k1 (selvage st)–65 sts remain.

Row 170: Slip 1 knitwise (selvage st), p1, work to last 2 sts, p1, k1 (selvage st).

Row 171: K1 (selvage st), k1, work to last 2 sts, k1, k1 (selvage st).

Row 172: Repeat Row 170.

Rows 173-176: Repeat Rows 169-172–64 sts remain.

Row 177: K1 (selvage st), sk2p, work to last 2 sts, k1, k1 (selvage st)–62 sts remain.

Rows 178-180: Repeat Rows 170-172.

Rows 181-192: Repeat Rows 169-172–59 sts remain.

Rows 193 and 194: Repeat Rows 177 and 178–57 sts remain.

Rows 195 and 196: Repeat Rows 171 and 172.

Rows 197-208: Repeat Rows 169-172–54 sts remain.

Rows 209 and 210: Repeat Rows 177 and 178–52 sts remain.

Rows 211 and 212: Repeat Rows 171 and 172.

Rows 213-224: Repeat Rows 169-172–49 sts remain.

Short Row Shoulder Shaping

Note: Stitch counts that follow are for all sts on the needle, including those that are left out of work while working short rows.

Row 225: K1 (selvage st), sk2p, work to last 5 sts, wrp-t–47 sts remain.

Row 226: Slip 1, work to last 2 sts, p1, k1 (selvage st).

Row 227: K1 (selvage st), k1, work to last 10 sts, wrp-t.

Rows 228, 230, 232, 234, 236, and 238: Repeat Row 226.

Row 229: K1 (selvage st), skp, work to last 15 sts, wrp-t–46 sts remain.

Row 231: K1 (selvage st), k1, work to last 21 sts, wrp-t.

Row 233: K1 (selvage st), skp, work to last 27 sts, wrp-t–45 sts remain.

Row 235: K1 (selvage st), k1, work to last 33 sts, wrp-t.

Row 237: K1 (selvage st), k1, work to last 39 sts, wrp-t.

Row 239: K1 (selvage st), k1, work to last 2 sts, working wraps together with wrapped sts as you come to them, k1, k1 (selvage st).

BO all sts purlwise, except first and last sts, which should be worked knitwise.

Left Front

Using size US 6 circ needle, Long-Tail CO and MC, CO 91 sts.

Establish Pattern

Row 1 (RS): Change to size US 5 needle. P1 (selvage st), work in Moss st to last 3 sts, k3 (selvage sts).

Row 2: [Slip 1 purlwise tbl, slip 1, p1] (selvage sts), work in Moss st to last st, k1 (selvage st).

Row 3: Slip 1 purlwise tbl (selvage st), work in Moss st to last 3 sts, [slip 1, k2] (selvage sts).

Row 4: [Slip 1 purlwise tbl, slip 1, p1] (selvage sts), work in Moss st to last st, k1 (selvage st).

Repeat Rows 3 and 4 twice.

Row 9 (RS): Change to size US 6 needle. Work even for 135 rows (piece should measure approximately 17¾" from the beginning).

Shape Armhole

Row 145 (RS): K1 (selvage st), sk2p, work to last 3 sts, [slip 1, k2] (selvage sts)–89 sts remain.

Row 146: Slip 1 purlwise tbl, slip 1 purlwise, p1 (selvage sts), work to last 2 sts, p1, k1 (selvage st).

Rows 147-148: Repeat Rows 145 and 146–87 sts remain.

Shape Neck

Row 149: K1 (selvage st), sk2p, work to last 4 sts, ksp, ssk (selvage st)–83 sts remain.

Row 150: K1 (selvage st), p1, work to last 2 sts, p1, k1 (selvage st).

Row 151: K1 (selvage st), sk2p, work to last 2 sts, k1, k1 (selvage st)–81 sts remain.

Rows 152, 154, 156, 158, 160, 162, 164, 166, and 168: Repeat Row 150.

Row 153: K1 (selvage st), sk2p, work to last 3 sts, ksp, k1 (selvage st)–78 sts remain.

Row 155: Repeat Row 151–76 sts remain.

Row 157: K1 (selvage st), skp, work to last 3 sts, ksp, k1 (selvage st)–74 sts remain.

Row 159: K1 (selvage st), skp, work to last 2 sts, k1, k1 (selvage st)–73 sts remain.

Row 161: K1 (selvage st), skp, work to last 3 sts, sskp, k1 (selvage st)–70 sts remain.

Row 163: Repeat Row 159–69 sts remain.

Row 165: Repeat Row 157–67 sts remain.

Row 167: Repeat Row 159–66 sts remain.

Row 169: Slip 1 purlwise tbl (selvage st), k1, work to last 3 sts, ksp, k1 (selvage st)–65 sts remain.

Row 170: K1 (selvage st), p1, work to last 2 sts, p1, p1 (selvage st).

Row 171: Slip 1 purlwise tbl (selvage st), k1, work to last 2 sts, k1, k1 (selvage st).
Row 172: Repeat Row 170.
Rows 173-176: Repeat Rows 169-172–64 sts remain.
Row 177: Slip 1 purlwise tbl (selvage st), k1, work to last 4 sts, sskp, k1–62 sts remain.
Rows 178-180: Repeat Rows 170-172.
Rows 181-192: Repeat Rows 169-172–59 sts remain.
Rows 193 and 194: Repeat Rows 177 and 178–57 sts remain.
Rows 195 and 196: Repeat Rows 171 and 172.
Rows 197-208: Repeat Rows 169-172–54 sts remain.
Rows 209 and 210: Repeat Rows 177 and 178–52 sts remain.
Rows 211 and 212: Repeat Rows 171 and 172.
Rows 213-220: Repeat Rows 169-172–50 sts remain.
Rows 221-223: Repeat Rows 169-171–49 sts remain.

Short Row Shoulder Shaping
Note: Stitch counts that follow are for all sts on the needle, including those that are left out of work while working short rows.
Row 224: K1 (selvage st), p1, work to last 5 sts, wrp-t.
Row 225: Slip 1, work to last 4 sts, sskp, k1 (selvage st)–47 sts remain.
Row 226: K1 (selvage st), p1, work to last 10 sts, wrp-t.
Row 227: Slip 1, work to last 2 sts, k1, k1 (selvage st).
Row 228: K1 (selvage st), p1, work to last 15 sts, wrp-t.
Row 229: Slip 1, work to last 3 sts, ksp, k1 (selvage st)–46 sts remain.
Row 230: K1 (selvage st), p1, work to last 21 sts, wrp-t.
Rows 231, 235, and 237: Repeat Row 227.
Row 232: K1 (selvage st), p1, work to last 27 sts, wrp-t.
Row 233: Repeat Row 229–45 sts remain.
Row 234: K1 (selvage st), p1, work to last 33 sts, wrp-t.
Row 236: K1 (selvage st), p1, work to last 39 sts, wrp-t.
Row 238: K1 (selvage st), p1, work to last 2 sts, working wraps together with wrapped sts as you come to them, p1, p1 (selvage st).
BO all sts knitwise, except first and last sts, which should be worked as p1-tbl.

Sleeves (make 2)
Using size US 6 circ needle, Long-Tail CO and MC, CO 103 sts.

Establish Pattern
Row 1 (RS): Change to size US 5 needle. P1 (selvage st), k1, work in Moss st to last 2 sts, k1, p1 (selvage st).
Row 2: Slip 1 knitwise (selvage st), p1, work in Moss st to last 2 sts, p1, k1 (selvage st).
Row 3: Slip 1 purlwise tbl (selvage st), k1, work in Moss st to last 2 sts, p1, p1 (selvage st).
Row 4: Slip 1 knitwise (selvage st), p1, work in Moss st to last 2 sts, p1, k1 (selvage st).

Shape Sleeve
Row 5: Slip 1 purlwise tbl (selvage st), k1, m1p, work to last 2 sts, m1p-l, k1, p1 (selvage st)–105 sts.
Row 6: Slip 1 knitwise (selvage st), p1, work in Moss st to last 2 sts, p1, k1 (selvage st).
Row 7: Slip 1 purlwise tbl (selvage st), k1, work in Moss st to last 2 sts, k1, p1 (selvage st).
Rows 8, 10, and 12: Repeat Row 6.
Row 9 (RS): Change to size US 6 needle. Repeat Row 7.
Row 11: Repeat Row 7.
Row 13: Slip 1 purlwise tbl (selvage st), k1, m1r, work to last 2 sts, m1, k1, p1 (selvage st)–107 sts.
Rows 14- 20: Repeat Rows 6 and 7, ending with Row 6.
Rows 21-68: Repeat Rows 5-20–119 sts.
Rows 69-80: Repeat Rows 5-16–123 sts.

Shape Cap
Row 81: K1 (selvage st), sk2p, work to last 4 sts, sskp, k1 (selvage st)–119 sts remain.
Row 82: K1 (selvage st), spp, work to last 3 sts, psp, k1 (selvage st)–117 sts remain.
Rows 83-108: Repeat Rows 81 and 82–39 sts remain.
BO all sts knitwise.

FINISHING
Wash and block all pieces to measurements.

Shoulder Join
RS facing, using size US 0 circ needle and A, pick up and knit 59 sts along left Front shoulder edge. Do not break yarn. Using second needle and continuing with yarn from left Front shoulder edge pick-up, repeat for left Back shoulder edge. With left Front shoulder sts on front needle and left Back shoulder sts on back needle, and with WS's together, using size US 3 needle and yarn attached to back needle, join shoulders using Reverse Joinery BO. Fasten off final st. Repeat for Right shoulder.

Armhole/Sleeve Joins
RS facing, using size US 0 circ needle and A, pick up and knit 176 sts along left Sleeve cap shaping. Do not break yarn. Using second needle and continuing with yarn from left Sleeve cap pick-up, pick up and knit 176 sts from beginning of left Front armhole shaping, over left shoulder, to beginning of left Back armhole shaping. Set aside; do not break yarn. With Sleeve Cap sts on front needle and armhole sts on back needle, and with WS's together, using size US 3 needle and yarn attached to back needle, join shoulders using Reverse Joinery BO. Fasten off final st. Repeat for Right armhole/Sleeve Cap.

Neck Edging

RS facing, using size 0 circ needle and A, beginning at bottom of right Front neck edge, pick up and knit 255 sts along neck shaping, as follows: 102 sts to shoulder seam, 1 st in shoulder seam, 6 sts to beginning of right Back neck shaping, pm, 1 st in right Back neck corner, pm, 35 sts to left Back neck corner, pm, 1 st in left Back neck corner, pm, 7 sts to left shoulder seam, 1 st in shoulder seam, 101 sts to bottom of left Front neck edge.

Row 1 (WS): Change to size US 1 needle. K1 (selvage st), knit to 1 st before first marker, dcd (removing markers), knit to 1 st before next marker, dcd (removing markers), knit to last st, p1 (selvage st)–251 sts remain.

Row 2: Slip 1 purlwise tbl (selvage st), purl to last st, k1 (selvage st).

Row 3: Slip 1 knitwise (selvage st), knit to last st, p1 (selvage st).

Row 4: Repeat Row 2.

Using size US 2 needle, BO all sts knitwise. Weave in Neck Edging tails only.

Sleeve Edging

RS facing, using size 0 circ needle and A, pick up and knit 135 sts along CO edge of right Sleeve.

Row 1 (WS): Change to size US 1 needle. K1 (selvage st), knit to last st, p1 (selvage st).

Row 2: Slip 1 purlwise tbl (selvage st), purl to last st, k1 (selvage st).

Row 3: Slip 1 knitwise (selvage st), knit to last st, p1 (selvage st).

Row 4: Repeat Row 2.

Using size US 2 needle, BO all sts knitwise. Break yarn, leaving 6" tail. Repeat for left Sleeve.

Side/Sleeve Joins

RS facing, using size 0 circ needle and A, pick up and knit 227 sts along left Front side and Sleeve, as follows: 145 sts along left Front, from CO edge to beginning of armhole shaping, 1 st in left Front armhole join, 81 sts along left edge of left Sleeve. Do not break yarn. Using second needle and continuing with yarn from Front side and Sleeve pick-up, repeat for left Back side and Sleeve, as follows: 81 sts along right edge of left Sleeve, beginning at CO edge, 1 st in left Back armhole join, 145 sts along left Back side, from armhole shaping to CO edge. Set aside; do not break yarn. With left Front side and left Sleeve edge sts on front needle and left Back side and right Sleeve edge sts on back needle, and with WS's together, using size US 3 needle and yarn attached to back needle, join pieces using Reverse Joinery BO. Fasten off final st. Repeat for right side and Sleeve.

Finishing

Weave all loose ends into selvage sts. Wash and block piece.

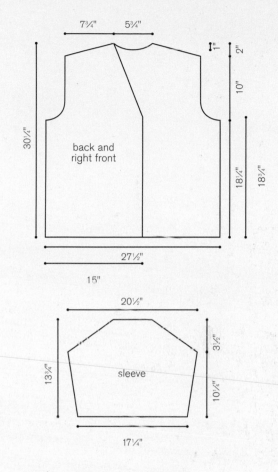

Note: Measurements shown are after blocking.

Bridget
Marrin

From 2001 to 2006, Bridget Marrin's knitting studio was a twelve-by-sixteen-foot lab filled with gas cylinders, where she worked as a gas analyst for a company that manufactures simulated smog for air pollution control research. Finished knitted projects hung on the walls above her, yarn sat in cardboard boxes at her feet, and works in progress rested on top of her gas chromatograph. It was probably the last place you'd have expected to find knitted clothes and houses, though you might have been slightly less startled by knitted regulators and other scientific gadgets. The eclectic studio was just one example of how Bridget, a polymath who has studied fine art, model-making, nursing, robotics, and biology, has used knitting to connect her disparate fields of interest.

Bridget added knitting to her broad skill set in 1994, while she was attending Mount St. Mary's College in Los Angeles, pursuing a degree of her own design in bio-art. "My sister Tina hooked me," she says (see page 108). "We would hang out together, and knit and chat." Though Tina only showed her how to knit and purl, Bridget was ready to start knitting an Aran sweater of her own design just a month later.

"Bridget is the kind of person who goes for things full force," Tina says. "She used to wake up, drive an hour and a half to work, drive home after working in the lab for eight hours, build a shed in her backyard, and bake dozens of quiches with vegetables she grew in her own garden. My friends and I would be tired just from making the quiches, but Bridget has tons and tons of energy."

The same year she learned to knit, Bridget started working at the Museum of Jurassic Technology, a unique museum with its own distinguished ability to reconcile seemingly incompatible subject matter, by presenting offbeat exhibitions relating to natural history, the history of science, and the history of art. Museum founder and director David Wilson had worked in Hollywood doing special effects, and he taught Bridget how to make the models that would go on display. She learned how to use materials like plaster, Celluclay, dirt, styrene, and PVC pipe to create lifelike representations for exhibits. "It wasn't just a job," Bridget says. "I was an art and biology major before I started working there, but my work at the museum really developed me as an artist." During her five years at the museum, Bridget created a dozen dioramas, a miniature model freeway, and a centerpiece based on a drawing by Athanasius Kircher, a seventeenth-century scholar of science. Creating these models also inspired Bridget to move into sculptural knitting at home, where she was knitting things like nativity scenes and knitted vases filled with bouquets of knitted flowers.

Always a little bit scatterbrained—apt to leave a stove or iron on while problem-solving six different ideas—Bridget refined her ability to bridge disciplines during college. She took a combination of ambitious pre-med classes while doing fine art coursework. "I was always interested in physiological mechanisms," she explains. "At the same time, I took photography and video. I also got credit for working at the Museum of Jurassic Technology." Her 1997 senior thesis was a show of

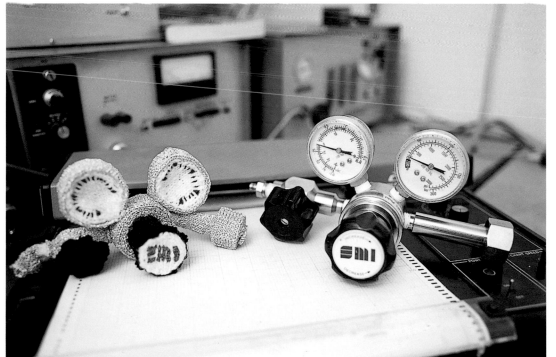

constructed minerals, a stained-glass window of herself, a diorama of a Los Angeles convent, and a video of herself and David Wilson performing an opera.

In 2000, Bridget quit her job at the museum to concentrate on making artwork for an exhibition at the Museum of Contemporary Art in San Diego. The curator there had seen her work at the Museum of Jurassic Technology and wanted to include her as an artist in his exhibit entitled, Small World: Dioramas in Contemporary Art. Bridget created a miniature diorama for the show called The Redlands Liberty Pole, based on a flagpole near her house. The piece included three-by-four-inch knitted flags connected to a motor that made the flags move as though they were outside in the wind, and it marked her first incorporation of knitting into her diorama projects. "Then, since I was knitting and model-making, it was the natural course of things to knit the models," she says.

After the exhibition at the Museum of Contemporary Art closed in 2001, Bridget began her job as a gas analyst and took an animation course at Glendale Community College. The class gave Bridget the tools she needed to begin an untitled long-term project about the adventures of a knitted girl who knits a boy who later comes to life. The stop-motion animation is shot on a miniature knitted set: a one-foot-tall house with two floors and a chimney from which tufts of smoke emerge. The fixtures inside the set are wired with lights that turn on and off, and the house stands on a bed of green mohair grass out of which grow conifer trees. Seven dolls perform as characters in the animation, and props like hands and flowers are used for cutaway scenes. Bridget describes the piece as inspired by the style of Czech animator Jan Svankmajer, but more homemade-looking. "Making knitted models is a very precise job," Bridget says. "I try to control the yarn, and sometimes I just can't. It doesn't always look as meticulous as I like, but it ends up looking charming."

In addition to completing the knitted girl animation, and building a deck for her boyfriend's backyard, Bridget has plans to make another film about nursing, based on her enrollment in nursing school at California State University, Los Angeles, in 2006. "I like to make art based on what I am actually doing with my life—basically, everything I do is for my art," Bridget says, sitting next to her elderly dog, Mary, who is wearing an Aran sweater of Bridget's design that matches the one Bridget wears. "I work with patients as a nurse practitioner, but I'm also doing research for my art. My film will be based on vignettes inside a hospital center, using latex models that wear hand-knit sweaters," she explains. With plans to teach knitting to patients who are bed-bound, Bridget has found a way to incorporate knitting into yet another endeavor.

Knitted Tube Dress

I really wanted a knitted dress and yet didn't want to wait a millennium to wear it, so I decided to find creative ways to speed up the process a bit. I experimented with larger needles and wasn't that impressed with the results, so I thought of a compromise between instant gratification and a nice piece, and came up with this little number. I think the bands, created by shifting back and forth between small and large needles, offers a sort of military/4-H element. The entire dress is worked in rib stitch, which lends it a clingy tube-dress-type fit.

— **Bridget Marrin**

SIZES
Small (Medium, Large)

FINISHED MEASUREMENTS
24 (26, 28)" chest, stretches to fit 34 (37, 40)" bust

YARN
Jamie Pompadour Bonus Bundle (85% sayelle, 15% rayon; 675 yards / 6 ounces): 1 ball #262 Jack and Jill

NEEDLES
One pair straight needles size US 2 (2.75 mm)
One pair straight needles size US 15 (10 mm)
Change needle size if necessary to obtain correct gauge.

NOTIONS
Stitch markers

GAUGE
24 sts and 28 rows = 4" (10 cm) in 1x1 Rib using smaller needles

---

NOTES
1x1 Rib
(multiple of 2 sts; 1-row repeat)
Row 1 (RS): *K1, p1; repeat from * across [ending k1 if there are an odd number of sts].
Row 2: Knit the knit sts and purl the purl sts as they face you.
Repeat Row 2 for 1x1 Rib.

DRESS
Back and Front (both alike)
Using smaller needles, CO 72 (78, 84) sts. Begin 1x1 Rib; work even for 15 rows.
**(WS) Change to larger needles. *P3tog; repeat from * across—24 (26, 28) sts remain.
(RS) Change to 1x1 Rib; work even for 15 rows, ending with a RS row.
(WS) Change to smaller needles. *P1-f/b, m1; repeat from * to last st, p1-f/b—71 (77, 83) sts.
(RS) Change to 1x1 Rib, increase 1 st at end of row—72 (78, 84) sts. Work even for 14 rows, ending with a RS row.
Repeat from ** once.
(WS) Change to larger needles. *P3tog; repeat from * across—24 (26, 28) sts remain.
Shape waist (RS): Change to 1x1 Rib, decrease 1 st each side—22 (24, 26) sts remain.
(WS) Work even for 14 rows, ending with a RS row.
(WS) Change to smaller needles. P1, *m1, p1-f/b; repeat from * to last st, m1—63 (69, 75) sts.
(RS) Change to 1x1 Rib. Work even for 15 rows, ending with a RS row.
(WS) Change to larger needles. *P3tog; repeat from * across—21 (23, 25) sts remain.
(RS) Change to 1x1 Rib; work even for 1 row.
(WS) Work even for 14 rows, ending with a RS row.
(WS) Change to smaller needles. *P1-f/b, m1; repeat from * to last st, p1-f/b—62 (68, 74) sts.
(RS) Change to 1x1 Rib, increase 1 st at end of row—63 (69, 75) sts. Work even for 14 rows, ending with a RS row.
(WS) Change to larger needles. *P3tog; repeat from *

across—21 (23, 25) sts remain.
(RS) Change to 1x1 Rib; work even for 1 row.

Shape armhole (WS): Decrease 1 st each side this row—19 (21, 23) sts remain. Work even for 13 rows, ending with a RS row.
(WS) Change to smaller needles. P1, *m1, p1-f/b; repeat from * to end—55 (61, 67) sts.
(RS) Change to 1x1 Rib; work even for 15 rows, ending with a RS row.
BO all sts.

Sleeves (make 2)
Using smaller needles, CO 36 (39, 42) sts. Begin 1x1 Rib; work even for 15 rows.
(WS) Change to larger needles. *P3tog; repeat from * across—12 (13, 14) sts remain.
(RS) Change to 1x1 Rib, increase 1 st each side—14 (15, 16) sts. Work even for 14 rows, ending with a RS row.
****(WS) Change to smaller needles. P1-f/b, *m1, p1-f/b; repeat from * to end—41 (44, 47) sts.
(RS) Change to 1x1 Rib, increase 1 st at end of row—42 (45, 48) sts. Work even for 14 rows, ending with a RS row.
(WS) Change to larger needles. *P3tog; repeat from * across—14 (15, 16) sts remain.
(RS) Change to 1x1 Rib, increase 1 st each side—16 (17, 18) sts. Work even for 14 rows, ending with a RS row.
Repeat from ** once 18 (19, 20) sts.
(WS) Change to smaller needles. P1-f/b, *m1, p1-f/b; repeat from * to end—53 (56, 59) sts.
(RS) Change to 1x1 Rib, increase 1 st each side—55 (58, 61) sts.
(WS) Increase 1 st at end of row—56 (59, 62) sts. Work even for 13 rows, ending with a RS row.
BO all sts.

FINISHING
Block pieces lightly. Sew top of Back and Front together for 1" in from each side, for shoulders. Set in Sleeves. Sew side and Sleeve seams.

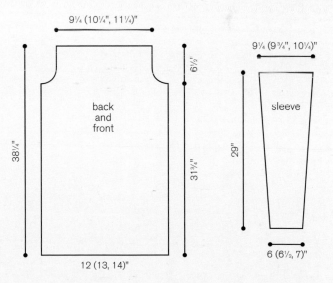

9¼ (10¼", 11¼)"

6½"

back and front

38¼"

31¾"

9¼ (9¾", 10¼)"

sleeve

29"

6 (6½, 7)"

12 (13, 14)"

Note: Measurements shown are before stretching; garment will stretch significantly. As the width stretches wider to fit, the length will be shortened.

Tina
Marrin

Tina Marrin learned to knit when a friend who was knitting a pair of powder pink angora breasts dragged her to lessons while they were in graduate school at the California Institute of Arts. Tina loved knitting so much that she spent an entire year doing it, forsaking work on her thesis art show. When the MFA class of 1995 exhibition arrived, Tina had only completed two artworks—both hooked rugs, one featuring a gothic chandelier, and the other depicting Debbie Harry's face. Worried that she hadn't made enough art to graduate, Tina displayed her rugs on a white wall and then plopped her knit projects, all of them hats, into a mound in the middle of the gallery floor in hopes that her professors wouldn't think she'd been idle. Her professors liked her work, describing it as ghostlike, as if someone had once worn all of Tina's hand-knit clothing and then evaporated or disappeared. Tina got her degree.

A lithe, spirited, thirty-something Californian who makes an impact in her flirty knit designs, Tina applies her fine art background to knitting projects that are beautiful, imprecise, and completely innovative. An accountant by day, she knits garments and creates hooked rugs during evenings and weekends on the top floor of a suburban Riverside, California, home, where she lives above her landlords. Tina mostly works in her bedroom in surroundings that reflect her eclectic nature, knitting on a large, yellow 1960s couch that she bought on eBay. The room is carefully adorned in Tina's personal color scheme: peach walls, a red bedspread, cream-colored curtains, and a blue yoga mat, rolled up neatly. Art collectors and fashion enthusiasts have purchased the hooked rugs and knit garments that she makes here, but Tina also trades her creations for other people's artwork, or for favors. In exchange for some of Tina's knitted crowns, which are worn on cold days to keep ears warm, a friend made Tina business cards that encapsulate Tina's take on knitting. Above her phone number, each one makes a different proclamation: "Tina knits flutter into butter," "Tina knits the wind in the trees," and "Tina knits valentines to rainbows."

Tina mostly designs freeform knitted garments in response to needs in her own life, like the pair of bright green knitted boots she made from high-heeled pumps that she never wore. Those boots spawned a whole group of other knitted shoe designs, and the work was so well received that Tina was invited to share her patterns with viewers of the television show *Knitty Gritty* and the readers of *Interweave Knits* and *Craft* magazines. For a while, she knit tops decorated with Braille messages like "You are the one," "Knitting IS Nourishment" and "I listen to Ed Tyll," which she does, on the radio, while she knits. Another interactive garment is her Scrabble Sweater, which functions as a portable version of the game. An intarsia Scrabble board is knit onto the front of the sweater and one arm unbuttons to act as a grab bag for the knitted letters.

Not everyone endorses Tina's knitting style, which is renegade and largely self-taught, but her process—complete with mistakes—is integral to her final product. "I used to go into yarn stores and show them what I had knit, and they were not impressed," Tina says, shrugging. "They picked out the mistakes and said things like, 'You're not supposed to knit at that gauge with that yarn,' or 'Don't worry, you'll get better.' But I like the way my stuff looks!" Tina never rips out stitches and starts over. If projects don't go as planned, she cuts them up, felts them, uses safety pins to hold them together, or makes even more mistakes as design solutions.

"A classic example is my Unravel Sweater," Tina says. "I was trying to do Elizabeth Zimmermann's percentage system for sweaters, but I did it wrong. It was really tight under the arms and on the upper arms. So in those areas, I cut stitches and let them unravel into ladders. That opened the area up. Then I knitted color panels and sewed them in behind the ladders. And it looks really good!" Her Tickle Dress, so named by an onlooker at The Showdown, a fashion show at the Center for Art and Architecture's MAK Center in Los Angeles, where Tina's knitting was featured in 2004, is a gray and beige angora dress that Tina accidentally shrank when washing. "So I cut slices around the waist and crocheted around the slices," she says. When Tina stained a skein of yarn with markers, she simply unwound it and colored over the yarn, length by length. "Mistakes are opportunities," she declares.

Though Tina plans to further study knitting through The Knitting Guild of America's Master Knitting Program, she doesn't think becoming a "better" knitter will affect her process of designing based on mistakes. "I think I'll just learn more ways to screw things up!" she declares. She'll apply her methodology to her upcoming projects, which include producing kits based on designs for entire knitted outfits, publishing patterns as tiny handmade books, starting her own yarn line, making a series of hand-knit dolls, and taking commissions to make photorealistic, knitted portraits of people's faces.

Facing page
Tina in her home in Riverside, California.

Below
Detail from Tina's Braille Sweater that reads "You are the one."

Ankle Boot

The idea for knitted boots came one month after I dropped a mint on a brand new pair of very expensive gold high-heel pumps. Buying the gold pumps was my attempt to be more flashy, but they just weren't me. Rather than cast-off (ha!) the shoes to the local thrift store, I figured I'd try to engulf the shoes in beautiful yarn, hopefully producing something as gorgeous as a couple of parade floats swathed in carnations. Before the inspiration left me, I grabbed my dad's power drill and made holes near the base of each shoe for cast on stitches—the result was what turned out to look more like spike heel mukluks. I wore the hell out of them, eventually retiring the shoes after the heel cracked on a day trip to the Angeles National Forest.
— **Tina Marrin**

SIZE
To fit size US 5½-7 (7½-9, 9½-11) woman's shoe

YARN
Brown Sheep Yarns Burley Spun (100% wool; 130 yards / 8 ounces): 1 skein BS110 orange you glad

NEEDLES
One set of 25 (27, 29) double-pointed needles (dpn) size US 9 (5.5 mm)
Change needle size if necessary to obtain correct gauge.

NOTIONS
One pair size US 5½-7 (7½-9, 9½-11) heeled shoes (Capezio's Jr. Footlight #550 were used here); crochet hook size US E/4 (3.5 mm); ³⁄₈" wide low-tack tape; flexible measuring tape; power drill and ³⁄₃₂" and ⁵⁄₃₂" drill bits; permanent marker of similar color to yarn used

GAUGE
8 sts and 10 rows = 4" (10 cm) in Stockinette stitch (St st)

NOTES
Because of the shape and contour of the shoes, the cast-on row may be worked on as many as 12 (13, 14) dpns. The cast-on and subsequent rows will be tight, so sts on the first several rows will be worked using a crochet hook to "knit" the sts onto a new needle. Adjust the number of dpn if desired, as you work up the Boot.

You may want to work both Boots simultaneously to ensure that all shaping happens in the same place.

To prepare yarn, wind 2 center-pull balls of equal length from 1 skein.

To prepare shoes, cut off ankle strap if necessary. Run tape along bottom of upper, from front to back of shoe, just above sole and heel; this will give you a ³⁄₈" line around the bottom of the shoe. *Note: You may have to tear the tape into smaller pieces to follow the curves of the shoe.*

Using marker, mark center of toe box, just above tape line. Place a mark every ½", just above the tape line, beginning left of the center mark, and ending before the heel seam. You should have 22 (24, 26) marks. Repeat for the right side of the shoe. *Note: Do not mark any seams.* You should have a total of 43 (47, 51) marks.

Using power drill and ³⁄₃₂" drill bit, drill hole through the upper at each mark, being careful to avoid drilling into seams or any insole or midsole materials, especially in the toe box. You may want to insert a thick piece of leather or suede into the toe box to protect the insole near the toes from the moving drill bit. DO NOT put your fingers near the moving drill bit. Once you've drilled all the holes, insert the ⁵⁄₃₂" drill bit and drill all holes slightly larger. *Note: The larger bit "grabs" more forcefully and quickly than the smaller bit; be careful when depressing the drill trigger. Clean out any drill dust and loose materials from the inside of the shoe.*

BOOT
CO 43 (47, 51) sts as follows: Beginning at center back seam of shoe, with yarn to inside of shoe, *insert crochet hook into first hole to left of center back seam, draw through a loop and place it on dpn. Repeat from * until all holes have a loop coming out of them. *Note: Do not pull sts too tightly; place 3-5 sts on each dpn. Break yarn, leaving tail to inside of shoe.*

Rnd 1: Using crochet hook and beginning with yarn to inside of shoe, draw up a loop in first st, and place it on new dpn; *draw up a loop in next st and transfer to same dpn; repeat from * for all sts on first dpn. Repeat for remaining needles, CO 1 st at end of rnd using Backwards Loop CO (see Special Techniques, page 172)–44 (48, 52) sts.
Rnd 2: Repeat Rnd 1, omitting last CO st.
Rnds 3 and 4: Repeat Rnd 2, changing to dpn instead of crochet hook when sts are loose enough.
Rnd 5 (Decrease Rnd): Work to 2 sts before center toe st, ssk, k1, k2tog, work to end–42 (46, 50) sts remain.
Note: Adjust number of dpns used as needed.
Rnds 6-8: Repeat Rnd 5–36 (40, 44) sts remain. Weave loose ends in and out through drilled holes.
Rnds 9-15 (17, 19): Repeat Rnd 5–22 sts remain. Break yarn. Weave in loose end.

Shape Front Ankle: Place 5 center front sts (center st and 2 sts to either side of it) on 1 dpn for ankle shaping. Join yarn and k5, turn.
Row 1 (WS): *Transfer 1 st from dpn on either side of center needle to center needle, purl across sts on center needle, turn.
Row 2: Transfer 1 st from dpn on either side of center needle to center needle, knit across center sts, turn. Repeat Rows 1 and 2 once; DO NOT turn on last row–13 sts on center needle.

Begin Ribbing (RS): Working in-the-round, *p1, k1; repeat from * around. Work even for 6 rnds. BO all sts in pattern. Weave in all loose ends.

Rachael
Matthews

Rachael Matthews lives by herself in London's East End, in a three-story house built by an architect who hoped the design would woo his sea-loving sweetheart. It didn't work, so he sold the house to Rachael. With sloping floors, porthole windows, moody wall treatments, and a generally unanchored feeling, it's doubtful that anyone but Rachael could have turned his vessel into a residence. Directly across the street from the London Buddhist Centre, Rachael's front door opens to a hallway that either leads to a guest bedroom that doubles as a sewing room, or a second, foreboding space too filled with old junk and knitting-event relics to walk through. Up a charmingly awkward and narrow staircase, the second floor reveals a kitchen filled with an equal amount of real and knitted food, and a combination dining/living/work room flush with books, records, a spinning wheel, a laptop computer, an overstuffed armchair, a knitted disco ball, and panes of colored glass meant to be placed in front of windows at different times of day to flood the interior with various mood lighting. Above this space is Rachael's loftlike bedroom, from which she rises each morning to dance. Rachael says, in her much-noted high-pitched voice, that she dances to warm up her muscles for daily jogs she takes to alleviate knitting-related repetitive-strain injuries. In addition to being a knitter, Rachael is also a teacher, an artist, a designer, a performer, and a socialite. Those who know Cast Off, a knitting club she runs to promote the craft as a healthy, contemporary, and creative pastime, call Rachael the foundation of London's revitalized knitting scene.

Rachael learned to knit when she was nine years old. The first thing she made after she picked up the basics from a close family friend was a long, turquoise straight line. She continued to knit throughout her childhood, and decided to study textile design as an undergraduate at Central Saint Martins College of Art and Design, a prestigious art school in London. There, she avoided knitting classes because she wanted to try out other art forms, and after she graduated in 1996, she freelanced as a textile printer and designer. Rachael also started making high end rag dolls to sell at fashion boutiques and at Spitalfields market, a vibrant indoor arena of books, food, crafts, and collectibles in East London. "My granny was cleaning out her cupboard," Rachael says, "so I took her old fabrics and made rag dolls out of them. I also did guitar and amp bags from old bits of fabric. I would look at a piece of fabric and think, what kind of music does it fit?"

By 2000, she had gotten sick of using her sewing machine. "There wasn't much knit around London then, but I spotted a garter stitch, chunky-yarn jumper at a store. It was totally fresh." Inspired, Rachael started

knitting coats out of bits of old rope, but she soon got lonely in her studio. "So I took my work to a pub and started knitting with other people," she says. Her boyfriend at the time was a musician, so she and her friend Amy Plant, whose boyfriend played music, too, would sit at their rock shows and knit. A couple of their friends wanted to learn, so she and Amy invited them to a local park for a knitting lesson. Continuing to knit with those friends, and friends of friends, at increasingly public places, Rachael and Amy developed a knitting club named Cast Off and wrote out a constitution, which reads, in part:

"Cast Off activities provide an alternative to the usual and often alienating networks in the world of handicrafts, by arranging fun and adventurous knitting meetings and workshops in a range of unusual public settings. Cast Off aims to introduce a wide cross section of people to the craft by providing materials and tuition to beginners and more advanced knitters. Cast Off aims to educate and spread the creative potential of knitting. Cast Off aims to include people of all backgrounds in its activities and no one is excluded from the club."

Facing page
Rachael prepares her kitchen for a feast of knitted food.

Below
Flyer for a Cast Off event.

"Our first flyer said, 'sponsored by no one,'" Rachael explains. "It was an educational, activist thing, a way to reclaim knitting as a positive social force." Deciding that they would never knit in the same place twice, Cast Off gathered in growing numbers at far-flung locations like Brighton Beach, the Hackney City Farm, the furniture section of a John Lewis department store, the Alexandra Palace Ice Rink, and the Tate Museum. One November day, at noon, 3 p.m., and 5 p.m., they met at a fruit and vegetable stand near the Liverpool Street tube station and waited for people to show up. They took a megaphone and their knitters down to the tube and knit through an entire round on the Circle Line. "Bring sandwiches, tea, and friends," their flyer read, "It takes forty-five minutes to knit all the way round." A small text circle on the flyer announced: "We think knitting is good for you." As the subway car made its stops, the group knitted intensely and created a giddy atmosphere. Newly made pom-poms were tossed around, one woman worked at her spinning wheel, and observers who edged closer to watch were invited to join in. Onlookers stayed past their subway stop to learn to knit, and disbelieving tourists snapped photos. *The Independent,* a London newspaper, wrote a story about the event, calling Cast Off members "guerilla knitters."

"We chose slightly daft places," Rachael explains. "Once we knit where some flats were being torn down. We never got permission to knit anywhere." The Savoy, a luxury hotel in London's West End theatre district, kicked them out for gathering there. "A waiter freaked out at the boys who were knitting," Rachael remembers. "He said boys shouldn't knit, and he told us we should

be knitting at home. Hotel guests were sympathetic to us; they thought it was outrageous." The event made all the local papers and even showed up in a few gossip columns.

Publicity resulted in bigger gigs and a bigger club to maintain. Cast Off grew from a group of Rachael's artist, musician, clothing designer, and political activist friends to include all kinds of people—students, professionals, beginning knitters, and longtime crafters. The Victoria and Albert Museum invited Cast Off over; Rachael estimates that four thousand knitters joined them there. Next they were invited to knit at the Palais de Tokyo, a contemporary art museum in Paris. They also went to Ireland. "Then I started feeling like a tour guide, so we went back to knitting in pubs," Rachael says.

After several television appearances and a thick book of press, the Cast Off mailing list got so big it wasn't a club anymore. "Free fun is hard to find, especially in London," Rachael says, guessing at the source of the group's popularity. "I also think that people got pissed off with shopping and the pressure to buy things. In the early days of Cast Off, everyone would be touched by the gorgeous things that people knit. They were genuinely moved by them. And people went home happy having made something." Saying it had nothing to do with celebrities who were reported to love the craft— "reporters would ask us about Madonna, and we would say, 'we don't know anything about that, sorry!'"— Rachael guesses a more likely reason for London's embrace of knitting had to do with the fact that many people worked jobs where they never saw the end result of their labor. "Knitting is a portable hobby you can do anywhere, and then use it or give it away," she says.

Though Rachael herself was working on Cast Off every day, she wasn't making any money teaching people how to cast on, so she started selling knitting kits. Her first kit featured a cigarette done in a stockinette stitch, and she went on to develop kits for a big toe protector, an exfoliating sponge cover, a blindfold, a first-aid kit, and a dishcloth. As the Cast Off meetings waned in frequency, the kits continued her sense of public engagement. "I would think, what do people need? What will make them laugh? I would think about the places I liked to go and would wonder what kind of kit would fit there," she says. Her kits eventually resulted in a book called *Knitorama*, which was published in 2005 and packed with patterns for unusual designs like fried-egg earmuffs, a hand grenade, and knitted cakes. Rachael's crochet follow-up, *Hookerama*, came out a year later.

Rachael continues to knit in public but hasn't been organizing as many Cast Off events. "There are too many members for the same kinds of meetings. So I use the mailing list so that everyone can work on making something, like with the knitted wedding," Rachael says, referring to an event she organized in 2005. When artist Freddie Robins (see page 162) invited Rachael to contribute to an exhibition on ceremony that she was curating for the Pump House Gallery on the banks of the lake at London's Battersea Park, Rachael proposed an all-knit wedding—featuring Freddie and her longtime partner, artist Ben Coode-Adams. Though Freddie says that she may have been Rachael's muse for the project, Rachael says that she thinks Freddie offered to get married because she was

worried no one else would volunteer to be a bride in an art project. Rachael made an invitation with patterns for knitted sandwiches, flowers, bows, candles, and other wedding-related items, then sent it out to her Cast Off mailing list and to all the guilds and colleges she thought would spread the word. Her patterns were meant to be a guide, but people were invited to knit whatever they wanted. "They did a thorough job," Rachael says. "You can really trust knitters!" They sent her an abundance of knitted cameras, food, champagne, and doves—even a three-tiered wedding cake. All the work was credited in a slide show during the wedding reception and late-night dance party.

Rachael continues to create knitted landscapes and other art projects, and is considering opening the bottom storage room of her house to knitting meetings, events, and parties, but she has to clean it up and get the proper zoning permits first. Until the next big event, Cast Off's website entertains its members through chat rooms, message boards, and short films made by Rachael like *Cast Off Club Clips* and *Gary,* a piece about a friend of hers who can knit while bicycling. "What is Cast Off?" Rachael herself wonders. "It's art, and fashion … it's both, and neither."

Knitted Boxing Match

Every knitter knows that our hobby is a great way to make unwanted demons go away. And if you have knitted through the night with your friends you also know how important it is to take breaks every few rows to stretch your body, get your circulation going, and to say what is on your mind. Play-fighting in your knitting circle can really open up the conversation.

Boxing can help boost self-confidence, common sense, strength, a sense of calm under pressure—in fact, all the qualities you get from knitting but with the added bonuses of working up a sweat, losing weight, and, hopefully, ending up on the floor screaming at the mercy of your friends.

The boxing gloves can also be worn as real gloves on cold days when you don't need to use your hands. The knitted whistle doesn't really work, but you can make a whistle-like noise and just hold it to your mouth. The knitted gum shields, however, are very good for protection and dramatically change your facial expressions.

— Rachael Matthews

FINISHED MEASUREMENTS
16" hand circumference, stuffed

YARN
Hayfield Bonus Toytime DK Yarn (100% acrylic; 76 yards / 25 grams): #977 signal red (MC), 11 balls; #965 black (A), 1 ball; #961 white (B)
Crystal Palace Yarns Party Ribbon (100% nylon ribbon; 87 yards / 50 grams): #207 cloud cream (C), 1 ball

NEEDLES
One pair straight needles size US 2 (2.75 mm)
One pair straight needles size US 3 (3.25 mm)
One pair straight needles size US 5 (3.75 mm)
One pair straight needles size US 6 (4 mm)
   for Gum Shields
One pair double-pointed needles size US 8 (5 mm),
   for I-cord laces
Change needle size if necessary to obtain correct gauge.

NOTIONS
Stitch markers; stitch holders; crochet hook size US F/5 (3.75 mm); stitch holder; 1 yard ½"-thick foam; small amount of polyester fiberfill or sponge; French knitting mill, spool knitter, or I-cord maker (optional)

GAUGE
18½ sts and 25½ rows = 4" (10 cm) in Stockinette st (St st) using size US 5 needles and MC

STITCH PATTERN
1x1 Rib
(multiple of 2 sts)
All Rows: *K1, p1; repeat from * to end of row.

GLOVES (make 2 pair)

RIGHT GLOVE
Right Inner Mitten
Using size US 3 needles and MC, CO 48 sts. Begin 1x1 Rib; work even for 18 rows.
Change to size US 2 needles and St st; work even for 10 rows.

Thumb Gusset
Increase Row 1 (RS): K24, place marker (pm), k1-f/b, k1, k1-f/b, pm, k21–50 sts. Work even for 3 rows.
*Increase Row 2 (RS): Work to first marker, slip marker (sm), k1-f/b, work to 1 st before next marker, k1-f/b, sm, work to end–52 sts. Work even for 3 rows.
Repeat from * 4 times–60 sts.

Thumb
Row 1 (RS): K25, place sts on holder for back of hand, k14, turn, place remaining sts on holder for front of hand.
Row 2: CO 2 sts, p14, turn–16 sts.
Row 3: CO 2 sts, k16–18 sts.
Continuing in St st, work even on these 18 sts for 2¼", ending with a WS row.

Shape Thumb
Decrease Row 1 (RS): K1, *k2, k2tog; repeat from * to last st, k1–14 sts remain.
Decrease Row 2 (RS): *K2tog; repeat from * to last 4 sts, k4–9 sts remain.
Break yarn, thread through remaining sts, pull tight and fasten off. Sew thumb seam.

Hand
Join yarn to sts on holder for back of hand, work to thumb, pick up and knit 4 sts along base of thumb (2 sts on either side of seam), work across sts on holder for front of hand–50 sts.
Continuing in St st, work even for 4", ending with a WS row.

Shape Hand

Row 1 (RS): K2, [skp, k18, k2tog, k2] twice—46 sts remain.
Row 2 and all WS Rows: Purl.
Row 3: K2, [skp, k16, k2tog, k2] twice—42 sts remain.
Row 5: K2, [skp, k14, k2tog, k2] twice—38 sts remain.
Row 7: K2, [skp, k12, k2tog, k2] twice—34 sts remain.
Row 8: Purl. BO all sts. Sew side seam. Weave in all loose ends.

Right Outer Glove
Outer Punch Piece
Using MC and size US 5 needles, CO 43 sts.

Begin Pattern
Rows 1 and 3 (RS): Knit.
Rows 2 and 4: Purl.
Row 5: Using Intarsia method (see Special Techniques, page 000), k10 with MC, k23 with A, k10 with MC.
Row 6: P10 with MC, p23 with A, k10 with MC.
Rows 7-18: Repeat Rows 5-6.
Row 19: Rep Row 5.
Rows 20 and 22: With MC, purl.
Row 21: Knit.
Row 23: Change to B and knit.
Row 24: Change to MC and purl.
Row 25: Knit to end, CO 9 sts—52 sts.
Rows 26, 28, 30, 32, 34, 36, 38, 40, 42, and 44: Purl.
Row 27: Knit to end, CO 3 sts—55 sts.
Row 29, 33, 37, 41, 43, and 45: Knit to end, CO 1 st—61 sts after Row 45.
Rows 31, 35, and 39: Knit.
Row 46: P26, turn, transfer remaining 35 sts to st holder for fingers.
Rows 47, 49, 51, 53, 55, 57, 59, 61, and 63: K2tog, knit to end—9 sts remain after Row 63.
Rows 48, 50, 52, 54, 56, 58, 60, 62, and 64: P2tog, purl to end—8 sts remain after Row 64.
BO all sts.

Fingers
Rejoin yarn to sts on holder, purl to end.
Row 47 (RS): Knit.
Row 48: Purl.
Row 49: Knit to last st, m1, k1—36 sts
Row 50: Purl.
Rows 51-58: Repeat Rows 49-50—40 sts.
Rows 59-76: Work even in St st.
Row 77: K2tog, knit to end—39 sts remain.
Rows 78-82: Work even in St st.
Row 83: K2tog, knit to end—38 sts remain.
Rows 84-86: Work even in St st.
Row 87: K2tog, knit to last 2 sts, ssk—36 sts remain.
Row 88: P2tog, purl to end—35 sts remain.
Rows 89-98: Repeat Rows 87 and 88—21 sts remain.
BO all sts.

Palm Piece
Left Side
Using MC and size US 5 needles, CO 15 sts.
Begin Pattern:
Row 1 (RS): Knit.
Rows 2-8: Work even in St st.
Row 9 (Eyelet Row): K3, yo, k2tog, knit to end.

Rows 10-14: Work even in St st.
Rows 15-44: Repeat Rows 9-14.
Row 45: Repeat Row 9. Break yarn and transfer sts to st holder.

Right Side
Using MC and size US 5 needles, CO 15 sts.
Begin Pattern:
Row 1 (RS): Knit.
Rows 2-8: Work even in St st.
Row 9 (Eyelet Row): K11, yo, k2tog, knit to end.
Rows 10-14: Work even in St st.
Rows 15-32: Repeat Rows 9-14.
Row 33: BO 3 sts, k8, yo, k2tog, knit to end—12 sts remain.
Row 34, 36, 38, 40 and 42: Purl to last 2 sts, p2tog—5 sts remain after Row 42.
Row 35 and 37: K2tog, knit to end—8 sts remain after Row 37.
Row 39: P4, yo, k2tog, k1.
Rows 41 and 43: Knit.
Row 44: Purl to end, CO 11 sts—16 sts.
Row 45: K13, yo, k2tog, k1, CO 2 sts, knit across 15 sts from holder for Left Side—33 sts.
Rows 46-48: Work even in St st.
Row 49: K2tog, work to last 2 sts, k2tog—31 sts remain.
Row 50: Purl.
Rows 51-54: Repeat Rows 49-50—27 sts remain after Row 53. BO all sts.
Row 55: Repeat Row 49—25 sts remain.

Inner Palm Piece Edging: With RS of Palm Pieces facing, using size US 5 needles, pick up and knit approximately 80 sts along inside edges of pieces, beginning at CO edge of one side piece, and ending at CO edge of other side piece. Beg Rev St st. Work even for 5 rows. BO all sts. Fold Edging to WS and sew to WS, making sure sts do not show on RS

Palm Backing Piece
Using MC and size US 5 needles, CO 6 sts. Begin St st; work even for 45 rows. BO all sts.

Inner Thumb Piece
Using MC and size US 5 needles, CO 2 sts.
Begin Pattern:
Rows 1, 3, 5, 7, and 9 (RS): Knit.
Rows 2 and 4: P1, m1p, purl to end—4 sts.
Row 6: P1, m1p, purl to last st, m1p, p1—6 sts.
Row 11: K1, m1, knit to last st, m1, k1—8 sts.
Rows 12–15: Work even in St st.
Row 16: P1, m1p, purl to last st, m1p, p1—10 sts.
Rows 17-20: Work even in St st.
Row 21: K1, m1, knit to last st, m1, k1—12 sts.
Rows 22-25: Work even in St st.
Row 26: P2tog, purl to end—11 sts remain.
Row 27: Knit to last 2 sts, k2tog—10 sts remain.
Rows 28-35: Repeat Rows 26 and 27—2 sts remain. BO all sts.

LEFT GLOVE
Left Inner Mitten
Work as for Right Inner Mitten to beginning of Thumb Gusset, ending with a WS row.

Thumb Gusset

Increase Row 1 (RS): K21, place marker (pm), k1-f/b, k1, k1-f/b, pm, knit to end–50 sts. Work even for 3 rows.
***Increase Row 2 (RS):** Work to first marker, slip marker (sm), k1-f/b, work to 1 st before next marker, k1-f/b, work to end–52 sts. Work even for 3 rows.
Repeat from * 4 times–60 sts.

Thumb

Row 1 (RS): K21, place sts on holder for back of hand, k14, turn, place remaining sts on holder for front of hand.
Row 2: CO 2 sts, p14, turn–16 sts.
Row 3: CO 2 sts, k16–18 sts.
Complete as for Right Inner Mitten

Left Outer Glove

Work all pieces as for Right Outer Glove, reversing all shaping.

FINISHING

LACES (make 2 per pair)

Note: You may use a French knitting mill, spool knitter, or I-cord maker, if you have one.
Using dpn and A, CO 4 sts. work I-cord (see Special Techniques, page 172) 20" long.

Block pieces flat. Lay Outer Punch Pieces on foam (making sure there is room to trace other pieces) and trace around piece for stuffing. Carefully cut foam.

Thread lace through eyelets in Palm Piece as if lacing a shoe, beginning at top of piece. Sew Palm Piece to Palm Backing Piece. Using B, work decorative stitching in two sets of parallel lines on front of Palm Piece, the first just above the laces, and the second 1" below the BO edge, as follows: Thread single strand on tapestry needle and, beginning at either edge, thread yarn across piece, through every other stitch (see photo). Sew bottom edge of Palm Piece to bottom edge of Inner Mitten,

gathering edge as necessary to fit. Sew Inner Thumb Piece to thumb edge of Palm Piece.

Sew top edge of Outer Punch Piece to top edge of Palm Piece, gathering Outer Punch Piece tightly to fit Palm Piece as you sew. Sew bottom edge of Outer Punch Piece to bottom edge of Inner Mitten, gathering edge as necessary to fit. Stuffing pieces as you continue sewing, sew thumb edge of Outer Punch Piece to Inner Thumb Piece. Sew thumb side of Palm Piece to Outer Punch Piece. Sew side seam on opposite side. Sew top edge of Thumb to top edge of Palm Piece. Note: On leather boxing gloves, this is done to protect the thumb; on these gloves, it is done for shaping.

REFEREE WHISTLE (make 1)
Band
Using B and size US 5 needles, CO 10 sts. Begin St st; work even for 50 rows. BO all sts.

Crochet Circle (make 2)
Rnd 1: Using B and crochet hook, ch 4, 9 dc in 4th ch from hook jn with sl st to top of ch–10 dc.
Rnd 2: Ch 3 (counts as dc), dc in same st, 2 dc in each st around, join–20 dc.
Rnd 3: Repeat Rnd 2—30 dc.
Fasten off.
Fold Band in half lengthwise. Beginning at CO/BO edge, sew one long side together for 1¼". Insert one Crochet Circle into remaining opening and sew around Circle. Repeat for other side.

GUM SHIELD
Using C and size US 6 needles, CO 20 sts. Begin St st; work even for 20 rows.
Fold in half length wise, stuff with fiberfill or sponge, and sew closed.

Cat
Mazza

Troy, New York, is home to Uncle Sam, many closed textile mills, and Rensselaer Polytechnic Institute, where activist knitter Cat Mazza got her master's degree and now teaches classes in media studio imaging and interactivity. She and her filmmaker boyfriend, Jim Finn, live in a duplex apartment downtown, right above the First United Presbyterian Church's pastor's office. Cat works on the first floor of their apartment, out of an L-shaped studio with sliding wooden doors that are always open to a view of two pet guinea pigs in a homemade cage. A typical day in her studio can involve grant writing, working on software prototypes, some machine- or hand-knitting, having friends over for photo shoots of knitted clothing, and e-mailing someone across the world who discovered her through her website, microRevolt (www.microrevolt.org), and who also wants to get involved with her activist projects, which use forms of handmade resistance— like knitting—to educate others about sweatshop labor.

As early as college, at Carnegie Mellon University in Pittsburgh, Cat was involved in tactical media art, in which artists hack or disrupt media in order to insert an oppositional view. While pursuing her BFA in studio art with a specialization in electronic media, Cat worked with an activist art group called Carbon Defense League (CDL), whose projects included reprogramming Game Boy cartridges to add commentary on the stereotypical characters in the games. In doing so, Cat developed an art practice concerned with technology, computer programming, and activism.

In 1999, after she received her BFA, she headed to New York City for an education job at Eyebeam, a non-profit art and technology center. "I was doing a lot of technology work there," she explains, "and I started getting to know other new media artists who were thinking and talking about new media as an emerging genre." Cat had an hour-long subway ride home each day, and she wanted to find something tactile to do when she left her screen-based computer work, so she took a special trip to her grandmother's Connecticut home one weekend to learn to knit. "It became a fierce obsession straight away," she describes. "I knitted a scarf and then free-styled this really complex baby hat for my friend's newborn the same month." As she produced more clothing during her commutes, Cat became interested in knitting as an abandoned skill that was practiced before garments were made through feminized sweatshop labor. Cat found the overlaps between textiles and technology compelling. "It was one thing to learn that hand-knitting and loom technology were analyzed and

explored when people came up with the first computer," she says. "It was another thing to understand that once technologies advanced textile production so that it became mechanized, labor abuses started."

In 2003, Cat went to the University of Maine in Orono on a six-month fellowship for gender studies and globalization research. There, she started to integrate her love of knitting, her background in new media technologies, and her commitment to socially sound art production through small, conceptual gestures that call attention to the labor involved in mass-produced garments. Her first art piece was a hand-knit sweater vest featuring a Nike swoosh. "Knitting logos into garments is an absurd act that simultaneously glorifies and assaults corporate logos' symbolic power," she says.

She decided to try out knitting's ability to function as a campaign against sweatshop labor by encouraging other knitters to "logoknit," and by educating them about sweatshop abuses. While in Maine, she created her website microRevolt, named after an idea of molecular revolutions developed by French philosopher Felix Guattari. "He talks about how social change happens through small acts of resistance," Cat explains. "Knitting is just a small act of resistance against the fact that mostly women work in horrible conditions to make the products that we consume. If only two percent of Americans demand that garments be made in fair working conditions, the corporations that capitalize the most on cheap labor would have to change their policies."

In fall 2003, Cat started a master's program in electronic art at the Rensselaer Polytechnic Institute in Troy. There she developed a computer program that could automate knit patterns and make logoknitting easily approachable. She worked with a computer science undergraduate named Eric St. Ong to develop a piece of software that she named knitPro, which lets browsers turn any image saved as a GIF, JPEG, or

PNG file into a free chart. "It takes a high-resolution image and then lowers the resolution and maps a graph over it, which becomes a chart that a fiber hobbyist can read," Cat explains. "One stitch is one pixel. You can upload a picture of your dog and then make it into a cross-stitch project, frame it, and put it up in your kitchen—or knit it onto a sweater." KnitPro celebrates the tradition of early craft circles that freely passed down patterns from generation to generation and mimics this tradition through free, digital distribution. Her software received an honorable mention for the "digital communities" award at the prestigious Prix Ars Electronica Festival, an international cyber arts competition, in 2005.

Though the web page offering Cat's knitPro software averages an astounding 400 hits per day, Cat says that so far, no one has used it to knit logos. (Because the images crafters send in for conversion are uploaded through her program, she sees them all.) "Logoknitting is my art practice," she says. "But I encourage people to use knitPro to knit anything they want."

Many knitPro users have gotten involved in Cat's other art projects, however, like her blanket petition. Since 2003, Cat has been collecting small knitted and crocheted squares that each act as a signature on a petition for fair labor policies. People have mailed in 4x4-inch squares from more than twenty countries and almost every U.S. state. "Knitting seemed like a more hands-on, genuine way of creating a signature," Cat explains. Currently fourteen-by-nine feet, the blanket is in the shape of the Nike swoosh, and, when completed, will be sent to the CEO of Nike along with a letter demanding that Nike apparel be manufactured in accordance with established International Labor Organization conventions. In 2004, Cat took the blanket on a tour that stopped at knitting circles in Pittsburgh, Cleveland, and Chicago, and since then the blanket has been shown at art exhibitions and schools in Brazil, Scotland, Italy, England, New York, and California. Further tackling the relationships between production

and consumption, Cat has created a video documentary of interviews with people who have been working in anti-sweatshop activism, like Marieke Eyskoot, the European coordinator of the Clean Clothes Campaign, an anti-sweatshop nonprofit focused on global solidarity. She used the footage to try out a new software she created called knitoscope, a moving-image offshoot of her freeware knitPro, which takes digital video and alters it into images of various stitches. The name knitoscope is based on Edison's early animation technology the kinetoscope, predecessor to the modern movie projector from the late 1800s. Cat's documentary, *Talking Stitch,* turns regular footage of talking heads into moving stitch patterns that are flat, pulsating, abstract textiles.

"I like to combine aesthetics with activism," Cat says when describing *Talking Stitch.* "Other artists might focus on the aesthetic issues, and I think that making beautiful things is totally valid, but activism is important to me."

Cat's long-term goal is to network cells of hand-knitters and other craft hobbyists involved in DIY apparel production. She calls the project NARCA, which stands for New American Radical Craft Alliance. "A cell could be a college fashion class, a women's center venue, a co-op, a makeshift lab, or a craft store," Cat explains. Having started a microRevolt reblog, which is a weblog with curated content instead of original posts, Cat has posted links to projects made by other DIY crafters. "I see all these hobbyists out there making things," she says. "They could be networked, which could provide a viable, sustainable alternative to purchasing mass-produced clothing," Cat says. She hopes that creating a powerful microeconomy might tip the balance of power toward fair labor. "NARCA is intended to create an alternative to sweatshops, not compete with them, as that would be too optimistic," she says. "It's just one small drop in the bucket toward change."

Barbie Fair Isle Logoknit Legwarmers

After developing a freeware program called knitPro, a web application that translates digital images into needlecraft patterns, I started making graphs of apparel logos as a way of crafting commentary on corporate labor exploitation. This design has the 'B' in the Barbie logo, and a pattern inspired by infinite fill graphics. I liked the blend of traditional Fair Isle stitching with a digital logo recognizable to consumers.
— **Cat Mazza**

FINISHED MEASUREMENTS
15" circumference; 22" length

YARN
Caprendoose Hills Farm Wool (100% wool; 200 yards / 4 ounces): 2 hanks pink (MC); 1 hank each purple (A), magenta (B), and red (C).

NEEDLES
One 12" (30 cm) circular needle size US 6 (4 mm)
Change needle size if necessary to obtain correct gauge.

NOTIONS
Stitch marker

GAUGE
16 sts and 20 rows = 4" (10 cm) in Stockinette stitch (St st)

STITCH PATTERN
2x2 Rib
(multiple of 4 sts; 1-rnd repeat)
All Rnds: *K2, p2; repeat from * around.

LEGWARMERS
Left Leg
Using MC, CO 60 sts. Join for working in the rnd, being careful not to twist sts; place marker (pm) for beginning of rnd. Begin 2x2 Rib. Work even for 6 rnds.
Begin St st and Chart A using Stranded Colorwork Method (see Special Techniques, page 172). Work even for 42 rnds, changing colors as indicated in the Chart.
Continuing in MC and St st, work even for 7 rnds.
Begin Chart B. Work even for 30 rnds, changing colors as indicated in the Chart.
Continuing in MC and St st, work even for 5 rnds.
Begin Chart A. Work even for 21 rnds, changing colors as indicated in the Chart.
Change to 2x2 Rib. Work even for 7 rnds. BO all sts in pattern.

Right Leg
Work as for Left Leg until 42 rnds of Chart A have been completed.
Continuing with Chart A, work even for 63 more rnds.
Change to 2x2 Rib. Work even for 7 rnds. BO all sts in pattern.

FINISHING
Weave in all loose ends. Block pieces if desired.

Key
- Knit using MC
- Knit using A
- Knit using B
- Knit using C

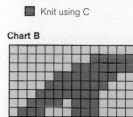

Chart A — 21-row repeat — 5 3 1 — 6-st repeat

Chart B — 29 27 25 23 21 19 17 15 13 11 9 7 5 3 1 — 19 17 15 13 11 9 7 5 3 1

Mandy McIntosh

As an artist born into a family who knitted out of economic necessity, Mandy is ambivalent when speaking about the craft. She first insists that knitting is secondary to her media art practice, and then she says that it's a very deep part of her family history and something to which she will always return. Mandy's mother, the most talented knitter in a large Irish family that emigrated from Donegal, Ireland, to Glasgow, Scotland, in the 1940s, taught her how to knit squares at a young age. As an adult, Mandy tried to turn her heritage into a career as a knitwear designer, but after becoming disillusioned with the fashion industry, she started exploring the anthropological and artistic aspects of knitting instead. This led to an expanded art and design practice encompassing computer animation, Internet art and graphic design, and the establishment of a studio in downtown Glasgow. While directing variable creative projects in conjunction with other artists, specialists, and communities on a project-by-project basis, Mandy continues to use knitting to expand the boundaries between art, craft, and design.

In 1981, when Mandy was fourteen years old, she won an award for excellence in English in a school contest, and she chose the 1979 hardcover *Wild Knitting*, edited by Angela Jeffs, as her prize. She was captivated by the book, which she terms "a post-punk call to arms." The book demonstrated how to knit three-dimensional objects and included patterns for cocktail hats, a raincoat knit from strips of polyethylene sheets, a shoulder wrap in the shape of an armadillo, and a "ragbag top" made from scraps of fabric and leftover yarn.

The book inspired Mandy to knit all of her own clothing. She was into the local Glasgow new romantic punk scene, Adam Ant was her hero, and she wanted to be completely original. Striving for a style she remembers as a "hybrid of romance and edgy plastic," Mandy wore frilly white blouses with pixie ankle boots, or Aran sweaters with yellow fisherman's trousers. When an aunt gave her a bag of old mohair and acrylic yarn, the first thing she made was a turquoise mohair top: essentially two squares sewn together with a slash neck, gaps for arms, and lots of embroidery. She worked her way toward knitting entire outfits. "I would spend a week knitting a new thing for each weekend," she says. "I'd start knitting a sweater dress, but it would be all different colors and textures." A Debbie Harry look-alike at Mandy's high school asked if she could buy some of Mandy's clothes, and soon Mandy was selling knitted garments to a boutique in Glasgow.

When Mandy finished high school, she didn't immediately go to college, choosing instead to take a few classes at a textile industry school. Afterward, she applied to the British art and textile school Trent Polytechnic (since renamed Nottingham Trent University) where she received a degree in knitwear design. During her third year of school, she learned to write patterns during an internship at the head office of Emu, a yarn company in London.

Right out of school, Mandy got a coveted job as a knitwear designer for the Paris-based fashion house Kenzo. She worked there for two years, climbing from a position as an assistant to a knitwear designer to head designer of a children's line of knit clothes. It was a mixed experience. "I learned discipline, and that was very important," Mandy recalls. "It was glamorous at times, with the runway shows and the champagne. But conceptually, it was not interesting. And I only got paid minimum wage, even though I had a very prestigious job as a designer. I worked in an office above a Kenzo boutique, and I couldn't afford to buy any of the clothes that were sold downstairs." It was hard for her to leave such an esteemed position; her former classmates thought she was crazy when she resigned. "I'm a socialist at heart," she insists, "and the politics of the fashion world really disturbed me. I quit because they started to use fur and also because they sacked a whole atelier of seamstresses in one fell swoop with no notice. It all just felt very stilted and uncreative—the profit margin was more important than innovation. I was very depressed by how limited the parameters were there."

Inspired by a Bruce Chatwin novel called *The Songlines,* in which the main character seeks to save the endangered Aboriginal cultures of Australia, Mandy embarked on a one-year trip to the northern region of

Australia. There she worked odd jobs for a traveling carnival as a way to access permit-only Aboriginal communities. "It was a means to an end," Mandy explains—a way to expose herself to Aboriginal culture. "The Aboriginal communities were still expressing themselves in craft, making bark paintings and decorative narrative-based artifacts to sell. It was all very raw and basic—sitting in the shade, making stuff from what was around—and it was such a different world from fashion and surface and all that crap. It inspired me to start painting and drawing again."

When she came home, Mandy needed a new direction, one consonant with her experiences abroad. She found a course on interdisciplinary art with a focus on philosophy and anthropology at the Glasgow School of Art, where she trained as a designer. She continued studying at the school, completing a master's degree in design. For her final project, Mandy presented a metal object and a knitted garment. "All the objects needed to have some functionality, but I pushed that as far as I could," she explains. "The metal box was a huge pram object which could be pushed, and it was all built around a tiny hand-drawn paper face I found in the street." The knitted garment was a coat based on that of Little Red Riding Hood, with a cabled hood and knitted pleats.

Next, Mandy jumped into filmmaking, intending to explore the history and meaning of knit fabric through that medium. Her 1996 experimental film *Donkey Skin,* shot on location in County Galway, Ireland, examined the symbolism in traditional Aran knitting. It was partially autobiographical in its focus on Mandy's mother and grandmother, but it also detailed the symbolism of knit cables and the semantics of knit stitches, portraying the way knit cables once acted as talismans and maps. A main scene, in black and white, features a woman in a long dress made entirely of white Aran sweaters sewn together.

When Mandy finished the film, she put knitting aside. "Sometimes knitting is the most incredible thing. Sometimes it's just not what I want to be doing," she explains, citing her years working in the fashion industry as influencing her tendency to look for something completely fresh after becoming oversaturated. She spent time creating computer animations and also completed a series of public art projects, like a museum commission in which she worked collaboratively with schoolchildren on a radio play that was streamed over the Internet.

Three years later, when she was offered an art residency in Australia, Mandy came across a women's organization that started her thinking about knitting again. She was inspired to create a website that linked three islands where knitting formed part of the local economy—it would become her most ambitious knitting venture. Mandy visited Tasmania, Fair Isle, and Newfoundland to record knitters speaking about their shops and co-ops, then posted text, images, video, sound recordings, and a traditional fisherman's trigger mitt pattern, all collected during her travels, to a website she titled Woolworld (www.hamandenos.com/woolworld/woolworld.html), teaching herself web design in the process.

Four years later, she expanded Woolworld, adding text and patterns based on her travels to America. In 2004, she received another residency, this time in New York City, where she was stunned by knitting's popularity. "Little knit boutiques started appearing in all sorts of locations, one in my street even, called Purl," (see page 80) she writes in the online journal she kept as the first recipient of the Scottish Arts Council's research opportunity. "The reason these boutiques are so enticing to me is because in Glasgow it's very difficult to find any kind of place that sells wool, the craft has completely declined there. There it was pragmatic and cost effective to knit. Here it's aspirational." Inspired by the knitting scene in Manhattan, and responding to high emotions over the recent presidential election, she designed a sweater based on a pair of vultures she studied at the Bronx Zoo. Vulture, Bronx Zoo, a political fashion piece, is a sweater pattern with instructions that include interpretive text:

> "At the Bronx Zoo in New York City, a pair of cinereous vultures are neighbours to a solitary golden eagle. I have visited them several times. They are two outlandish Isabellas next to the clichéd classicism of the eagle (which no-one really pays that much attention to because the vultures are more arresting) … When we look at a vulture we know we will die, and if we were to die and if the vulture was there, it would most certainly eat us. It's the vulture that we imagine can almost supernaturally sense our dying, circling the lost, water starved cowboys we are. The cinereous vultures at the Bronx Zoo are super-cool, striking birds. Beside the eagle, a symbol of supremacy, the motif of the avenger, the vulture signifies more than this nation. In a time of hawks and doves, the vulture is a mute itinerant."

The second free pattern she added to Woolworld was also based on her experiences in the United States: a cotton tie made from a discolored skein of Lily cotton yarn that she found in a Salvation Army store. Struck by the graphic design of the paper label, and how the "L" of Lily bloomed into an exquisitely drawn flower, Mandy researched the brand, discovering that it was produced by the first cotton mill operated exclusively by emancipated African American workers. (Until the 1950s, most mills employed only whites, leaving black people to do the less lucrative and backbreaking work of farming cotton.) The resulting design is based on the history of the Lily Cotton Mill in North Carolina, and includes, like many of her patterns, text that explains her inspiration: "I decided on the bus back downtown that I would knit a tie from the Lily cotton. I think this was because I had spent days absorbed in photographs of very dignified and elegantly dressed people from the history of the Civil Rights Movement."

To further expand Woolworld, Mandy created a link to Radiant Circle, a web project she had undertaken a few years earlier. "I reknitted it," she explains. Radiant Circle is a fictional band of knitters that urge browsers to spin, dye, and knit their own clothes. With free patterns for knitted face masks, provocative text, and colorful, psychedelic images of young children wearing elaborate hoods that Mandy knitted herself, the site evokes the social movements of the 1960s through a contemporary tool for social action: the Internet. Woolworld is a dynamic digital meeting place for handcraft and anthropology; it's a project that Mandy intends to keep expanding with more clothing designs that explore knitting's relationship to local politics and economies.

"I love knitting. I love knitted objects and garments and it's really a thrill every time I'm in a situation where I'm about to knit something," says Mandy. "Shopping for yarn is total joy and also, when I find an amazing pattern or some really great pure wool in a thrift store, I get a real kick out of that. I see everything else I do as an extension of knitting because in a way it was like my first love: the drawing, the filmmaking, the thinking, the way of being an artist … it all comes out of that first compulsion to pick things out of a bag and join them together to make something else."

Some of the Fish I Ate in Portugal

In Lagos, I bought three fish in the market. Then I bought capers, pine nuts, lemons, sun-dried tomatoes, and herbs to put in their bellies. Paula filleted one of the fish in the kitchen of where we were staying, and she did a good job because she had learned to do it in catering college. I prepared the other two, slashed them, stuffed them, and roasted them in the oven. They were amazing. When we were clearing up afterwards, my dad found a stain on the roasting tray that was in the shape of Africa.

Caitlin was learning about the history of slavery in school. Lagos turned out to be a European port of call for slave ships in the 18th century so Paula took a picture of the converted slave market for Caitlin to show her teacher. There was a display of local crafts for sale inside the old slave market. It had cool, whitewashed walls and tiny barred windows.

Later that year, in Porto, I had some fish in a large cafe with paintings of Aboriginal artifacts on the walls. The waiters looked like admirals in white coats with brass buttons.

We took a short train ride to Espinho for an animation festival and found a little restaurant by the beach where we had fried fillets of white fish and potatoes. The owner let us try some seasonal wine with roasted chestnuts. We went back there twice because the man was so nice. It was his wife who fried the fish and she did a good job. We had the same meal every time.

We also had horrible fish at a restaurant by the river in Porto. It made us bicker and we bickered even more the next day at the gypsy market. We were so traumatized by the horrible fish that we were scared to eat. The gypsy market was interesting—there were lots of homemade implements, wooden spoons in particular, also ceramics.

Then we saw an older Portuguese woman having quite an ostentatious lunch on the patio of a small restaurant, so we went in there because from where we were standing, her food looked delicious. We were the last people to be served in the restaurant; they were winding down. A man took our order and a woman prepared some amazing fish for us in a very nonchalant way.

The woman who had cooked the fish took off her apron and came in to slump at a table and watch a wall-mounted television. She didn't have much time to relax because her son appeared. She jumped up to give him her seat, disappearing back into the kitchen and then returning with a mountain of some kind of pasta. He ate his food without talking to her and swilled it down with Pepsi. She hovered, but he ignored her.

She went back to watching the television; a Portuguese language drama serial was on. It was a period piece, featuring African slaves and their Portuguese masters. At one point the camera cut to an elderly black woman with white hair whose head was constrained by some kind of metal muzzle. She was crying and she seemed to be encouraging a young black man to make a bolt for freedom.

On our last day in Porto, I bought the yellow wool from a wool shop we had seen on the first day. The wool was spun for making carpets but it was soft enough to wear.

— **Mandy McIntosh**

FINISHED MEASUREMENTS
37" chest

YARN
Tricots Brancal, Arraiolos; Fio de la para tapetes (yarn for carpets) (100% pure wool; 66 yards / 50 grams): 13 skeins, bright yellow.
Note: If desired, substitute any bulky 100% wool yarn for the yarn used; just be sure to match the stitch gauge given.

NEEDLES
One pair straight needles size US 10½ (6.5 mm)
One 32" (80 cm) circular (circ) needle size US 10½ (6.5 mm)
Change needle size if necessary to obtain correct gauge.

NOTIONS
Stitch markers

GAUGE
13 sts and 18 rows = 4" (10 cm) in Stockinette stitch (St st)

NOTES
The Sleeves are worked from the top down, then sewn together at the sides to form the neckband. The Back and Front are picked up separately from the Sleeves, then worked down to the armholes, where they are joined for the Body, then worked from the top down in-the-round.

STITCH PATTERN
Double Herringbone Mesh
(panel of 21 sts; 12-row repeat)
Rnd 1: K2, [yo, ssk] 3 times, yo, sk2p, [yo, k2tog] 4 times, yo, k2.
Rnd 2 and all even numbered Rnds: Knit.
Rnd 3: K3, [yo, ssk] 3 times, yo, sk2p, [yo, k2tog] 3 times, yo, k3.
Rnd 5: K4, [yo, ssk] twice, yo, sk2p, [yo, k2tog] 3 times, yo, k4.
Rnd 7: K2, k2tog, yo, k1, [yo, ssk] twice, yo, sk2p, [yo, k2tog] twice, yo, k1, yo, ssk, k2.
Rnd 9: K1, k2tog, yo, k3, yo, ssk, yo, sk2p, [yo, k2tog] twice, yo, k3, yo, ssk, k1.
Rnd 11: K2tog, yo, k5, yo, ssk, yo, sk2p, yo, k2tog, yo, k5, yo, ssk.
Rnd 12: Knit.
Repeat Rnds 1-12 for Double Herringbone Mesh.

DRESS
Sleeves (make 2)
Note: Sleeve is worked from the top down.
Using Cable CO (see Special Techniques, page 172), CO 55 sts.
Row 1 (RS): Knit.
Row 2 and all WS rows: Purl.
Row 3: K27, yo, k1, yo, knit to end of row—57 sts.
Row 5: K27, yo, k3, yo, knit to end of row—59 sts.
Row 7: BO 16 sts (1 st rem on right-hand needle), k10, yo, k5, yo, knit to end of row—45 sts remain.
Row 8: BO 16 sts, purl to end—29 sts remain.
Row 9: K1, skp, k6, yo, [k1, yo] twice, k7, yo, [k1, yo] twice, k6, k2tog, k1—33 sts

Row 11: K1, skp, k5, yo, k3, yo, k1, yo, k9, yo, k1, yo, k3, yo, k5, k2tog, k1—37 sts.
Row 13: K1, skp, k4, yo, k5, yo, k1, yo, k11, yo, k1, yo, k5, yo, k4, k2tog, k1—41 sts.
Row 15: K1, skp, k3, yo, k7, yo, k1, yo, k13, yo, k1, yo, k7, yo, k3, k2tog, k1—45 sts.
Row 17: Knit.
Row 19: K20, skp, place marker (pm), k1, k2tog, knit to end—43 sts remain.
Row 21: K1, skp, work to 2 sts before marker, skp, k1, k2tog, work to last 3 sts, k2tog, k1—39 sts remain.
Rows 23-38: Repeat Rows 21 and 22 eight times—7 sts remain.
Row 39: K1, skp, k1, k2tog, k1—5 sts remain.
Row 41: K1, dcd, k1—3 sts remain.
Sew Sleeves together along each side, from CO edge to BO sts of Rows 7 and 8, so that the CO row now becomes the neckline of the Dress, the BO sts of Rows 7 and 8 form the Yoke from which the Dress will be picked up, and the fastened-off st of each Sleeve is pointing down. The seams will become the center Front and Back

Body
Front
Note: Front is picked up from Sleeves, and worked from the top down, to the armhole, where it is joined with the Back for the Body.
RS facing, pick up and knit 16 sts along the BO sts of the left side of one Sleeve/Neckband, pm, 1 st in the center seam, pm, and 16 sts along the BO sts of the right side of the other Sleeve/Neckband (see Assembly Diagram)—33 sts.

Begin Fish Head:
Row 1 and all WS Rows: Purl.
Row 2: Begin St st. Knit to first marker, slip marker (sm), yo, k1, yo, sm, knit to end—35 sts.
Row 4: Continuing in St st, work to first marker, sm, yo, work to second marker, yo, sm, work to end—37 sts.
Repeat Row 4 every other row 5 times, ending with a WS row—47 sts.
Break yarn and place sts on holder for Body.

Back
Work as for Front until there are 45 sts.

Shape Armholes
Next Row (RS): CO 11 sts for armhole, work to marker, sm, yo, work to next marker, yo, sm, work to end—58 sts.
Next Row: CO 11 sts for armhole, work to end, turn work—69 sts.

Body
Join Back and Front: RS facing, continuing across Back sts and working sts onto circ needle, *knit to marker, sm, yo, knit to next marker, yo, sm, work to end; DO NOT TURN. Working across Front sts from holder, repeat from * once—120 sts.
Join for working in the rnd, pm for beg of rnd. Knit 1 rnd.
Next Rnd: Work to marker, *sm, yo, work to next marker, yo, sm; repeat from * once, work to end—124 sts. Knit 1 rnd.
Repeat last 2 rnds twice, removing all markers on last rnd, except beg of rnd marker and marker before Fish Head on Front—132 sts.

Begin Fish Body: *Note: Fish Body will be worked on Front only.* Knit to first marker, remove marker, k1, pm, work Double Herringbone Mesh across 21 sts, knit to end of rnd. Work even until 4 repeats of Double Herringbone Mesh have been completed.

Begin Fish Tail and Shape Skirt:

Setup Rnd: K1, m1, [k5, m1] 16 times, k6, m1, knit to 1 st before marker, move marker 1 st to the right, k2tog, yo, k6, pm, yo, k2tog, yo, k3, yo, pm, ssk, yo, k6, yo, pm, ssk, k6, m1, k6, m1, knit to end of rnd–154 sts.

Rnd 1: Knit.

Rnd 2: Work to 1 st before marker, move marker 1 st to the right, k2tog, yo, knit to next marker, sm, yo, k2tog, yo, knit to next marker, yo, sm, ssk, yo, knit to next marker, yo, sm, ssk, knit to end of rnd–156 sts.

Rep Rnds 1 and 2 four times–164 sts.

Inc Rnd: [K1, m1] twice, [k5, m1, k1, m1] 16 times, knit to 1 st before marker, move marker 1 st to the right, k2tog, yo, knit to next marker, sm, yo, k2tog, yo, knit to next marker, yo, sm, ssk, yo, knit to next marker, yo, sm, ssk, knit to last 5 sts, m1, k1, m1, knit to end of rnd–202 sts.

Repeat Rnds 1 and 2 once–204 sts.

End Fish Tail: Knit to first marker, purl to next marker, sm, p2, knit to next marker, sm, purl to next marker, sm, knit to end of rnd. Knit 1 rnd. Rep last 2 rnds once, removing all markers except beg of rnd marker. Knit 7 rnds.

Dec Rnd 1: K2, k2tog, [k6, k2tog] 16 times, knit to last 6 sts, k2tog, knit to end–186 sts rem. Knit 7 rnds.

Dec Rnd 2: K1, k2tog, [k5, k2tog] 16 times, knit to last 6 sts, k2tog, knit to end–168 sts rem. Knit 7 rnds.

Dec Rnd 3: K2tog, [k4, k2tog] 16 times, knit to last 6 sts, k2tog, knit to end–150 sts rem. BO all sts.

FINISHING

Sew side of Sleeves to side of Yoke. Weave in all ends. Lightly block piece if desired.

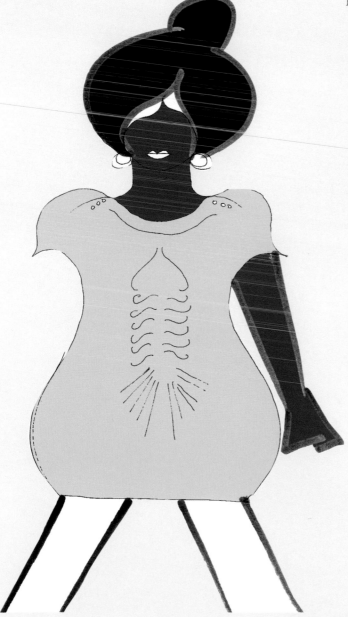

Mandy's sketch for her Some of the Fish I Ate in Portugal design.

Althea
Merback

Althea Merback knits conceptual clothing; it would never fit on anyone's body. You could maybe wear a pair of her gloves on your two front teeth. Very tightly, you could button one of her cardigans around two of your fingers. Though her garments are measured in millimeters, they are huge when gauged by time invested. One sweater, smaller than a quarter and boasting inset pockets, cabled pleats, and a complicated Fair Isle design, took her about five hundred hours to make. When you first see these clothes, you don't ask how long they took to make or even what size they are—you just want to know how they could possibly have been made by hand. Working out of the living room of her Bloomington, Indiana, home, Althea knits while wearing a pair of flip-down magnifying visors, and submits her finished work to her four children for their scrutiny. Only one small glove has failed their rigorous testing, and it was quietly fed to the family's dog.

Although Althea's exceptional skill in knitting on a miniature scale evolved over many quiet years of working by herself, she attributes much of her progress to the friends and colleagues who have pushed her to develop along the way. Althea first learned to knit from a friend in college at Ohio State University, where she studied to be a respiratory therapist. After graduating in 1988 and taking a job in a hospital, Althea knit during long night shifts, working sweaters with complicated patterns and multiple color changes while listening to the quiet breathing of the sleeping patients for whom she was responsible.

Then she gave a knitting lesson to a certain friend. "She was this wild, crazy woman," Althea recalls. "She was an installation artist, and she never conformed to anything. She found patterns repugnant. She said to me, 'Why do you follow patterns? That's not real knitting.' Those words just stuck in my head."

It took Althea a couple of years to summon the courage to create and finish her very first original design—a pair of gloves—in 1999, the same year she gave birth to triplets. As Althea labored over those gloves, another friend introduced her to the world of miniature. "My friend Emily showed me a dollhouse she had rescued from the garbage," she says. "And when I saw it, I was totally amazed. Something clicked. I went home and made my own dollhouse, which is still in an unfinished state in my basement." Her out-of-the-blue fascination with building the dollhouse quickly diminished as she became obsessed with the idea of filling it with tiny furniture. Then, while Althea was browsing eBay for one-inch-scale couches, she came upon a miniature sweater. "There was something in me that said 'I can do that,'" she says, "and I instantly turned the computer off, grabbed the smallest knitting stuff I could find, and made a sweater. I still have that sweater, and I look at it now, and it seems huge. But at the time, it was tiny!" Measuring only two by two inches, the sweater itself was about the correct dimensions to fit the miniature standard of $\frac{1}{12}$th scale, but the stitches were far too large—even though Althea had knit about twenty stitches per inch using size 0 needles and baby-weight yarn.

Althea spent the next few months intensely knitting miniature garments of her own design: sweaters, skirts, gloves, hats, vests, a wool dress, and a chenille robe with a fluffy collar. Once she had completed several small items, she decided that she needed further guidance. "I had never been exposed to the world of miniatures," Althea explains. "I knew there were famous artists within the field who made furniture and dolls because I had read about them on my Internet searches, but I had never seen good-quality miniature pieces, and was it a mind-blower when I finally did. This wasn't just girly doll stuff; there was room for truly talented artists in this field."

Althea placed a few examples of her work into a cigar box and drove to the nearest miniature shop, which was two-and-a-half hours away from her home. The shopkeeper praised Althea's designs, but confirmed that she had to make smaller stitches in order to get her work to the right scale, which meant using smaller threads and thinner needles. She settled on Gütermann silk sewing thread and first tried knitting it with sharpened doll needles she bought from a craft store. The work was still too big, so she tried tatting needles before deciding that she had to make her own to get the range of sizes she needed to do the work she had in mind. Althea is now equipped with knitting needles of varying sizes, all made from medical wire about the diameter of a 100-weight silk sewing thread, the tips ground and polished to a point. A spare bit of wire or a small sewing needle serves as a cable needle.

Most miniature artisans reproduce traditional garments that have some kind of utilitarian purpose (items for a Victorian dollhouse or infant christening gowns, for example), but Althea's garments eschew practical concerns for the artistic endeavor of developing a visual theme that wraps around a tiny garment. For example, Lucas Cranach's sixteenth-century painting *The Golden Age*—a surreal composition of a lost, ideal time when naked men and women danced ecstatically through the Garden of Eden—inspired one of Althea's first miniature projects. Within Althea's one-inch-wide translation of Cranach's work, reinterpreted on a tiny sweater, a girl picks tulips under an apple tree as birds fly above. A starry sky curves around the neck. A man fishes off a tiny island surrounded by waves, and a woman in striped tights smells a huge flower, on sleeves that are merely one inch long. The diminutive sweater, now in the permanent collection of the Kansas City Toy and Miniature Museum, utilized twenty-two different colors of thread as well as intarsia and Fair Isle color techniques.

Althea included the cardigan, titled Earth to Sky, among the pieces she submitted when applying for membership in the International Guild of Miniature Artisans in 2003. Achieving Artisan status through the guild helped Althea move her knitting from a hobby into a profession, earning her the opportunity to show and sell her work at all guild events. She also became eligible to attend the guild's school in Maine, which she did as soon as she received her Artisan status. The school became her introduction to the world of miniature artists: Althea describes it as "a sort of art camp for people who make miniatures." Though her family had always been enthusiastic about her miniatures, Althea's new friends at art camp gave her the support and encouragement she needed to take her knitting more seriously as a profession. The guild school, she says, was where she started to feel like an artist.

Althea now makes a living by selling her work to museums and private collectors, as well as at the Artisan Guild show held yearly in New York City and other miniature events throughout the United States. In preparation for the Chicago International Miniature Show, the world's largest miniature event (with over 250 exhibitors from twenty countries and thousands of attendees), Althea completed an ancient Egyptian-themed cardigan inspired by the tomb paintings and treasures of King Tut. At the same time, she knit a pullover inspired by ancient Greek pottery, which has Greek imagery knitted into it and is shaped like a Greek vase. Plotting out an Andy Warhol pop art vest and a Frank Lloyd Wright cardigan, Althea plans to complete the pictorial art history series she initiated with her Earth to Sky Cardigan.

Constantly trying "to get more detail into each and every thing" she makes, Althea works as much pictorial detail as possible and as many stitches per inch as she can manage into each garment. She has pushed herself from knitting forty stitches an inch to creating "micro sweaters" that are made from an astounding eighty stitches per inch. These ¼44-scale cardigans, which Althea refers to as "dollhouse for a dollhouse," are smaller than a dime. Watching the 2004 Olympic athletes inspired her to create these tiny items. "They struggle through almost unbearable physical strain in order to break world records," she says of the athletes, sympathizing. A few years ago, because of a pinched nerve in her neck that caused her hand to go numb, Althea had to rig a hanging arm support from the ceiling of her garage so she could continue with her knitting.

Though knitting painfully small items may not seem enjoyable, Althea insists that "creating an object for a physical world that is so small it is almost beyond our grasp" is a thrilling experience. Because she likes challenges, she rarely knits the same pattern twice, preferring instead to move from one design idea to the next without repeating something she has already finished. This is also why Althea doesn't normally accept commission work—too often people want a repeat of something she has already made. Because each piece takes months to make, she would rather spend that time creating a new design that is fresh and challenging. Her latest challenge is particularly broad in scope, and may take her beyond the typical world of miniatures: She has been hired to knit garments for a feature-length animated film, the first, she hopes, of many opportunities to find other avenues where she can explore and expand her technical skills and design ideas.

Spread left to right
On the left, a Bavarian cardigan made with hand-dyed wool and inset pockets has a cabled pleat in the back. On the right, Althea's Country-City vest; a country theme knit with a cityscape on the back.

Althea's knitted gloves fit in the palm of a hand.

Mini Sweater Earrings

I remember as a child watching a Loony Tunes cartoon where Bugs Bunny tricks Elmer Fudd into thinking he's sick and tells him that his tongue is "coated." When Elmer sticks out his tongue, it is indeed clad in a tiny coat.

In keeping with the fanciful sense of style only found in cartoons or childhood fiction, this tiny $1/44$ scale pair of sweaters can be worn on your ears. If after making one of them you decide it would be absolute insanity to make another—no worries, you can wear one as a pendant.
— **Althea Merback**

FINISHED MEASUREMENTS
¾" chest

YARN
YLI Silk Thread (100% silk; 219 yards): 1 spool each black (A), white (B), and #256 rust (C)

NEEDLES
One set of four size 8.0 (00000000 / .5 mm) needles (available at www.bugknits.com)
Change needle size if necessary to obtain correct gauge.

NOTIONS
Stitch markers *(Note: You may want to use contrasting color thread);* small gauge sewing needle; 2 small glass bottles with cork stoppers (available at www.bythebaytreasures.com); 2 earring posts with loop at bottom; clear thread; jeweler's glue

GAUGE
55 sts = 1" (2.5 cm) in Stockinette stitch (St st)

STITCH PATTERNS
1x1 Rib
(multiple of 2 sts; 1-row repeat)
All Rows: *K1, p1; repeat from * across.

Stripe Sequence
*Work 2 rows in B, then 2 rows in A. Repeat from * for entire garment.

2-Color Rib
(multiple of 2 sts)
Row 1 (WS): *K1 using A, p1 using B; repeat from * across.
Row 2: *K1 using B, p1 using A; repeat from * across.
Row 3: Repeat Row 1.

BLACK AND WHITE SWEATER
Sleeves (make 2)
Using A, CO 10 sts, leaving a 6" tail. Begin 1x1 Rib. Work even for 4 rows.
Shape Sleeve (RS): Change to St st and Stripe Sequence, increase 1 st each side–12 sts. Work even for 1 row.
Continuing in Stripe Sequence as established, repeat last 2 rows twice–16 sts. Work even for 4 rows.
Shape Cap: BO 3 sts at beginning of next two rows–10 sts remain. Break yarn. Using CO tail, sew Sleeve seam from CO edge to beg of cap shaping. Set aside, leaving sts on needles.

Body
Note: Body is worked back and forth in one piece, then Sleeves are joined and piece is worked back and forth to Neckband.
Using A, CO 30 sts. Begin 1x1 Rib. Work even for 4 rows.
Increase Row (RS): Change to St st and Stripe Sequence, increase 10 sts evenly across first row–40 sts. Work even for 10 rows, ending with a RS row.
Shape Armholes (WS): BO 3 sts, p14, BO 6 sts, p17.

Yoke
Join Sleeves (RS): Continuing in St st and Stripe Sequence, BO 3 sts, k14, place marker (pm), knit across 10 sts from first

Sleeve, pm, k14, pm, knit across 10 sts from second Sleeve–48 sts. Purl 1 row.
Shape Raglan (RS): Decrease 8 sts this row, then every other row 3 times, as follows: [K1, k2tog-tbl, knit to 3 sts before marker, k2tog, k1, sm] 3 times, k1, k2tog-tbl, knit to last 3 sts, k2tog, k1–16 sts remain.
Neckband (RS): Change to A; break B. Knit 1 row.
Next Row: Change to 1x1 Rib. Work even for 4 rows. BO all sts in pattern.

FINISHING
Sew side, raglan and armhole seams. With clear thread, securely tie inside of front and back of Neckband together, making sure thread does not show on RS; do not cut thread. Using small crochet hook or tapestry needle, carefully insert sweater into bottle, leaving loose end of thread outside of bottle. Draw needle through cork stopper from bottom to top; insert stopper into bottle; secure to bottle with small dot of glue. Tie knot at top of stopper so that sweater hangs approximately in the middle of the bottle. Tie thread to loop of earring post with small knot. Secure knots with small dots of glue.

RUST SWEATER
Sleeves (make 2)
Using A, CO 10 sts, leaving a 6" tail. Begin 1x1 Rib. Work even for 1 row.
Change to 2-Color Rib; work even for 3 rows. Break B.
Shape Sleeve (RS): Change to St st, increase 1 st each side–12 sts.
Change to C; work even for 1 row.
Continuing in St st and C, repeat last 2 rows twice–16 sts. Work even for 4 rows.
Shape Cap: BO 3 sts at beginning of next two rows–10 sts remain. Break yarn. Using CO tail, sew Sleeve seam from CO edge to beg of cap shaping. Set aside, leaving sts on needles.

Body
Note: Body is worked back and forth in one piece, then Sleeves are joined and piece is worked back and forth to Neckband.
Using A, CO 30 sts. Begin 1x1 Rib. Work even for 1 row.
Change to 2-Color Rib; work even for 3 rows. Break B.
Increase Row (RS): Change to St st, increase 10 sts evenly across first row–40 sts.
Change to C; work even for 10 rows, ending with a RS row.
Shape Armholes (WS): BO 3 sts, p14, BO 6 sts, p17.

Yoke
Join Sleeves (RS): Continuing in St st and C, BO 3 sts, k14, place marker (pm), knit across 10 sts from first Sleeve, pm, k14, pm, knit across 10 sts from second Sleeve–48 sts. Purl 1 row.
Shape Raglan (RS): Decrease 8 sts this row, then every other row 3 times, as follows: [K1, k2tog-tbl, knit to 3 sts before marker, k2tog, k1] 3 times, k1, k2tog-tbl, knit to last 3 sts, k2tog, k1–16 sts remain.
Neckband (RS): Change to A; break C. Knit 1 row.
Next Row (WS): Change to 2-Color Rib. Work even for 3 rows. Break B.
Continuing in A, BO all sts in pattern.

FINISHING
Finish as for Black and White Sweater.

Annie Modesitt

Many knitters learn their basic skills from their mothers, grandmothers, or family friends, but Annie Modesitt mostly taught herself. After decades of working with intuitive movements that other knitters constantly told her were wrong, Annie searched her lineage for hints that someone in her family had been good with fiber, hoping to pedigree her knitting style. Her last name implies an ancestry of garment production: Modesitt comes from the French word *modiste*, meaning one who makes fashionable clothes and hats for women. Yet it was another term that empowered Annie, one she stumbled upon in a magazine article that detailed three major knitting methods. Once Annie learned that her knitting style was named combination knitting, and was a legitimate practice, she allowed herself to pursue an illustrious knitting career.

Annie first learned the knit stitch from a friend when she was in her early twenties. Before she could learn to purl, Annie was transferred from New York to Texas by *Time* magazine, where she worked in image production. "I didn't like it there," Annie admits, "but I had time to perfect my unique way of knitting." Through instinctive motions, Annie taught herself how to purl and soon became a fast knitter, completing her first sweater—an intarsia pullover—in just a weekend. When Annie returned to New York in 1984, one year after she had moved to Texas, she sent some of her sketches and schematics to *Vogue Knitting* for review. The company contacted her, but not to take her designs; instead, they hired her as a technical writer. During her six-month tenure at the magazine, however, Annie came to realize that her self-taught knitting style was unusual, and a bad fit for the job. She couldn't use her knitting to interpret someone else's work, and she wasn't able to write patterns for the standard knitter because she didn't knit the standard way.

Still, Annie found design success with other major knitting magazines and yarn companies. She also knitted for Fifth Avenue fashion designers, creating samples for them to send to China to be copied. Every morning, Annie took the subway from her Brooklyn home into Manhattan, where she sat in a different art museum and knit all day long. Though Annie describes these years as idyllic, she also says that she became increasingly discouraged by the feedback she got that her knitting technique was "wrong." "One unforgettable experience was the woman on a train in Cologne who *took my knitting out of my hands* to show me the correct way to knit," Annie recalls in her blog. After five years, Annie decided to abandon the craft. She completed a master's degree in costume and set design at Rutgers University, and then worked as a milliner for movies and plays. For most of the 1990s, Annie didn't knit.

When Annie was pregnant with her second child, she and her husband moved from Brooklyn to New Jersey, and the advent of family life renewed her interest in knitting. In the fall of 2000, she read an article in *Interweave*

Knits magazine that detailed three major knitting styles: western, which creates open loops; eastern, which creates a dense fabric; and combination, which looks just like western but works the purl stitch in the eastern mode, and perfectly described Annie's way of knitting. "It was one of the happiest days of my life," Annie says.

Empowered, Annie returned to knitting full time, equally distributing her talents among designing, teaching, and writing. Informed by her background in costume design, Annie regularly researches garments from fashion history to cull shapes and silhouettes for knit garments, and often applies the same approach when designing knitted jewelry, furniture, and hats. Along with *Knitting Millinery,* which explores knitting hats using millinery techniques, Annie has published three other pattern books: *Twist and Loop, Men Who Knit and the Dogs Who Love Them,* and *Romantic Hand-Knits.* She also compiled *Cheaper Than Therapy,* a group of essays on dealing with grief through fiber craft. Her first and most personal book, *Confessions of a Knitting Heretic,* is a patchwork compilation of reflective essays, technical lessons, and original patterns that clearly capture her personality and teaching style. Six feet tall with bright red hair, Annie charms her students with a steady flow of easy jokes, encouraging words, and lucid technical explanations. She's just as likely to equate a half double crochet stitch with a *ménage à trois* as she is to make a sincere statement about the importance of self-acceptance. She advises knitters to be adventurous, patient, and flexible, all the while stressing that there are different and equally valuable ways of forming a stitch.

Annie works out of her home while her two children are at school and her husband is at work. She knits at an incredible speed, utilizing all sorts of self-taught techniques for working through problems in her characteristic style, assigning personality quirks to her fabric "as a new way to approach a recalcitrant cable or an unhappy cast-on" or personifying what she calls the "generations of rows" on her needles. And perhaps most pleasing, after years of struggling with the legitimacy of her knitting style, she enters a frame of mind she calls "compulsive calmness," in which the rhythmic motions of her needles free her mind into a suspended state, enabling her to infuse her stitches with a steady peacefulness.

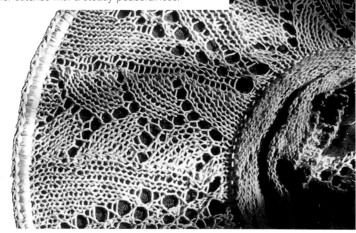

Esther

Back in the 1940s and 1950s, when dinosaurs ruled the Earth, women swam in girdles masquerading as bathing suits. Even so, they managed to look sexy (maybe all that lifting and separating wasn't such a bad thing).

By using a double strand of a cotton/lycra blend yarn I've created a very firm yet rather elastic fabric for this suit. The fit is enhanced by the 2x2 ribbing around the back and sides, a flattering detail for all body types.

As long as you follow the yarn manufacturer's washing instructions, this suit should work well for you both in and out of the water!

— Annie Modesitt

SIZES
To fit 33 (33¾, 34¾, 37¼, 40, 44½, 48, 52½)" bust; 34¼ (35, 36, 38¾, 41¼, 45¾, 49¼, 53¾)" hips. *Note: This swimsuit is designed to fit very closely, and the ribbing stretches quite a bit.*
Swimsuit shown measures 34¾" at chest

FINISHED MEASUREMENTS
27 (27¾, 28¼, 30½, 32¾, 36¼, 39¼, 43)"chest, unstretched;
33 (33¾, 34¾, 37¼, 40, 44½, 48, 52½)", stretched
28 (28¾, 29½, 31¾, 33¾, 37½, 40¼, 44)" hips, unstretched;
34¼ (35, 36, 38¾, 41¼, 45¾, 49¼, 53¾)", stretched

YARN
Cascade Yarns Fixation (98.3% cotton / 1.7% elastic; 100 yards / 50 grams): 6 (6, 8, 8, 8, 10, 10, 12) balls #8001 white

NEEDLES
One 24" (40 cm) circular (circ) needle size US 5 (3.75 mm)
One set of five double pointed needles (dpn) size US 5 (3.75 mm)
Change needle size if necessary to obtain correct gauge.

NOTIONS
Contrasting crochet cotton or ravel cord for Provisional CO; stitch markers (including 1 in contrasting color); stitch holder; tapestry needle; 12" strong crochet cotton

GAUGE
22 sts and 36 rows = 4" (10 cm) in 2x2 Rib, using 2 strands of yarn held together, unstretched
18 sts and 28 rows = 4" (10 cm) in 2x2 Rib, using 2 strands of yarn held together, stretched

NOTES
I-Cord BO: Using Cable CO (see Special Techniques, page 172), CO 2 sts, *k2, k2tog-tbl, slip 3 sts from right-hand needle back to left-hand needle; pulling yarn tight across back of work, repeat from * until 3 sts remain, k3tog-tbl.
Unless otherwise indicated, slip all sts purlwise with yarn in back.

STITCH PATTERN
2x2 Rib
(multiple of 4 sts; 2-row (rnd) repeat)
Row (Rnd) 1: *K2, p2; repeat from * across.
Row (Rnd) 2: Knit the knit sts and purl the purl sts as they face you.
Repeat Row (Rnd) 2 for 2x2 Rib.

ABBREVIATIONS
M1-b (lifted increase): To work the increase on a knit st, insert the right-hand needle, from the top down, into the st below the first st on the left-hand needle, knit this st, then knit the first st. To work the increase on a purl st, insert the right-hand needle, from the top down, into the top loop of the st just below the first st on the left-hand needle, purl this st, then purl the first st.

BATHING SUIT
Front Crotch
Using dpn and Provisional CO (see Special Techniques, page 172), and 2 strands of yarn held together, CO 14 (14, 18, 18, 18, 18, 18, 18) sts.

Establish Pattern and Shape Crotch:
Row 1 (WS): P4, m1-b, purl to end–15 (15, 19, 19, 19, 19, 19, 19) sts.
Row 2: K3, slip 1, m1-b, knit to last 4 sts, slip 1, k3–16 (16, 20, 20, 20, 20, 20, 20) sts.
Row 3: Purl.
Row 4: K3, slip 1, knit to last 4 sts, slip 1, k3.
Repeat Rows 1-4 3 (4, 4, 5, 5, 5, 5, 5) times–22 (24, 28, 30, 30, 30, 30, 30) sts.
Next row (WS): P4, m1-b, purl to end–23 (25, 29, 31, 31, 31, 31, 31) sts.
Next row: K3, slip 1, m1-b, knit to last 4 sts, slip 1, k3–24 (26, 30, 32, 32, 32, 32, 32) sts.
Repeat last 2 rows 7 (9, 9, 11, 11, 11, 11, 11) times–38 (44, 48, 54, 54, 54, 54, 54) sts. Work even until piece measures 6¼ (6½, 6¾, 7, 7, 7¼, 7¼, 7½)" from the beginning, ending with a RS row, CO 23 (20, 20, 19, 23, 27, 31, 37) sts at end of last row–61 (64, 68, 73, 77, 81, 85, 91) sts.

Shape Thigh (WS): Purl to end of row, CO 23 (20, 20, 19, 23, 27, 31, 37) sts—84 (84, 88, 92, 100, 108, 116, 128) sts. Work even for 3 rows, omitting slipped sts.

Next row (Turning Row) (WS): Change to circ needle, k23 (20, 20, 19, 23, 27, 31, 37), p38 (44, 48, 54, 54, 54, 54, 54), knit to end. Transfer sts to st holder for Body.

Center and Back Crotch

Carefully unravel Provisional CO and place 14 (14, 18, 18, 18, 18, 18, 18) sts on dpn.

Establish Pattern

Row 1 (WS): Using 2 strands of yarn held together, purl.
Row 2: K3, slip 1, knit to last 4 sts, slip 1, k3.
Repeat Rows 1 and 2 until piece measures 2¾ (3, 3¼, 3½, 3½, 3¾, 3¾, 3¾)" from the beginning, ending with a WS row.

Shape Back (RS): K3, slip 1, yo, *p2, k2; repeat from * to last 6 sts, p2, yo, slip 1, k3—16 (16, 20, 20, 20, 20, 20, 20) sts.
Next row: P4, p1-f/b in yo, work to last 4 sts, p1-f/b in yo, work to end—18 (18, 22, 22, 22, 22, 22, 22) sts.
Repeat last 2 rows 4 (5, 4, 5, 6, 7, 7, 8) times, working increased sts in ribbing as established—34 (38, 38, 42, 46, 50, 50, 54) sts.
Next row: K3, slip 1, m1-b, work to last 4 sts, slip 1, k3—35 (39, 39, 43, 47, 51, 51, 55) sts.
Next row: P4, m1-b, work to last 4 sts, p4—36 (40, 40, 44, 48, 52, 52, 56) sts.
Repeat last 2 rows 21 (21, 21, 23, 23, 27, 31, 33) times, working increased sts in ribbing as established—78 (82, 82, 90, 94, 106, 114, 122). Work even until piece measures 9 (10, 9, 10, 11, 13, 14, 15)" from Provisional CO row, ending with a RS row.
Next row (WS): BO 4 sts, work to end—74 (78, 78, 86, 90, 102, 110, 118) sts remain.

Join Front and Back

Next row (RS): BO 4 sts, work 28 (28, 28, 32, 32, 36, 40, 44) sts, place marker (pm), work 14 (18, 18, 18, 22, 26, 26, 26) sts, pm, work 28 (28, 28, 32, 32, 36, 40, 44) sts, pm; continuing in 2x2 Rib as established on Back, work across 28 (28, 28, 32, 32, 36, 40, 44) sts from holder for Front, pm, k28 (28, 32, 28, 36, 36, 36, 40), pm, work across 28 (28, 28, 32, 32, 36, 40, 44) sts in 2x2 Rib, beg with k2—154 (158, 162, 174, 186, 206, 222, 242) sts. Join for working in the round; pm (contrasting color) for beginning of rnd. Work even for 4 rnds.

Shape Waist

Rnd 1: *Work to 2 sts before marker, k2tog-tbl, slip marker (sm), work to next marker, sm, k2tog; repeat from * once, work to end—150 (154, 158, 170, 182, 202, 218, 238) sts remain.
Rnd 2: Work even.
Rnd 3: *Work to 1 st before marker, slip 1, sm, work to next marker, sm, slip 1; repeat from * once, work to end.
Rnd 4: Work even.
Repeat Rnds 1-4 five times—130 (134, 138, 150, 162, 182, 198, 218) sts remain.
Repeat Rnds 3 and 4 until piece measures 7½ (7¾, 7¾, 8, 8, 8¼, 8¼, 8½)" from where Front and Back join.

Shape Bust

Rnd 1: *Work to 1 st before marker, slip 1, sm, work to marker, sm, slip 1; repeat from * once, work to end.
Rnd 2: Work to 1 st before marker, k1, sm, work to marker, sm, k1, work to 1 st before marker, m1-b, k1, sm, work to marker, sm, k1, m1-b, work to end—132 (136, 140, 152, 164, 184, 200, 220) sts.
Repeat Rnds 1 and 2 eight times, working increased sts in ribbing as established—148 (152, 156, 168, 180, 200, 216, 236) sts. Work even until piece measures 11½ (12, 12¼, 12¾, 13, 13½, 13¾, 14¼)" from where Front and Back join.

Shape Upper Back

Row 1 (RS): Work to 1 st before marker, slip 1, sm, work 7 (9, 9, 9, 11, 13, 13, 13) sts, turn.
Row 2: Working back and forth on needles, work to first marker, sm, p3tog, work to end—146 (150, 154, 166, 178, 198, 214, 234) sts remain.
Row 3: Work to first marker, k3tog-tbl, work to end—144 (148, 152, 164, 176, 196, 212, 232) sts remain.
Repeat Rows 2 and 3 18 (19, 20, 21, 22, 23, 24, 24) times—72 (72, 72, 80, 88, 104, 116, 136) sts remain.
Using I-Cord BO, BO all sts.

FINISHING

Turn hem at leg opening to WS at Turning Row and sew to WS, being careful not to let sts show on RS. Weave in all loose ends. Fold down "corners" of front edges if necessary to create smooth line along top of suit.

Front Gather

Mark center stitch of Front St st panel 3½" down from top of suit with safety pin. Using tapestry needle and strong crochet cotton, beginning on the WS, weave in and out of every other stitch in this column, working up to the top of the suit and leaving a 7" tail on the WS. Pull both ends of the cord to gather this center column and tie tightly in a knot, trim tails.

Tie

Using 2 strands of yarn held together, work 2-st I-Cord 6" long. Pull cord from back to front through lowest gathered st of Front Gather, up to top of suit to WS. Sew in place on WS, making sure to hide crochet cotton gathering cord.

Cross Back Straps

Mark points along top edge of suit, approximately 5" to either side of center Front and 3" to either side of center Back. Try suit on and measure from marked right Front point, over shoulder to marked left Back point. Using 2 strands of yarn held together, work two 2-st I-Cords 2" shorter than measurement. Sew to WS at markers, going from right Front to left Back and left Front to right Back.

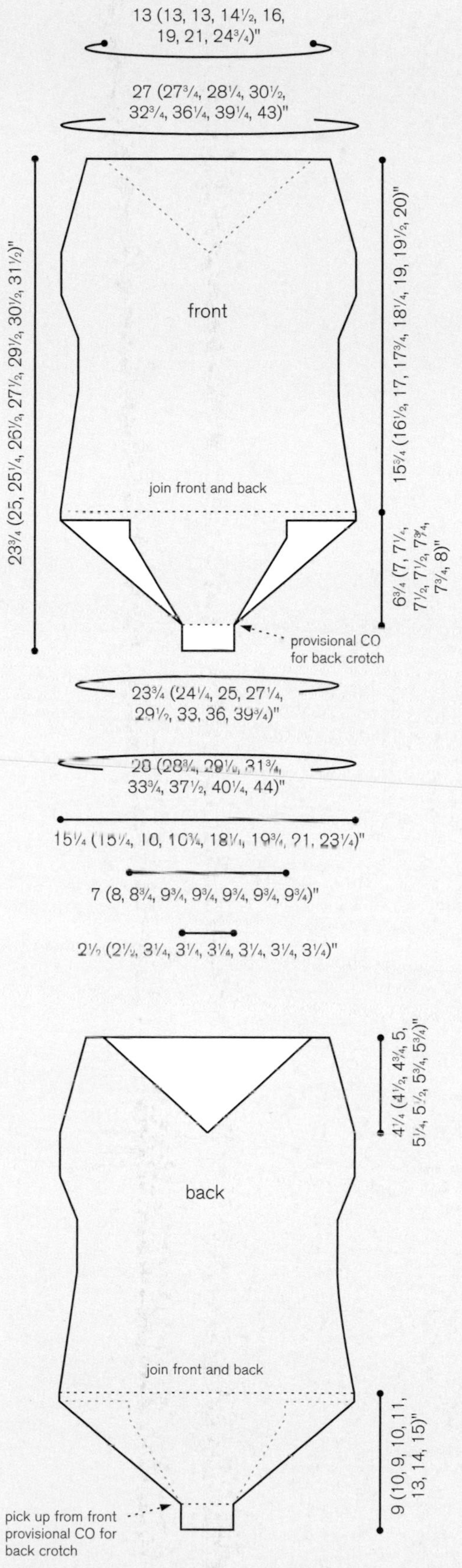
13 (13, 13, 14½, 16, 19, 21, 24¾)"
27 (27¾, 28¼, 30½, 32¾, 36¼, 39¼, 43)"
23¾ (25, 25¼, 26½, 27½, 29½, 30½, 31½)"
15¾ (16½, 17, 17¾, 18¼, 19, 19½, 20)"
front
join front and back
6¾ (7, 7¼, 7½, 7½, 7¾, 7¾, 8)"
provisional CO for back crotch
23¾ (24¼, 25, 27¼, 29½, 33, 36, 39¾)"
28 (28¾, 29½, 31¾, 33¾, 37½, 40¼, 44)"
15¼ (15¼, 16, 16¾, 18¼, 19¾, 21, 23¼)"
7 (8, 8¾, 9¾, 9¾, 9¾, 9¾, 9¾)"
2½ (2½, 3¼, 3¼, 3¼, 3¼, 3¼, 3¼)"
4¼ (4½, 4¾, 5, 5¼, 5½, 5¾, 5¾)"
back
join front and back
9 (10, 9, 10, 11, 13, 14, 15)"
pick up from front provisional CO for back crotch

Note: Measurements shown are unstretched.

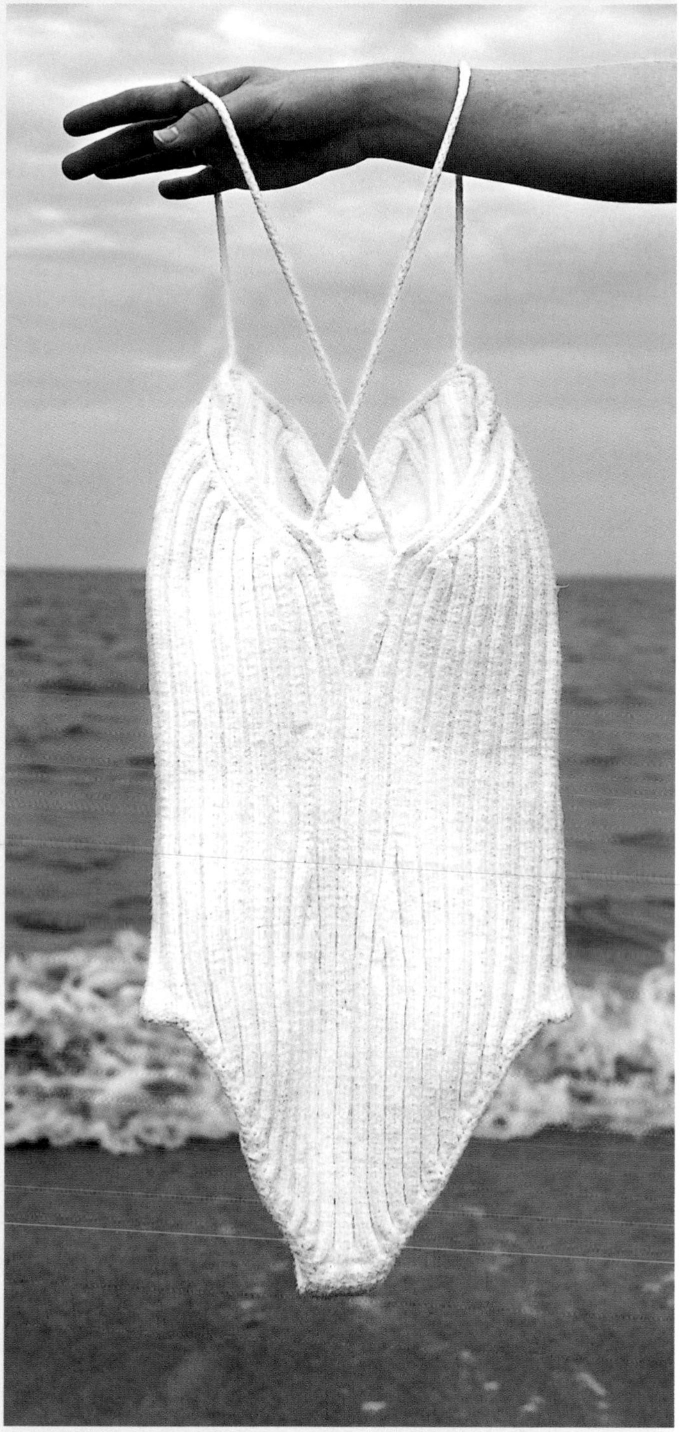

Debbie
New

Debbie New has no sentimental feelings toward her knit projects—garments, sculptures, vessels, even interpretations of scientific concepts—which look as though they should be carefully archived and housed within fine art, science, or craft museum collections. When a Canadian art gallery that had exhibited one of her pieces closed, and everything inside was confiscated, Debbie's reaction was unusual. "My husband was upset that I couldn't get my artwork back, but I didn't care," she says. "When I'm finished with something, it's done. Once I've made the work, that's it." Debbie's knitting reflects a wide, eclectic range of interests—biology, music, engineering, and boating—through which she initiates challenges that she works out by creating a knitted form. After that, she loses interest. She never knits the same thing twice, because there would be no point, the idea and its solution having already been mastered.

Debbie learned to knit in 1942, when she was four and a half and struck with the whooping cough. Because her infant brother was sick with pneumonia, Debbie was sent away to recuperate with family friends. They showed her how to knit what they called a doll scarf, but Debbie remembers it being much too small to function satisfactorily. A few years later, when Debbie's mother taught her how to read patterns, Debbie knit more practical clothing in order to fulfill the "social service projects" required by her Australian school. Starting at age ten and continuing all through high school, Debbie knit a garment each year to be sent to needy people living in developing countries.

For the next twenty years, Debbie delved into science, music, and childrearing, knitting only as an occasional hobby. In college at the University of Melbourne, Debbie studied pre-med her first year and then switched to microbiology for her bachelor's degree. She only knit two things during her college years: a sweater for herself and one for her future husband, John, whom she married in 1958, the same year she graduated. For her first six months out of school, Debbie worked as a university microbiologist, and for the next six months, Debbie did research in a hospital as a biochemist. Then she had her first baby. Over the next ten years, as John acquired a Ph.D. and took on numerous teaching jobs and fellowships, Debbie moved their growing family from Australia to Canada, then to the United States, next to England, and finally back to Canada, giving birth to a new child in each country. "I knitted for the family in fits and starts from then on," Debbie recalls.

When Debbie, John, and their four children moved to Canada so that John could teach at the University of Waterloo, Debbie started playing violin with a local symphony orchestra. She played "semi-professionally," as she puts it, performing regular concerts or recitals for about four years. She quit the symphony when she and her husband adopted a child. Family took over again as they adopted one child each of the following three years. Debbie mentions offhand that "sometime during this period, I built a harpsichord," and also remembers knitting sweaters for each child with emblems appropriate to them. "None of these were from patterns, but were doodled on odd bits of paper," she explains. "I also knit a few intarsia sweaters based on the children's own paintings."

In 1980, Debbie got a bachelor's degree in education with a concentration in special education. During the subsequent year, while the family lived in Cambridge, England, for her husband's one-year research fellowship, Debbie got a master's degree in the philosophy of education. "We had five children with us at that time,

Facing page
Debbie in the living room of her Waterloo, Canada, home, wearing her Ouroborus Jacket from her book *Unexpected Knitting*. Made out of a single closed ring (like the ouroborus symbol of a dragon or snake biting its tail), the jacket is worked in a large circle on 4 or 5 circular needles one after the other.

Below
"I arrange [my yarns] by color, as you can see. I think the way you choose to arrange your yarns exerts some influence on what you choose to make with them," Debbie says.

and I wrote my master's thesis in the bathtub, because it was the only quiet place in the house," she says. It was in Cambridge, working mostly at the kitchen table, that Debbie invented a speech reader for deaf babies. The device emitted a frequency range of colors in response to the frequency of sounds. "It was meant to encourage deaf children to play with sound," she explains. "It clears up things you can't read on lips." She patented her device in the United States, Europe, and England.

After returning to Waterloo and spending three years as a substitute teacher for special education and hearing-impaired classes, Debbie picked up work on her speech reader device again. She did research with children to see what the device could do, accruing credits she applied toward a Ph.D. in education and biomedical engineering at the University of Toronto. But two years into her degree, in 1989, her husband fell ill and was forced to retire. Debbie quit her Ph.D. work to stay home with him.

She started knitting again, "for her own entertainment," as she puts it. With childlike curiosity, she experimented in her living room with unusual techniques, like knitting Fair Isle vertically rather than horizontally. The curving nature of stockinette stitch challenged her to

knit two different teacups that could be freestanding, yet not stiff. Other real-life objects Debbie knitted include a navigable boat, multiple Christmas tree ornaments, and a pitcher plant full of fireflies made from miniature filament lamps. She knit herself a short armored vest, hinged for access, out of cotton she then dipped into a bonding solution normally used on flooring and wall panels. She made a three-by-five-foot mosaic called Madonna and Child, stitched onto a canvas backing. She knit candy wrappers and duct tape into knee-length vests.

"Sometimes it is such a challenge that sets me going—the challenge to construct a complex garment out of a circle; the challenge to simplify that technique to its bare essentials; the challenge to complicate it and explore its potential," Debbie says. "Must we knit in straight lines, must we knit with yarns of similar weight? And what happens when we don't?" Some of her projects took weeks, some months, and others years to work through. Her knitting often engenders new techniques (which can be found in her book *Unexpected Knitting,* Schoolhouse Press), like an original three-needle bind off on two needles and a special increase for use in mitered corners. "I like to juxtapose disparate ideas and produce the unexpected," Debbie explains. "I could say that this is to startle viewers and make them think, but really it is just for the fun of it. I draw on ideas from other fiber arts, from music, from science, from mathematics. Sometimes I have something serious to do, but mostly, I play. It preserves me from taking myself too seriously!"

Having masterminded freeform techniques—like virtual knitting, which produces a knitted fabric on a removable backing using a threaded needle—Debbie started teaching knitting workshops. Since 1994, she has traveled around the world to teach people that, as she writes in *Unexpected Knitting*, "what you already know is sufficient for whatever plan you dream up." Even though her classes are advertised as exploring one particular topic, like her freeform or swirl knitting techniques, Debbie usually digresses. "I add things if they seem to need to be added," she says. "It goes wherever it goes."

Debbie's projects are strewn from room to room in the Waterloo home she has lived in since 1970, which can accommodate, at a squeeze, all eight children and sixteen grandchildren during Christmas visits. Her family and personal life inspire many of her projects. "One son is an engineer, and he always comes up with ideas he wants me to knit," Debbie explains. "He wanted me to knit something to show the stages of a mathematical paradox that had to do with turning a sphere inside out without creating any crease." He later proposed that Debbie knit a pair of cipher sweaters, one with a public key for encoding messages and the other with a private key to decode them. A second son, a mathematician, sent her a tongue-in-cheek treatise titled "Coracular Applications of the Knitting of Hyperbolic Discs" after she had knitted her own coracle, a one-person boat. When she was looking for a way to knit a fractal, another son, a filmmaker, suggested she look at cellular automata. This, and perhaps her background in science, led her to her "Cellular Automaton" technique, which uses the biological concept that cells evolve according to a set of rules based on the states

of their surrounding cells. It results in an improvised pattern that is generated while the knitter knits. But while ideas may come from her children, "the knitted expressions come from me," she says. "The children just humor me."

Years after Debbie put her speech reader device away, she returned to ideas about visualizing sound by building a theremin, an electronic musical instrument that's played by moving one hand in front of one antennae to control pitch and the other hand in front of a second antennae to control volume. Debbie's theremin was meant to interpret the touch of knitted fabric. Her piece Duet for Thread and Theremin consists of an exquisite knit fabric hanging over a theremin's antenna; when viewers touch the fabric, their motions are translated into ethereal sounds. Debbie also hopes to invent a way to knit something that can change and move over time, like music, and she is contemplating ways to make a gallery installation of knits that can be acted upon and altered by visitors' touch.

Though Debbie's work connects the disparate fields of music, biology, handcraft, and engineering, among many others, she is happy to simply describe herself as a knitter. "If I think of myself as an artist," she says, "I feel I have to make a piece of art every time I work, and I have to develop a style that's uniquely mine. I don't want to place those constraints on myself—I don't want to have to fit into my century. I'd rather be a knitter. With knitting, I can go anywhere I want."

Scribble Lace Bolero

This bolero combines two techniques I have used elsewhere: scribble lace and labyrinth knitting. Scribble lace has a row of thick, textured yarn suspended between flimsy rows of thin yarn, allowing the featured yarn to scribble about as it celebrates its freedom. It reveals the whole length of an exotic yarn so it looks as handsome as it did in the skein. Labyrinthine paths fill a space and I usually knit them as very long rows. But here they are knit in short sections so they can be connected together while you work and a final step allows you to adjust the fit. Knitting a labyrinth can be as contemplative an experience as walking one. I have used some unusual stitches here as well to give a cast-on and bind-off that are firm enough to hold their own when knit on large needles and to allow the miter stitches to stretch the extra distance required of them.

The thicker yarns I have used from La Lana Wools are richly colored with natural dyes. It is best if the thin yarn is not too smooth and slippery and the Rowan Kidsilk serves that purpose.

The bolero shown is a medium size. There are suggestions for modifying the garment described at the end. The idea itself is quite general—a path that connects to itself as it grows. I hope it might tempt a few folk to wander off along a path of their own.

— **Debbie New**

SIZES
One size

FINISHED MEASUREMENTS
To fit 32-36" bust (see notes at right to adjust size)

YARN
La Lana Wools Dos Mujeres (55% mohair / 45% merino; 122 yards / 2 ounces): 2 hanks, kota I (A)
Rowan Yarns Kidsilk Haze (70% super kid mohair / 30% silk; 227 yards / 25 grams): 1 ball each #595 liqueur (B) and #578 swish (C)
La Lana Wools Handspun Mohair Bouclé (100% mohair; 96 yards / 8 ounces): 1 hank marigold (D)
Note: There is enough yarn here to make the bolero in the size shown or a size larger.

NEEDLES
One 24" (40 mm) circular (circ) needle size US 11 (8 mm)
Change needle size if necessary to obtain correct gauge.

NOTIONS
Crochet hook size US L/11 (8 mm) (optional); stitch marker

GAUGE
8 sts and 11½ rows = 4" (10 cm) in Stockinette stitch (St st) using D

NOTES
Refer to Working the Bands and Assembly Diagram.
You may work this Bolero with or without Sleeves.

Either Body or Sleeves can be shortened or lengthened by changing all the CO numbers equally (for instance, if you want to add 3 sts, make sure you add 3 sts to each CO number). However, you must not change the 5-st Twice-Knit CO's. Remember that if you add or subtract CO numbers, this will also change the number of loops that you must pick up from the Backwards Loop CO of the previous Band.

The width of the Body can also be increased or decreased by easing less or more fabric when sewing Bands 1 and 13 along the bottom edge. Note that if you increase the width significantly, you will at the same time shorten the length, so you may wish to add sts to all the Bands.

You may work Bands 1 and 13 of the Body to make a tie across the front of the piece rather than sewing them along the bottom to the back. See instructions at the beginning of Bands 1 and 13.

Each row is knit in the same direction, using a separate ball of yarn. To do this, when you complete a row, DO NOT turn your needle; simply slip the stitches back to the right-hand end of the needle to work the next row. *Note: The only time you will turn your work is after working the Twice-Knit CO, as indicated in the instructions.*

You will have eight balls of yarn trailing from your work, but since you never turn your needles (except following the Twice-Knit CO), your balls of yarn can be neatly lined up along the left-hand edge, to keep them from tangling. They should never be twisted around each other and should stay in the same order from beginning to end. If you work from the center of center-pull balls, it will keep the strands neater. The yarns are only cut after finishing the whole body and at the end of each sleeve, so there are very few ends to deal with.

All Bands are worked in the same Color Sequence, using the same strand of yarn from one Band to the next. For instance, when you begin to CO sts for Band 2, you will continue with the same strand of A that you used to CO sts for Band 1; then when the Band 2 CO is complete, slide these sts back to the right-hand end of the needle and use the strand of B that you used for Row 1 of Band 1 to work Row 1 of Band 2 (see illustration). Continue to work in this manner throughout the entire piece.

When working purl rows, you are working with very thick and very thin yarns. When working the thick yarn, make sure you draw each stitch through fully so the thin yarn lies at the base of the stitch and is not dragged up by the more textured yarn. When working the thin yarn, make sure that the new stitch both enters and leaves at the top of the stitch below it; you may need to tug the work down gently to do this.

Increases and decreases are all double knit to elongate them and allow the miters to stretch further. You may find it easier to work the increases if you don't drop the original stitch from the left-hand needle until you have completed the increase.

Twice-Knit CO: *Note: You will have to turn your work before working this CO, then turn it again once you've worked the number of sts required in this CO.* Beg with sl st on needle *K1, transfer st back to left-hand needle purlwise, knit into the st on the left-hand needle, draw up a loop but do not drop st from left-hand needle; place new loop on left-hand needle; repeat from * for remaining sts to be CO.

Pick Up and Purl: Pick up and purl into horizontal loop between sts in CO edge. *Note: When this pick-up is used, be sure to pick up only from those CO sts that were worked using the Backwards Loop CO. There will be an easily visible horizontal bar or loop between these CO sts.*

Twice-Knit BO: Pass next-to-last st on right-hand needle over last st, *transfer st to left-hand needle, k2, pass next-to-last st on right-hand needle over last st; repeat from * to end or for number of sts to be BO, transfer st to left-hand needle, k1.

Twice-Knit Joined BO: *Transfer st from right-hand needle to left-hand needle, k2tog, pass next-to-last st on right-hand needle over last st, transfer st back to left-hand needle, k1; repeat from * to end or for number of sts to be BO. *Note: When working this BO, the sts after the marker on the left-hand end of the Band will be BO together with the sts before the marker, so that a portion of the Band will curve back on itself.*

Kk2 (single increase): *K1, transfer st back to left-hand needle, k1*, with left-hand needle, lift the st from the row below the st you just worked, repeat from * to *.

Kk3 (double increase): *K1, transfer st back to left-hand needle, k1*, **with left-hand needle, lift the st from the row below the st you just worked, k1, transfer st back to left-hand needle, k1**; repeat from ** to ** once.

Kk2tog (single decrease): K2tog, transfer st back to left-hand needle, k1.

Kk3tog (double decrease): K3tog, transfer st back to left-hand needle, k1.

Color Sequence
Each Band uses the same color sequence, as follows:
CO: A.
Row 1: B.
Row 2: Second ball of B.
Row 3: C.
Row 4: D.
Row 5: Second ball of C.
Row 6: Third ball of B.
BO: Second ball of A.

BOLERO
Prepare the yarn by winding 3 separate same-sized balls of B, and 2 separate balls each of C and A.

Body
Note: All Bands follow the same Color Sequence. After completing a row, do not turn your work, unless instructed to. Slip sts back to beginning of needle to work next row. When working a row with a strand that has been used previously in the Band, make sure to pull the last st of the previous row firmly.

Band 1
Note: If you want to work Bands 1 and 13 to make a tie across the front of the piece rather than sewing them along the bottom to the back, work kk2tog instead of kk2 at the end of Row 2; do not work any increases or decreases in Row 6.

Working the Bands

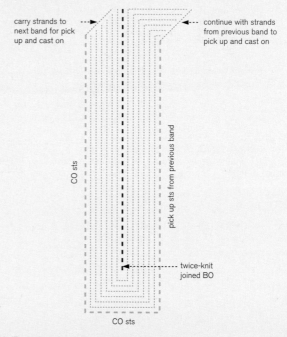

carry strands to next band for pick up and cast on

continue with strands from previous band to pick up and cast on

CO sts

pick up sts from previous band

twice-knit joined BO

CO sts

This illustration gives a general view of how the Bands will be worked. Note that a number of the Bands will have slightly different dimensions, but will be worked in a similar manner. Green lines indicate the pick-up/CO row; orange lines indicate Rows 1-6; the red line indicates the Twice-Knit Joined BO row that causes Row 6 to fold over on itself; and blue lines indicate that strands were used from the previous Band to work the pick-up/CO row for this Band, and will be used in the next Band for the pick-up/CO row. Sharp angles in the orange rows indicate where sts are increased to create mitered corners.

Using Twice-Knit CO and A, CO 35 sts; turn work.

Row 1: Change to B; knit.

Row 2: Change to second ball of B, knit to last st, kk2—36 sts.

Row 3: Change to C; knit.

Row 4: Change to D; purl.

Row 5: Change to second ball of C; purl.

Row 6: Change to third ball of B, knit to last st, kk2—37 sts. Change to second ball of A; k1, transfer st back to left-hand needle, k2, BO all sts using Twice-Knit BO. Secure last st without breaking yarn, by passing the ball through the st.

Band 2

Working Color Sequence as for Band 1, using Backwards Loop CO (see Special Techniques, page 172), CO 23 sts.

Rows 1, 3, 4, and 5: Work as for Rows 1, 3, 4, and 5 of Band 1.

Row 2: Kk2, knit to last st, kk2—25 sts.

Row 6: Kk2, knit to end—26 sts.

Using right-hand needle, pick up last BO st from Band 1, k1 from left-hand needle, BO all sts using Twice-Knit BO. Secure last st without breaking yarn.

Band 3

Using Backwards Loop CO, CO 1 st, pick up and purl 23 sts from loops of Backwards Loop CO sts of previous Band, place marker (pm), turn work, CO 5 sts using Twice-Knit CO, turn work, CO 28 sts using Backwards Loop CO—57 sts.

Rows 1, 3, 4, and 5: Work as for Rows 1, 3, 4, and 5 of Band 1.

Row 2: [Kk3] twice, knit to 2 sts before marker, [kk2tog] twice, k1, [kk2tog] twice, knit to last st, kk2—58 sts.

Row 6: K2, kk2, kk3, knit to 2 sts before marker, kk2tog, kk3tog, kk2tog, knit to last st, kk2.

Using right-hand needle, pick up last BO st from previous Band, k1 from left-hand needle, BO 5 sts using Twice-Knit BO, knit to marker, k1, work Twice-Knit Joined BO until there are no remaining sts on right-hand needle, work Twice-Knit BO to end. Secure last st without breaking yarn.

Band 4

CO 1 st, pick up and purl 28 sts from loops of Backwards Loop CO sts of previous Band, pm, turn work, CO 5 sts using Twice-Knit CO, turn work, CO 8 sts using Backwards Loop CO—42 sts.

Rows 1, 3, 4, and 5: Work as for Rows 1, 3, 4, and 5 of Band 1.

Row 2: Kk3, kk2, knit to 2 sts before marker, [kk2tog] twice, k1, [kk2tog] twice, knit to last st, kk2.

Row 6: Kk2, k1, [kk2] twice, knit to 2 sts before marker, kk2tog, kk3tog, kk2tog, knit to last st, kk2.

Using right-hand needle, pick up last BO st from previous Band, k1 from left-hand needle, BO 25 sts using Twice-Knit BO, knit to marker, k1, work Twice-Knit Joined BO to end. Secure last st without breaking yarn.

Band 5

CO 1 st, pick up and purl 8 sts from loops of Backwards Loop CO sts of previous Band, pm, CO 5 sts using Twice-Knit CO, CO 28 sts using Backwards Loop CO—42 sts.

Rows 1, 3, 4, and 5: Work as for Rows 1, 3, 4, and 5 of Band 1.

Rows 2 and 6: Work as for Band 4.

Using right-hand needle, pick up last BO st from previous Band, k1 from left-hand needle, BO 5 sts using Twice-Knit BO, knit to marker, k1, work Twice-Knit Joined BO until there are no remaining sts on right-hand needle, work Twice-Knit BO to end. Secure last st without breaking yarn.

Bands 6, 7, and 8

CO 1 st, pick up and purl 28 sts from loops of Backwards Loop CO sts of previous Band, pm, turn work, CO 5 sts using Twice-Knit CO, turn work, CO 28 sts using Backwards Loop CO—62 sts.

Rows 1, 3, 4, and 5: Work as for Rows 1, 3, 4, and 5 of Band 1.

Rows 2 and 6: Work as for Band 4.

Using right-hand needle, pick up last BO st from previous Band, k1 from left-hand needle, BO 5 sts using Twice-Knit BO, knit to marker, k1, work Twice-Knit Joined BO to end. Secure last st without breaking yarn.

Assembly Diagram

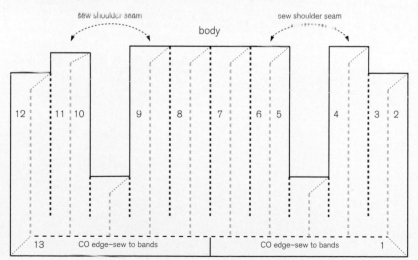
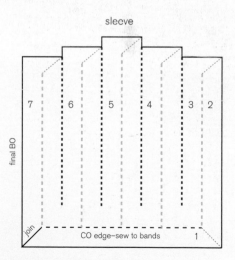

The yellow lines indicate where the CO edges of Body Bands 1 and 13 are sewn to Body Bands 3-11, and where the CO edge of Sleeve Band 1 is sew to Sleeve Bands 3-6.

Band 9

Work as for Band 4.

Band 10

Work as for Band 5.

Band 11

CO 1 st, pick up and purl 28 sts from loops of Backwards Loop CO sts of previous Band, pm, turn work, CO 5 sts using Twice-Knit CO, turn work, CO 23 sts using Backwards Loop CO–57 sts.

Rows 1, 3, 4, and 5: Work as for Rows 1, 3, 4, and 5 of Band 1.
Row 2: Kk3, kk2, knit to 2 sts before marker, [kk2tog] twice, k1, [kk2tog] twice, knit to last st, kk3–58 sts.
Row 6: Kk2, k1, [kk2] twice, knit to 2 sts before marker, kk2tog, kk3tog, kk2tog, knit to last st, kk3–59 sts.
Using right-hand needle, pick up last BO st from previous Band, k1 from left-hand needle, BO 8 sts using Twice-Knit BO, knit to marker, k1, work Twice-Knit Joined BO to end. Secure last st without breaking yarn.

Band 12

CO 1 st, pick up and purl 23 sts from loops of Backwards Loop CO sts of previous Band–24 sts.
Rows 1, 3, 4, and 5: Work as for Rows 1, 3, 4, and 5 of Band 1.
Row 2: Kk3, kk2, knit to last st, kk2–28 sts.
Row 6: Kk3, k2, knit to last st, kk2–31 sts.
Using right-hand needle, pick up last BO st from previous Band, k1 from left-hand needle, BO all sts using Twice-Knit BO. Secure last st without breaking yarn.

Band 13

Note: If you want to work Bands 1 and 13 to make a tie across the front of the piece rather than sewing them along the bottom to the back, work kk2tog instead of kk2 at the beginning of Row 2; do not work any increases or decreases in Row 6.
Using Twice-Knit CO, CO 35 sts.
Rows 1, 3, 4, and 5: Work as for Rows 1, 3, 4, and 5 of Band 1.
Rows 2 and 6: Kk2, knit to end–37 sts.
Using right-hand needle, pick up last BO st from previous Band, k1 from left-hand needle, BO all sts using Twice-Knit BO. Secure last st without breaking yarn.

Sleeves (make 2)

Note: Use the same color sequence and method of working as for Body.

Band 1

Using Twice-Knit CO, CO 30 sts.
Row 1: Knit.
Row 2: Knit to last st, kk2–31 sts.
Row 3: Knit.
Row 4: Purl.
Row 5: Purl.
Row 6: Knit to last st, kk2–32 sts.
K1, transfer st back to left-hand needle, k2, BO all sts using Twice-Knit BO. Secure last st without breaking yarn.

Band 2

Using Backwards Loop CO, CO 20 sts.
Rows 1, 3, 4, and 5: Work as for Rows 1, 3, 4, and 5 of Band 1.
Rows 2 and 6: Kk2, knit to last st, kk2–24 sts after Row 6.

Using right-hand needle, pick up last BO st from previous Band, k1 from left-hand needle, BO all sts using Twice-Knit BO. Secure last st without breaking yarn.

Band 3

CO 1 st, pick up and purl 20 sts from loops of Backwards Loop CO sts of previous Band, pm, turn work, CO 5 sts using Twice-Knit CO, turn work, CO 21 sts using Backwards Loop CO–47 sts.
Rows 1, 3, 4, and 5: Work as for Rows 1, 3, 4, and 5 of Band 1.
Row 2: Kk3, kk2, knit to 2 sts before marker, [kk2tog] twice, k1, [kk2tog] twice, knit to last st, kk2.
Row 6: Kk2, k1, [kk2] twice, knit to 2 sts before marker, kk2tog, kk3tog, kk2tog, knit to end–46 sts remain.
Using right-hand needle, pick up last BO st from previous Band, k1 from left-hand needle, BO 5 sts using Twice-Knit BO, knit to marker, k1, work Twice-Knit Joined BO to end. Secure last st without breaking yarn.

Band 4

CO 1 st, pick up and purl 21 sts from loops of Backwards Loop CO sts of previous Band, pm, turn work, CO 5 sts using Twice-Knit CO, turn work, CO 23 sts using Backwards Loop CO–50 sts.
Rows 1, 3, 4, and 5: Work as for Rows 1, 3, 4, and 5 of Band 1.
Row 2: [Kk3] twice, knit to 2 sts before marker, [kk2tog] twice, k1, [kk2tog] twice, knit to last st, kk2–51 sts.
Row 6: K2, [kk3] twice, knit to 2 sts before marker, kk2tog, kk3tog, kk2tog, knit to last st, kk2–52 sts.
Using right-hand needle, pick up last BO st from previous Band, k1 from left-hand needle, BO 5 sts using Twice-Knit BO, knit to marker, k1, work Twice-Knit Joined BO to end. Secure last st without breaking yarn.

Band 5

CO 1 st, pick up and purl 23 sts from loops of Backwards Loop CO sts of previous Band, pm, turn work, CO 5 sts using Twice-Knit CO, turn work, CO 21 sts using Backwards Loop CO–50 sts.
Rows 1, 3, 4, and 5: Work as for Rows 1, 3, 4, and 5 of Band 1.
Row 2: Kk3, kk2, knit to 2 sts before marker, [kk2tog] twice, k1, [kk2tog] twice, knit to last st, kk3–51 sts.
Row 6: Kk2, k1, [kk2] twice, knit to 2 sts before marker, kk2tog, kk3tog, kk2tog, knit to last st, kk3–52 sts.
Using right-hand needle, pick up last BO st from previous Band, k1 from left-hand needle, BO 5 sts using Twice-Knit BO, knit to marker, k1, work Twice-Knit Joined BO to end. Secure last st without breaking yarn.

Band 6

CO 1 st, pick up and purl 21 sts from loops of Backwards Loop CO sts of previous Band, pm, turn work, CO 5 sts using Twice-Knit CO, turn work, CO 20 sts using Backwards Loop CO–47 sts.
Rows 1, 3, 4, and 5: Work as for Rows 1, 3, 4, and 5 of Band 1.
Row 2: Kk3, kk2, knit to 2 sts before marker, [kk2tog] twice, k1, [kk2tog] twice, knit to last st, kk2.
Row 6: Kk3, knit to 2 sts before marker, kk2tog, kk3tog, kk2tog, knit to last st, kk3.
Using right-hand needle, pick up last BO st from previous Band, k1 from left-hand needle, BO 5 sts using Twice-Knit BO, knit to marker, k1, work Twice-Knit Joined BO to end. Secure last st without breaking yarn.

Band 7

Turn work; using Twice-Knit CO, CO 31 sts; turn work.

Rows 1, 3, 4, and 5: Work as for Rows 1, 3, 4, and 5 of Band 1.

Row 2: Kk2, knit to last 2 sts, kk2, kk3–35 sts.

Row 6: Kk2, knit to last 4 sts, [kk2] twice, k1, kk2–39 sts.
Using right-hand needle, pick up last BO st from previous Band, k1 from left-hand needle, BO all sts using Twice-Knit BO. Secure last st without breaking yarn.

FINISHING

Body

Note: See Assembly Diagram.

Using A, sew top of Bands 3 and 4 to top of Bands 5 and 6 for right shoulder. Repeat for Bands 8 and 9, and 10 and 11 for left shoulder.

Note: If you have chosen to work Bands 1 and 13 to make a tie across the front of the piece rather than sewing them along the bottom to the back, work a row of single crochet along the bottom of the piece for a clean edge.

Bands 1 and 13 are longer than the other Bands to allow you to adjust their placement for proper fit. Try the piece on and pin these 2 Bands in place along the bottom of the Bolero,

from front to back. Sew in place, then trim ends of Bands about an inch past where they meet. Unravel ends back to where Bands meet, and secure ends of both Bands together, as follows, so they don't unravel further: For A, B and C, knot ends together and weave in. For D, unravel thinner strand from thicker strand; knot thin strand and weave in. Taper ends of thick strand, then, using tapestry needle, run each piece through a piece of the strand on the opposite Band to secure.

The back neck should be narrow enough to hold the shoulders in place. If not, work 1 row single crochet across the neck to decrease the width.

Sleeves

Set in Sleeves so that the square corners of the Sleeve fit into the square corners of the armhole. Sew sleeve seams. Band 1 is longer than needed to allow you to adjust the bottom of the Sleeve for a comfortable fit. Sew Band to bottom of Sleeve, then trim end a few inches past where it meets its other end. Unravel the ends back to where the ends meet, and finish as for Bands 1 and 13.

Debbie explains, "My yarn collection is an odd assortment of things I have picked up on sale, things people have passed on to me, the occasional exotic fiber that has got the better of me, and a few yarns that were so incredibly ugly I couldn't resist them."

Eugene Ong

Facing page
Eugene in his Los Angeles apartment with his cat Malachy.

Left
A dress from Eugene's 2007 fall/winter collection.

Eugene Ong grew up designing. As a child, he made elaborate paper airplanes that actually flew. He drew buildings, particularly hotels in tropical resorts and shops in urban settings. Using a professional, computer-aided drafting program his father taught him to operate in grade school, he redesigned logos for existing brands and created new ones for imaginary entities, including one for a company he called Ujein, a more symmetrical-looking version of his own name. Fifteen years later, he chose Ujein as the name for his line of hand-knit clothing.

As a teenager, Eugene's interests ran the gamut from fashion—he fell in love with Martin Margiela, Junya Watanabe, Comme des Garçons, Hussein Chalayan, and early McQueen and Galliano—to architecture. Initially, architecture won out. "I went to college right after high school and I didn't know exactly what I wanted to do," Eugene recounts. "Architecture seemed like a cool, creative, professional job. I don't think anyone goes into architecture school knowing exactly what it is." Nonetheless, he became one of the best students in his architecture classes at California Polytechnic State University in San Louis Obispo, California. "By my third year," he says, "I was doing really well." But during his fourth year, Eugene studied in Denmark, and things began to change. "I had always excelled, and then when I went to Denmark, everything flipped," he says. "They loved modernism, and I was anti-modernism for my own political reasons. I didn't agree with that design philosophy, and they couldn't respect mine. It was a hard year." The one positive experience in Denmark for Eugene was knitting, which his host mother taught him. "I would knit little segments of fabric using different techniques. That way, I could try different ideas without getting bored," he recalls.

When Eugene returned to the United States for his last year of architecture school, he continued to knit during his spare time. "I started with scarves, and then tops," he says. "Then I tried to incorporate knitting into my thesis. I made a tube as an entryway for a hypothetical store by knitting a plastic material. It was structural but flexible at the same time. The teacher really liked it." After he earned his degree in 2001, Eugene went to a job fair and was hired on the spot by a corporate firm that specialized in institutional buildings.

Eugene worked at the company for a year as the model shop manager, but he wasn't happy, so decided to take off seven months to experiment with clothing design, making knitted clothes he sold to local boutiques. He wasn't able to make a living though, so he went back to the architectural firm. "I really made a go of it," he says of returning to his job. "I told them I needed to learn a lot and to have more responsibility. But after a year, I realized I didn't really believe in it, and I wasn't making the world a better place, so I quit again."

A friend of Eugene's wanted to invest in a project, so together they came up with a line of silk-screened and embroidered T-shirts, which they created for two seasons. But, in 2004, when architect and curator Fritz Haeg asked Eugene to participate in Showdown Salon, a clothing exhibition and fashion show at the MAK Center for Art and Architecture's Schindler House in Los Angeles, Eugene chose to present hand-knitted sweaters instead of T-shirts. Those sweaters caught the attention of a clothing store owner, who then introduced Eugene to the director of a showroom in downtown Los Angeles. When Eugene showed the director and his business partner his work, they told him they wanted to back his line. "So I dropped everything else," Eugene says.

Eugene now develops two collections of about twenty hand-knit garments a year. He begins his design process with sketches, then moves into the trial and error of knitting. "First I produce an idea," Eugene says. "Then I make it in 3-D. It's like an architectural model." Often Eugene reinterprets how staple garments, like pullover sweaters or hooded sweatshirts, are created. "If I'm making a regular crewneck sweater, I usually don't think it has to be made up of a front, back, and two sleeves," Eugene explains. "The sleeves can be a modified raglan and start at the neckline and connect to the front and back panels. The sides of the garment can connect the front and side panel and attach at the armpit area of the sleeves. In some ways, it's like taking a whole predefined object and breaking it down into elementary geometric segments."

Eugene's work is rustic, but refined. It looks and feels like it's been made by hand, and it has: Each collection is hand-knit in a small town in central Italy. Eugene sends his samples to a main factory, which then distributes the work to local knitters who work out of their homes. For two years, his collections were made mostly from standard, commercially available natural fibers—mainly cotton and wool, with an occasional bit of stainless steel—but now all of Eugene's clothes are made with yarn produced in Argentina. "It's my own composition of dehaired llama and raw silk for fall, and raw silk, linen, and dehaired llama for spring," Eugene says. "Llama is called the cashmere of South America; it's very soft and warm." He makes the samples for each collection all in one color, then offers buyers a palette of colors from which to make individual choices.

Eugene knits samples for his collections in the living room of his Silver Lake, Los Angeles, apartment, with his cats Malachy and Caccia nearby. While he knits, he listens to indie rock music and watches soap operas like *Days of Our Lives* and *Passions*. Eugene is shy and quiet, and likes that knitting is something he can do in complete isolation. "I have never knit with anyone besides the Danish mom who taught me," he says. "Even though knitting is now my work, I still like it. Sometimes my hands hurt, and I hate deadlines, but the final product is worth it." The hands-on aspect of clothing design, as well as the instant satisfaction it offers, suits Eugene well. "Clothes are a lot quicker than architecture," he says. "Every six months, there is a new season, and you can keep exploring themes. Architecture is much slower, and it is client-driven," he continues. "I like to be able to completely control all aspects of a design, and I get a lot of pride from making something out of nothing. Knitting is building up a fabric. You can do something abstract and it still fits your body—it is abstract, but it has a purpose."

Ujein V-Neck Vest

The impetus of this design was to make a V-neck vest that was constructed differently than the classic one. Each panel of the vest is used in a three-dimensional manner, wrapping around the body, not constricting its use for only the front or the back of the garment. The ends of the panels interlock and stack in the front to form the V-neckline. The back of the garment is cut away and left loose to add some unexpected romance to such a classically conservative garment.

— Eugene Ong

SIZES

To fit 32 (34¾, 36½, 39)" bust, stretched

FINISHED MEASUREMENTS

28 (30½, 32, 34)" chest, unstretched

YARN

Heavy worsted-weight slub yarn with shiny binder: 225 (250, 275, 325) yards
Note: Any heavy worsted-weight slub yarn will give a similar effect, just be sure to match the stitch gauge given.

NEEDLES

One pair straight needles size US 13 (9 mm)
Change needle size if necessary to obtain correct gauge.

NOTIONS

Removable markers

GAUGE

12 sts and 16 rows = 4" (10 cm) in Stockinette st (St st), unstretched

----

NOTES

This piece is made up of 4 panels, each of which wrap from Front to Back or Back to Front, and which are then sewn together (see Assembly Diagram). Panel A forms the bottom left front half of the vest, and the long work-even portion wraps from front to back over the shoulder to form the left armhole; Panel B is the bottom right front half of the vest, and the long work-even portion wraps from back to front over the shoulder to form the right armhole; Panel C forms half of the center front neck, and wraps over the center of the shoulders to form the drapey portion of the back; Panel D forms the top portion of the center front neck, and wraps over the shoulders to form the back neck.

VEST

Panels A and B (both alike)
CO 27 (29, 31, 33) sts.

Establish Pattern:

Row 1 (RS): K5, *p1, k1; repeat from * to last 4 sts, k4.
Row 2: K4, *p1, k1; repeat from * to last 5 sts, p1, k4.
Repeat Rows 1 and 2 nine times.
Dec Row (RS): Knit to last 6 sts, k2tog, k4—26 (28, 30, 32) sts remain.
(WS) K4, purl to last 4 sts, k4.
Repeat last 2 rows 18 (19, 20, 21) times—8 (9, 10, 11) sts remain.
Place marker at right edge for armhole.
Continuing in Garter St (knit every row), work even for 84 rows.
BO all sts.

Panel C

CO 8 (9, 10, 11) sts. Begin Garter St. Work even for 200 (216, 232, 248) rows. BO all sts.

Panel D

CO 8 (9, 10, 11) sts. Begin Garter St. Work even for 100 (108, 116, 124) rows. BO all sts.

FINISHING

Note: Refer to Assembly Diagram. Lightly block pieces. RS facing, sew first 20 rows of left edge of A to first 20 rows of right edge of B (front seam). Sew first 20 rows of right edge of A to first 20 rows of left edge of B (back seam).

Fold the remaining portion of A to the back so that WS's are together, and so the top right corner of the BO edge meets the back seam. Sew the BO edge of A along 16 rows of the left side of B. Sew sides of A together from the BO edge up to the armhole marker. Repeat for B on the opposite side.

Sew the CO edge of C to the last 16 rows of B; sew the side edge of C along the edge of A; leave 17 rows of C (and 17 rows each of A and B at the base of the vee) unsewn, then continue to sew C to the side of B, beginning 17 rows up from the base of the back vee along B, and continuing over the shoulder, back to the front vee. Sew the BO edge of C to 16 rows of the side of C.

Sew the CO edge of D to the last 16 rows of C; sew the side edge of D along 46 rows of the edge of C; leave 17 rows of D (and approximately 86 rows of C) unsewn, then continue to sew D along the last 36 rows of C to the front vee. Sew the BO edge of D to 16 rows of the side of D.

Weave in all loose ends.

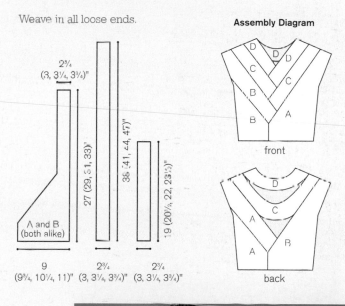

Assembly Diagram

front

back

Freddie Robins

Facing page:
Freddie stands in front of her knitted toy collection, on display in her bedroom. Some toys were purchased, others found, some given as gifts, a few knitted by former students and some she knitted herself.

Below:
Skin—A Good Thing to Live In, 2002. Machine-knitted wool, 83" x 75".

Freddie Robins lives in a two-story London apartment with her artist husband, Ben Coode-Adams; her daughter, Willa; and a dizzying collection of stuff. Though things like action figures, fishing tackle, fake food, miniature houses, stuffed animals, rubber lips, and American cereal boxes from the 1980s are crammed into every corner of the space, an initial impression of random junk gives way to subtle organizational techniques and overarching themes. A micro-collection of Shrek merchandise is gathered in one corner of the living room; international religious iconography is grouped together on the second-floor landing; taxidermy is presented in a hallway leading to the bathroom; and knitted toys are squashed into large wood and glass display boxes in the master bedroom. Everything in what Freddie and her husband call "the collection" has its place, and when smaller groupings are considered as a larger whole, they can be understood as an ambitious attempt to prioritize extreme, odd, irreverent, and macabre objects over everyday ones. Subverting notions of normality is also what drives Freddie's art practice.

Freddie learned to knit as a child, from her mother's best friend, Pamela Darking. "Pam was a great needlewoman who made fantastic things," Freddie says. "She really inspired me to work with textiles." From an early age, Freddie set challenging goals for herself, aspiring to make things as complicated as Patricia Roberts sweaters, which often include three-dimensional stitches, and as subversive as the designs featured in the 1979 book *Wild Knitting,* edited by Angela Jeffs, which include gigantic knitted fruit and knitted bat corsages. When she was sixteen years old, Freddie created a knitted mohair trompe l'oeil interpretation of a tuxedo and entered the design in a *Womancraft* magazine competition. She won first place in the contest's "Teenage

Jumper" category, along with a modest cash prize. With this early affirmation of her knitting talents, Freddie enrolled in Middlesex University to pursue a bachelor's degree in knitted textiles. "I was amazed at how right it was for me," Freddie says of the university. "It was so engaging and exciting. There was a heavy emphasis on research, and I really enjoyed being in London and seeing art, exploring shops and designers." During college, Freddie decided that she wanted to see designs through from beginning to end, rather than design fabric for someone else to construct or use, so she continued her training in knitted textiles by getting a master's degree at the Royal College of Art. "The Royal College was very intense," Freddie describes. "I was engaged with other ambitious people, and I had the time to develop a more sophisticated subversion in my work." Freddie developed a practice of using imagery not usually associated with textiles, like cow's organs and body scars, seeking to subvert the floral and Fair Isle patterning that people expected from knitting. She made use of junk and plastic, asserting them as materials of equal value to wool or cashmere. Although her work was well received at the college, Freddie didn't have a clear idea of what she wanted to do afterward. "I hadn't really worked out how I would exist outside school," she says. "I hate authority and hierarchy; it was a big battle to make my work in the world."

Upon graduation in 1989, Freddie took a position with Tait & Style, a design company based in the Orkney Isles, Scotland, founded by a former classmate, Ingrid Tait, and specializing in embroidered, knitted, and felted fabrics. "It was a fantastic learning experience," Freddie says of making fashion and furnishing accessories for the company, "and I got to see how to function as a creative person in the commercial world. But I lost a big engagement with my practice, and I wasn't

expressing what I wanted to express. I missed knitting." After working with Tait & Style for eight years, Freddie quit developing functional objects, gathered her thoughts about conformity, and applied herself toward more conceptually motivated textile projects—namely, her knitted art.

In 1998, Freddie received a Setting Up Award from the London-based Crafts Council that enabled her to establish her studio practice. She has worked since then to produce knitted projects that subvert cultural preconceptions of knitting as homey or benign. "A lot of my work looks at notions of the abnormal," Freddie explains, adding that her first group of knitted pieces were distorted and deformed gloves. Peggy, from that late-1990s series, is a machine knit glove with one finger missing—and a separate blood-stained knitted cover for the missing finger. (Peggy is Freddie's aunt, who had her finger bitten off by a horse.) A sweater series that Freddie produced a few years later features one sweater with a hood that covers the entire head as well as a sweater with two elongated sleeves that turn into socks at the ends. Other sinister, disconcerting, and anarchic knit works include Craft Kills, in which knitting needles pierce the fabric of a woolen body made in Freddie's own size, and a 2002 series of hand-knit and embroidered Knitted Homes of Crime. The small sculptures, approximately one foot high and reminiscent of ordinary tea cozies, are detailed portraits of homes associated with high-profile murders committed by women. They belie the notion of women as society's nurturers, and they are meant to be creepy. "Knitting is a friendly medium that can be used to engage your audience with a subject that might otherwise cause them to turn away," Freddie says. "I love that knitting is a common art because it comes with stereotypes that I can work against. Stereotypes give you power. They're useful."

In 2005, Freddie curated an exhibition for the Pump House Gallery in Battersea Park, London, entitled Ceremony, which subverted the paraphernalia and rituals associated with rites of passage. Rachael Matthews (see page 112), founder of the London knitting group Cast Off and one of the artists in the show, invited Freddie to be the bride in an all-knitted wedding. Freddie describes the wedding not as the occasion when she got married to her longtime partner, but as a "social investigation." "I walked in five minutes before the ceremony and got dressed really quickly, and everyone gushed and told me, 'You look so beautiful,' when I hadn't done a thing to prepare. But that's just what you're supposed to say to the bride at a wedding," she says. When the Craft Council asked Freddie to curate a show on knitting in 2005, she purposely chose only nonfunctional pieces, challenging the idea that knitting is normally used to make useful garments.

When she's not teaching constructed textiles at the Royal College of Art in London, Freddie makes her artwork out of a studio in the Dalston area of Hackney, London, where she researches freak shows, repellant objects, and other curiosities that she can incorporate into knit projects. "I like to look at things that frighten or disturb me," she says. "I've grown to love things I once hated or feared, like taxidermy. I am very object- and material-based. The collection and production of objects reassures me I'm alive." The actual act of knitting is as enjoyable to Freddie as researching lurid subject matter. "Creating a cloth out of nothing is an amazing process," she says. "I love color, and when you work with yarn, you work directly with color. I also love texture and working with my hands." Summarizing her own joyfully grim perspective on the craft, Freddie says that she has plans to knit her own coffin.

Ethel from Knitted Homes of Crime, 2002, commissioned by FirstSite and on display at the Minories Art Gallery, Colchester, England. Hand-knitted yarn, quilted lining fabric (10.24" x 7.09" x 6.30").

I'm So Angry Banner

I'M SO ANGRY is one of an ongoing series of hand-knitted banners that I have been making since 2000. I make them when I feel like it, or when I have something short and sharp that I need to say. The statements that I knit reflect the way that I feel about the human condition and myself. They are also a reflection of the way that I feel about knitting and the preconceptions surrounding it. Some of the other banners, I CAN'T REMEBE, I AM PERFET and DO I FIT IN are in private collections. I like the idea that I'M SO ANGRY can be in the collection of anyone who can maintain their anger long enough to knit it. I admit it; I am an angry knitter, too. If all the angry people sat down to knit, it might not make a better world but it would certainly be a warmer one.

— **Freddie Robins**

FINISHED MEASUREMENTS
Approximately 13½" wide x 37½" long

YARN
Rowan Yarns Yorkshire Tweed DK (100% wool; 123 yards /
50 grams): 1 ball each #347 skip (A) and #348 lime leaf (B);
2 balls #349 frog (C)
Debbie Bliss Merino DK (100% merino wool; 122 yards / 50
grams): 1 ball each #701 orange (D), #704 aubergine (E),
#503 lime (F), and #615 pale pink (G)
Jaeger Handknits Baby Merino DK (100% wool; 130 yards /
50 grams): 1 ball #231 red (H)

NEEDLES
1 pair straight needles size US 6 (4 mm)
Change needle size if necessary to obtain correct gauge.

GAUGE
20 sts and 32 rows = 4" (10 cm) in Stockinette st (St st)

NOTES
Changing colors as indicated, using separate balls of yarn for
each color, Intarsia Colorwork method (see Special Techniques,
page 172).

STITCH PATTERN
Seed Stitch
(multiple of 2 sts + 1; 1-row repeat)
All Rows: K1, *p1, k1; repeat from * across.

BANNER
Using A, CO 71 sts. Begin Seed St; work even for 10 rows.
(RS) Work 8 sts in Seed St, change to B and work 55 sts in Rev St
st, change to A and work in Seed St to end. Work even for 4 rows.
(WS) Work 8 sts in Seed St, change to B and work 4 sts in Rev
St st, work across 47 sts from Chart. Change to B and work 4
sts in Rev St st, change to A and work in Seed St to end. Work
even as established until entire Chart is complete.
(RS) Work 8 sts in Seed St, change to B and work 55 sts in Rev St
st, change to A and work in Seed St to end. Work even for 4 rows.
(WS) Continuing in A, work even in Seed St for 10 rows. BO all sts.

FINISHING
Block piece to measurements.

Beryl
Tsang

During the uncertain and complicated years following her breast cancer diagnosis at age thirty-seven, Beryl Tsang remained singularly focused on her myriad knitting projects as a way to cope. Knitting also helped ease the trauma of shopping for a prosthetic breast six months after her right breast was removed, when an invitation to a formal party sent her to every mastectomy boutique and medical supply store in Toronto. In desperation, she finally bought a mastectomy bra and a silicone breast advertised as the "lightest and most natural looking" on the market. When she got home, she put on the breast and bra, and promptly broke into tears.

Heading to her yarn stash for an uplifting knitting project, Beryl realized that she could knit herself a new breast to wear to the party. She finished an hour before the event and slipped it into one of her favorite underwire bras. Later, a friend at the party commented, "You really did a great job! Your left breast looks almost as good as the right one—a bit lumpy, but very realistic." "You know," Beryl corrected her, "It was my right breast that was removed." After knitting several more prostheses for women in her cancer support group, and receiving a name for her invention from a friend who spontaneously dubbed it "Tit-Bits," Beryl was inspired to create her website, www.titbits.ca, in 2005. While she hoped to sell the knitted prostheses, she also realized she could support women with breast cancer through discussion forums, free creative projects, links to medical resources, and her own wit and wisdom.

Born in 1966, Beryl has been knitting nearly her whole life. She first learned at age five, when her mother taught her the Continental style on a pair of chopsticks. Six years later, Beryl learned English-style, which she found much easier. She took to it in earnest, knitting throughout high school "as a diversion from studying," she says, belying her scholastic aptitude. After receiving a bachelor's degree in East Asian studies and a master's degree in history and culture, Beryl took a job at a youth drug prevention organization. Having since held a series of community service positions as a researcher or fundraiser, Beryl now works part-time as an equity and diversity consultant to several nonprofit organizations.

Knitting is linked to Beryl's not-for-profit career choice and giving nature—what she jokingly but somewhat earnestly calls her "Chinese need to feed everyone." Her renovated Victorian house in Toronto's historic Cabbagetown area is open every weekend to any friend who wants to drop by with a project in tow. Beryl also hosts a knitting club, The Secret Society for the Propagation of Fibre Pornography, which meets monthly in her home. As if all this organized crafting wasn't enough, Beryl also founded the Toronto Knit Rabble, which lets knitters claim Toronto's public transportation system as their territory during the twice-yearly Toronto Transit Commission Knit-A-Long.

It was natural, then, for Beryl to turn to her consuming hobby "for coping and for survival," as she puts it, after she was diagnosed with cancer. "Breast cancer is the result of a confluence of factors," Beryl explains, "and you can't control the outcome of a diagnosis. You can hope for the best, and you can control sock projects. Knitting made me wonder less, 'why me?'"

Knitting Tit-Bits with her friends helps keep Beryl upbeat. "I have a kooky, nutty bunch of paid knitters who help me make Tit-Bits," Beryl explains. "Jean Anne is a business analyst, Joyce is a video editor, Rosanne is a writer and artist, Selna's a bubbie, and Cheryl is a professional super-mum and crochet queen. We also call in members of the Secret Society for the Propagation of Fibre Pornography to help us when we get busy." They all gather in Beryl's loftlike bedroom, where a designated production manager assigns each of them a particular client. Together they knit an average of ten Tit-Bits per week, in three different categories: "everyday," made of cotton in various colors, "fancy," which may come in extra-soft cashmere, cream-colored stripes, or with curly trim, and "floosies," which are hot pink, red, or black, and made with confetti eyelash yarn. The most popular Tit-Bit is a buff color in a 36B or 34C cup.

When she's not knitting Tit-Bits, working in the nonprofit sector, shuttling her two kids around, or doing yoga, Beryl loves to correspond with her clients, whom she always befriends. She helps them figure out what kind of bra or what size Tit-Bit they need, and generally debriefs them about the breast cancer process. She usually mails out two or three Tit-Bits in one package so they can try different sizes and materials. She once placed someone's lucky golf ball inside a Tit-Bit, and she often sends her clients care packages. Former clients are now devoted pen pals, making Tit-Bits a community continually evolving around the use of knitting as a compassionate enterprise. On a more fundamental level, Tit-Bits are simply making women happy, filling a delicate need in a lighthearted but very effective way. As one client wrote to Beryl, in an e-mail titled "Woo-hoo": "Got 'em. Flaunting 'em as we speak. The hot ones are HOT! They're so soft and so dazzling and so BIG. I love the shells—imagine the strut. Thank you—thank you."

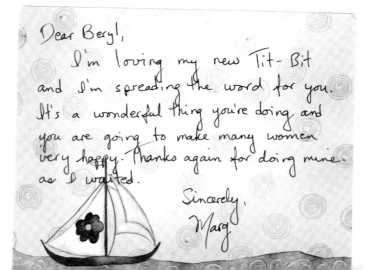

Breast Cancer Awareness Tit-Bit

When I first started Tit-Bits I envisioned women knitting them in black cashmere, fluffy confetti, and shocking fuchsia. But women sent me pictures of their bright white, buff, latte, milk and dark chocolate titties. None, it appeared, wanted to make wild titties.

One day an acquaintance asked me why I didn't make pink titties, since my logo has a pink Breast Cancer Awareness ribbon on it. I started making one, but couldn't seem to finish it. Then I stumbled across the website for Breast Cancer Action's Think Before You Pink Project, which urges women to ask some questions before purchasing products from corporations that exploit breast cancer to boost profits and then it hit me: I didn't want to be associated with the "Pink Parade." So I put away my pink titty.

Next, a longtime friend and radical eco-feminist called. She had had a mastectomy and, to cheer herself up, bought the most expensive and politically incorrect pink bra she could find—a lacy net confection with flowers.

"Please," she begged, "Won't you make me a pink titty to match my bra?"

I did and she flashes it everywhere she goes and then tells people about the Think Before You Pink Project and the real change that is needed to end breast cancer.

— Beryl Tsang

SIZES
To fit AA (A, low-B, high-B, low-C, high-C, D, DD and E+) bra sizes

FINISHED MEASUREMENTS
Approximately 3½ (4, 4½, 5, 5½, 6, 6½, 7¼, 7¾)" across

YARN
Crystal Palace Yarns Party (100% nylon; 87 yards / 50 grams): 1 hank #405 tulip petals (A) or #205 strawberry cream (B)
S.R. Kertzer Butterfly Super 10 (100% cotton; 250 yards / 125 grams): 1 hank #3446 shell pink (MC)

NEEDLES
One set of four double-pointed needles (dpn) size US 6 (4 mm)
One set of four double-pointed needles size US 5 (3.75 mm)
Change needle size if necessary to obtain correct gauge.

NOTIONS
Split ring marker; decorative shank button or bead for nipple (optional); cotton fleece or polyester fiberfill for stuffing; small weight (such as a smooth stone) to keep Tit-Bit from moving in bra.

GAUGE
22 sts and 24 rows = 4" (10 cm) in Stockinette st (St st) using larger needles and MC

NOTES
If necessary, adjust the number of stitches in the pattern to make a Tit-Bit that is the right size for you. Just make sure the total number of stitches is divisible by 3.

TIT-BIT (make 1 or 2 as needed)
Front
Using larger needles and A or B, CO 3 sts. Begin I-Cord (see Special Techniques, page 172). Work even for 2 rows. *[Optional. If you prefer not to use a button or bead nipple, work even until I-Cord measures 1¼–2".]*
**Increase Row: Continuing in I-Cord, *k1-f/b; repeat from * across–6 sts. Divide sts among 3 needles. Join for working in the round; place marker (pm) for beginning of rnd.
Increase Rnd: *Knit to last st on needle, m1, k1; repeat from * around–9 sts.
Sizes low-B (high-B, low-C, high-C, D, DD, E+): Repeat Increase Rnd twice–15 sts.
All sizes: Change to MC. Repeat Increase Rnd 15 (17, 16, 17, 19, 20, 22, 23, 25) times–54 (60, 63, 66, 72, 75, 81, 84, 90) sts. Purl 2 rnds. BO all sts.

Back
Using smaller needles and MC, CO 3 sts. Begin I-Cord. Work even for 1 row. Complete as for Front, beginning at **.

FINISHING
With wrong sides together, sew BO edges of Front and Back together, leaving an opening for stuffing.
Stuff Tit-Bit, using as much or as little stuffing as you like. The Back of the Tit-Bit should be flat, the Front perky but pliable. If it "stands at attention," or looks like a mutated balloon, you have overfilled it. Embed weight carefully in stuffing. Sew edge of Tit-Bit closed. Tack Front and Back together through the center, so that Back is concave and does not sit against the scar and chafe or irritate it. Attach a small decorative bead or button for the nipple, or knot the I-cord (if you chose to work the longer I-cord) and sew in place. Block Tit-Bit by soaking in warm water and soap flakes; rinse thoroughly, and gently squeeze and shape. Allow to dry completely. Pop it into your bra and wear it out!

Special Techniques

Backwards Loop CO

Make a loop (using a slip knot) with the working yarn and place it on the right-hand needle [first st CO], * wind yarn around left thumb clockwise, insert right-hand needle into the front of the loop on thumb, remove thumb and tighten st on needle; repeat from * for remaining sts to be CO, or for casting on at the end of a row in progress.

Cable CO

Make a loop (using a slip knot) with the working yarn and place it on the left-hand needle [first st CO], knit into slip knot, draw up a loop but do not drop st from left-hand needle; place new loop on left-hand needle; *insert the tip of the right-hand needle into the space between the last 2 sts on the left-hand needle and draw up a loop; place the loop on the left-hand needle. Repeat from * for remaining sts to be CO, or for casting on at the end of a row in progress.

Crochet Chain

Make a slip knot and place it on crochet hook. Holding tail end of yarn in left hand, *take hook under working end of yarn from front to back; draw yarn on hook back through previous st on hook to form new st. Repeat from * to desired number of sts or length of chain.

I-Cord

Using a double-pointed needle cast on or pick up the required number of sts; the working yarn will be at the left-hand side of the needle. * Transfer the needle with the sts to your left hand, bring the yarn around behind the work to the right-hand side; using a second double pointed needle, knit the sts from right to left, pulling the yarn from left to right for the first st; do not turn. Slide the sts to the opposite end of the needle; repeat from * until the cord is the length desired. Note: After a few rows, the tubular shape will become apparent.

Intarsia Colorwork Method

Use a separate length of yarn for each color section; you may wind yarn onto bobbins to make color changes easier. When changing colors, bring the new yarn up and to the right of the yarn just used to twist the yarns and prevent leaving a hole; do not carry colors not in use across the back of the work.

Kitchener Stitch

Using a blunt yarn needle, thread a length of yarn approximately 4 times the length of the section to be joined. Hold the pieces to be joined wrong sides together, with the needles holding the sts parallel, both ends pointing in the same direction. Working from right to left, insert yarn needle into first st on front needle as if to purl, pull yarn through, leaving st on needle; insert yarn needle into first st on back needle as if to knit, pull yarn through, leaving st on needle; *insert yarn needle into first st on front needle as if to knit, pull yarn through, remove st from needle; insert yarn needle into next st on front needle as if to purl, pull yarn through, leave st on needle; insert yarn needle into first st on back needle as if to purl, pull yarn through, remove st from needle; insert yarn needle into next st on back needle as if to knit, pull yarn through, leave st on needle. Repeat from *, working 3 or 4 sts at a time, then go back and adjust tension to match the pieces being joined. When 1 st remains on each needle, cut yarn and pass through last 2 sts to fasten off.

Kitchener Stitch with Bound-Off Stitches

Lay pieces to be grafted on a flat surface, with right sides facing up, and the edges to be grafted lying parallel to each other. Working from right to left, insert yarn needle into first loop of first st on piece closest to you (front piece) as if to purl, pull yarn through; insert yarn needle into first loop of first st on piece furthest from you (back piece) as if to purl, pull yarn through; *insert yarn needle into entire first st on front piece as if to purl, pull yarn through; insert yarn needle into entire first st on back piece as if to purl, pull yarn through. Repeat from *, working 3 or 4 sts at a time, then go back and adjust tension to match the pieces being joined. When all sts have been grafted, fasten off.

Long-Tail (Thumb) CO

Leaving tail with about 1" of yarn for each st to be cast-on, make a slipknot in the yarn and place it on the right-hand needle. Insert the thumb and forefinger of your left hand between the strands of yarn so that the working end is around your forefinger, and the tail end is around your thumb 'slingshot' fashion; * insert the tip of the right-hand needle into the front loop on the thumb, hook the strand of yarn coming from the forefinger from back to front, and draw it through the loop on your thumb; remove your thumb from the loop and pull on the working yarn to tighten the new st on the right-hand needle; return your thumb and forefinger to their original positions, and repeat from * for remaining sts to be CO.

Pompom

You can use a pompom maker or the following method: Cut two cardboard circles in the diameter of the pompom desired. Cut a 1" diameter hole in the center of each circle. Cut away a small wedge out of each circle to allow for wrapping yarn. Hold the circles together with the openings aligned. Wrap yarn around the circles until there is no room left in the center to wrap. Carefully cut yarn around outer edge of the cardboard circles. Using a 12" length of yarn, wrap around strands between the two circles and tie tightly. Slip the cardboard circles off the completed pompom; trim pompom, leaving the ends of the tie untrimmed. Using ends of tie, sew pompom to garment.

Provisional CO

Using waste yarn, CO the required number of sts; work in Stockinette st for 3-4 rows; work 1 row with a thin, smooth yarn (crochet cotton or ravel cord used for machine knitting), as a separator; change to main yarn and continue as directed. When ready to work the live sts, pull out the separator row, placing the live sts on a spare needle.

Reading Charts

Unless otherwise specified in the instructions, when working straight, charts are read from right to left for RS rows, from left to right for WS rows. Row numbers are written at the beginning of each row. Numbers on the right indicate RS rows; numbers on the left indicate WS rows. When working circular, all rounds are read from right to left.

Short Row Shaping

Work the number of sts specified in the instructions, wrap and turn [wrp-t] as follows:

Bring yarn to the front (purl position), slip the next st to the right-hand needle, bring yarn to back of work, return slipped st on right-hand needle to left-hand needle; turn, ready to work the next row, leaving remaining sts unworked.

When Short rows are completed, or when working progressively longer Short Rows, work the wrap together with the wrapped st as you come to it as follows:

If st is to be worked as a knit st, insert the right-hand needle into the wrap, from below, then into the wrapped st; k2tog; if st to be worked is a purl st, insert needle into the wrapped st, then down into the wrap; p2tog. [Wrap may be lifted onto the left-hand needle, then worked together with the wrapped st if this is easier.]

Stranded (Fair Isle) Colorwork Method

When more than one color is used per row, carry color(s) not in use loosely across the WS of work. Be sure to secure all colors at beginning and end of rows to prevent holes.

Tassel

Using color of your choice, wind yarn 20 times (or to desired thickness) around a piece of cardboard or other object the same length as desired for Tassel. Slide yarn needle threaded with matching yarn under the strands at the top of the tassel; tie tightly, leaving ends long enough for attaching Tassel to garment. Cut through all strands at the opposite end. Tie a second piece of yarn tightly around the Tassel several times, approximately 1/2" from top of Tassel; secure ends inside top of Tassel. Trim ends even; attach to garment.

Abbreviations

BO – Bind off
Ch – Chain
Circ – Circular
CN – Cable needle
CO – Cast on
Dc (double crochet) – Working from right to left, yarn over hook (2 loops on hook), insert hook into the next stitch, yarn over hook and pull up a loop (3 loops on hook), [yarn over and draw thorough 2 loops] twice.
Dcd (double centered decrease) – Slip next 2 sts together knitwise to right-hand needle, k1, pass 2 slipped sts over knit stitch.
Dpn – Double-pointed needle(s)
Hdc (half double crochet) – Yarn over hook (2 loops on hook), insert hook into next stitch, yarn over hook and draw up a loop (3 loops on hook), yarn over and draw through all 3 loops on hook.
K – Knit
K1-f/b – Knit into front loop and back loop of same stitch to increase one stitch.
K2tog – Knit 2 sts together.
K2tog-tbl – Knit 2 sts together through back loop.
K3tog – Knit 3 sts together.
Ksp – K1, transfer st back to left-hand needle, then pass second st on left-hand needle over st just worked, transfer st back to right-hand needle.

MB – Make bobble (as instructed).
M1-b (lifted increase) – To work the increase on a knit st, insert the right-hand needle, from the top down, into the st below the first st on the left-hand needle, knit this st, then knit the first st. To work the increase on a purl st, insert the right-hand needle, from the top down, into the top loop of the st just below the first st on the left-hand needle, purl this st, then purl the first st.
M1R (make 1-right slanting) – With the tip of the left-hand needle inserted from back to front, lift the strand between the two needles onto the left-hand needle; knit it through the front loop to increase one stitch.
M1 or M1L (make 1-left slanting) – With the tip of the left-hand needle inserted from front to back, lift the strand between the two needles onto the left-hand needle; knit the strand through the back loop to increase one stitch.
M1P (make 1 purlwise) – With the tip of the left-hand needle inserted from back to front, lift the strand between the two needles onto the left-hand needle; purl the strand through the front loop to increase one stitch.
P – Purl
P2tog – Purl 2 sts together.
P2tog-tbl – Purl 2 sts together through back loop.
P1-f/b – Purl the next st through the front of its loop, then through the back of its loop, to increase one st.
Pm – Place marker
Psso (pass slipped stitch over) – Pass slipped st on right-hand needle over the sts indicated in the instructions, as in binding off.
Rnd – Round
RS – Right side
Sc (single crochet) – Insert hook into next st and draw up a loop (2 loops on hook), yarn over and draw through both loops on hook.
Skp – (slip, knit, pass) – Slip next st knitwise to right-hand needle, k1, pass slipped st over knit st.
Sk2p (double decrease) – Slip next st knitwise to right-hand needle, k2tog, pass slipped st over st from k2tog.
Sl (slip) – Slip stitch(es) as if to purl, unless otherwise specified. Sl st (crochet slip stitch) – Insert hook in st, yarn over hook, and draw through loop on hook.
Sl st (crochet slip stitch) – Insert hook in st, yarn over hook, and draw through loop on hook.
Sm – Slip marker
Ssk (slip, slip, knit) – Slip the next 2 sts to the right-hand needle one at a time as if to knit; return them back to left-hand needle one at a time in their new orientation; knit them together through the back loop(s).
Sssk – Same as ssk, but worked on next 3 sts.
Ssp (slip, slip, purl) – Slip the next 2 sts to right-hand needle one at a time as if to knit; return them to the left-hand needle one at a time in their new orientation; purl them together through the back loop(s).
St(s) – Stitch(es)
K1-tbl – Knit one stitch through the back loop, twisting the stitch.
Tbl – Through the back loop
Tog – Together
WS – Wrong side
Wrp-t – Wrap and turn (see Techniques-Short Row Shaping)
Wyib – With yarn in back
Wyif – With yarn in front
Yb – Yarn back
Yf – Yarn front
Yo – Yarnover

Clockwise from top left
The view from Rachael Matthews' (page 112) house in London.

Flying into Glasgow.

It was so cold the day Kiriko photographed Lisa Anne Auerbach (page 08) that the Polaroids could hardly develop.

A Polaroid of Erika Knight (page 86) at the Waterloo train station.

Lunch in Paris with Kiriko and Risto Bimbiloski (page 26).

Facing page
Kiriko photographs Rachael Matthews (page 112) boxing with her two assistants, Annie and Naomi.

Thank You

I would like to thank:
All the knitters profiled in the book for allowing me into their homes, studios, histories, and projects.

Kiriko Shirobayashi, photographer, for her creativity, flexibility, and extreme work ethic. Half of this book belongs to her.

Melanie Falick, the book's editor, for providing a direction and a deadline, and for safeguarding and shaping the project with her vision and expertise.

Kevin O'Neill, graphic designer, for his talent, skill, and ambition, and for always ending e-mails with the word "awesome."

Sue McCain, pattern editor, for her knit pattern ingenuity, and her perfectionism, patience, and good humor.

Betty Christiansen, for generously and peacefully shaping my essays into cohesion.

Liana Allday, editor, who gracefully tied all of the book's loose ends together.

All of the book's models: Priscilla Alexandre, Genaro Ambrosino, Isy Crofton, Annie Doi, Jennifer Earle, Karen Eydie, Naomi Johnstone, Leah Mitchell, Karina New, Leni Niemegeers, Adjowii Ozemir, Rachel Rosenfield, Fiona Ryan, Iman Salim, and Kathryn.

Catherine Clark, who allowed us to photograph Beryl Tsang in the lovely Brooklyn General Store in Brooklyn: www.brooklyngeneral.com.

My family and Jason Spingarn-Koff, for their unrelenting faith; Emily Drury and Sara Grady, for everything they offered when *KnitKnit* was just an idea; all of *KnitKnit's* distributors and exhibitors, for their support; the MacDowell Colony, for the time and space to conceive of writing a book, and Lawrence Weschler, for writing "Seeing is Forgetting the Name of the Thing One Sees."

Designer Contact List

Lisa Anne Auerbach www.lisaanneauerbach.com, www.stealthissweater.com
Anna Bell www.needleandhook.co.uk
Isabel Berglund iberglund@hotmail.com
Risto Bimbiloski rbimbiloski@yahoo.com
Wenlan Chia www.twinklebywenlan.com
Dave Cole www.theknittingmachine.com, info@rotenberggallery.com
Liz Collins www.lizcollins.com
Jim Drain hellojimdrain@yahoo.com
Teva Durham www.loop-d-loop.com
Norah Gaughan www.norahgaughan.net
David Gentzsch Ozark Handspun, www.ozarkhandspun.com
Aimee Hagerty Johnson slavetotheneedles@sacbeemail.com
Joelle Hoverson www.purlsoho.com
Erika Knight www.erikaknight.com
Knitta www.knittaplease.com
Sarah Kohl www.knit-pics.blogspot.com
Catherine Lowe www.catherine-lowe.com, www.thecoutureknittingworkshop.com
Bridget Marrin bmarrin@hotmail.com
Tina Marrin www.tinamarrin.com
Rachael Matthews www.castoff.info
Cat Mazza www.microrevolt.org
Mandy McIntosh www.hamandenos.com
Althea Merback www.bugknits.com
Annie Modesitt www.anniemodesitt.com
Debbie New dnew@golden.net, www.schoolhousepress.com
Eugene Ong www.ujein.com
Freddie Robins www.freddierobins.com
Beryl Tsang www.titbits.ca

Photo and Illustration Credits

Cover image courtesy of Debora Smail. **4-5:** images courtesy of Molly Smith. **6 and 7:** images of Sabrina and *KnitKnit* #3 courtesy of Jason Spingarn-Koff. *KnitKnit* # 2 image courtesy of Cesar Lechowick. **7:** *KnitKnit* # 4 and 5 images courtesy of Sabrina Gschwandtner. **10-11, endpapers:** sweater image, zine covers and Freedom is Messy image courtesy of Lisa Anne Auerbach. **15, 18:** sketch courtesy of Anna Bell; button image and sweater image courtesy of Anna and Brad Bell. **21:** images courtesy of Mette Kjaer. **22-24:** knitted room images courtesy of Christoffer Askman. **27-29, endpapers:** images courtesy of Aleksandar Bimbil. **32, 33, 37:** rug image, childhood picture, and drawing courtesy of Wenlan Chia. **39, 42:** blanket and bear images courtesy of Dave Cole and Judi Rotenberg Gallery. **40-41:** images courtesy of Larry Smallwood and Dave Cole. **44-46, endpapers:** Samurai Coat, Skeleton Dress, and Vein Bustier images courtesy of Karen Philippi. **47:** images courtesy of Kim Stoddard. **51, 53:** images courtesy of Forcefield and Greene Naftali Gallery. **52:** images courtesy of Greene Naftali Gallery. **57, jacket flaps, endpapers:** sketch courtesy of Jim Drain. **59:** image courtesy of Sabrina Gschwandtner. **60-61:** Fair Isle Short Row Pullover and Zip-Off Color Block Yoke Sweater courtesy of Adrian Buckmaster, from *Loop-d-Loop* (Stewart, Tabori & Chang). **64, 66, 67:** Coastline Skirt, Starfish Shawl, Target Wave Mittens, and Cowl Pullover images courtesy of Thayer Allyson Gowdy, from *Knitting Nature* (Stewart, Tabori & Chang). **65, 69, endpapers:** sketches, childhood photo, and bag sketch courtesy of Norah Gaughan. **75-77, endpapers:** zine images courtesy of Aimee Hagerty Johnson. **81-82:** images courtesy of Anna Williams, from *Last-Minute Knitted Gifts* (Stewart, Tabori & Chang). **83:** Purl Soho image courtesy of Sabrina Gschwandtner. **87-88:** swatch and working board images courtesy of Erika Knight. **90-92:** sneaker, door handle, and night tagging images courtesy of Debora Smail. **91:** Great Wall of China image courtesy of MascuKnitity. **95:** sweater image courtesy of Catherine Lowe. **105:** knitted doll and knitted gloves images courtesy of Jeaneen Lund. **109:** image courtesy of Sabrina Gschwandtner. **113-115:** Cast Off flyer, Cast Off party, and knitted wedding images courtesy of Rachael Matthews. **122-123:** image courtesy of Bettina Escavriza. **126-129, 133, endpapers:** childhood photo, stills from *Electronic Fabric Film* and *Donkey Skin,* hood images, and sketch courtesy of Mandy McIntosh. **141:** Hat image courtesy of Annie Modesitt. **157:** image courtesy of Eugene Ong. **158-159:** wedding dress images courtesy of Jeaneen Lund. **163-165:** Skin-A Good Thing to Live in and Knitted Homes of Crime images courtesy of Douglas Atfield. **169:** card courtesy of Beryl Tsang. **174-175:** Glasgow, Paris lunch, Rachael Matthews' window, and Kiriko photographing boxers courtesy of Sabrina Gschwandtner. **Back Cover image** courtesy of Christoffer Askman. **Author Bio image** courtesy of Chris Habib.